Adolf

170

ESSAYS BY
PRESENT-DAY WRITERS

THE MACMILLAN COMPANY
NEW YORK · BOSTON · CHICAGO · DALLAS
ATLANTA · SAN FRANCISCO

MACMILLAN & CO., LIMITED
LONDON · BOMBAY · CALCUTTA
MELBOURNE

THE MACMILLAN CO. OF CANADA, LTD.
TORONTO

ESSAYS BY
PRESENT-DAY WRITERS

EDITED BY

RAYMOND WOODBURY PENCE 1885-

PROFESSOR OF RHETORIC AND ENGLISH COMPOSITION
IN DePAUW UNIVERSITY

New York
THE MACMILLAN COMPANY
1924

THE MACMILLAN COMPANY.

Set up and electrotyped.
Published April, 1924.

TO MY FATHER AND MOTHER

THIS BOOK IS INSCRIBED

PREFACE

The essay may be said to have been discovered—or invented—by Michel de Montaigne, who published the first two volumes of his *Essais* in 1580. He broke away from the impersonal moral disquisitions of his day and proceeded to write about himself, his own likes and dislikes, his foibles and idiosyncrasies. And one type of the essay—generally known as the Familiar Essay—has to the present time followed more or less closely Montaigne's model. A survey of the history of the essay will, of course, show that there is probably no form of writing with less clearly defined boundaries and limits. We think of the essay as including the short pithy epigrammatic utterance of Sir Francis Bacon, the formal literary criticism of Dryden, the chatty informal *Spectator* papers of Addison and Steele, the ponderous disquisitions of Dr. Samuel Johnson, the formal literary studies of Coleridge, Arnold, Pater, and Macaulay, the scientific treatises of Spencer, Darwin, Huxley, and Tyndall, the philosophical writings of Emerson, and the very informal, highly personal, chatty, whimsical conversation of Hazlitt, Leigh Hunt, Thackeray, Stevenson, and, above all, Charles Lamb. To this last group we may add our own Irving and Holmes. For convenience, then, we may recognize two fairly well defined types—the formal, impersonal, objective treatise and the very informal, personal, subjective. It is evident, of course, that no definite dividing line can be drawn between these two types.

A survey of what has been written in essay form since the beginning of the twentieth century shows that the formal type is very rapidly losing ground and that the informal is just about as rapidly gaining. It is not our purpose here to investigate reasons but simply to state facts. For practical purposes, then, we may say that the essay of the present-day is preëminently the familiar essay. And it is not strange that this is so. Somebody has said that the most interesting subject in the world is "I"; the next most interesting is "You"; much below either of these is the interest in "The Rest." Best of all we like to talk about ourselves; the next best thing is hearing somebody talk about himself. In the typical familiar essay, therefore, the pleasing egotism of the writer is matched by a healthy curiosity on the part of the reader in the personal experiences, embarrassments, confessions, mistakes, ludicrous and ridiculous blunderings of the writer. And the more personal they are the more we, the reader, like them, because in them we recognize ourselves and our own experiences; we come upon echoes of our own thoughts to which we have unfortunately never been able to give expression. And we are pleased, for we all enjoy saying, "How True!"

The rapid growth in popularity of the familiar essay has resulted in the use of the familiar-essay manner or technique in dealing with subjects that ordinarily would not be considered familiar-essay subjects. *Jungle Peace* and *Edge of the Jungle,* two volumes of scientific papers in the familiar-essay mood by the noted American scientist, William Beebe; the volumes of John Burroughs and John Muir; the volumes of literary essays by James Huneker, Brander Matthews, H. L. Mencken, A. Edward Newton, William Lyon Phelps, Stuart P. Sherman, and C. Alphonso Smith; the volumes of London sketches by Thomas Burke; books primarily of pedagogical interest, such as Henry S. Canby's *College Sons and College Fathers,* Thomas Arkle Clark's *Discipline and the Derelict,* William T. Foster's *Should Students Study?*— all of these are examples of more or less serious matters treated in an informal, familiar manner. In fact, one of the most popular books of the present time—H. G. Wells'

Outline of History—is nothing but history written in a familiar-essay manner. The same is true of Hendrik van Loon's *Story of Mankind.* An interesting thing is the newness of this method of approach; for such a combination of serious matter and a light, informal, familiar manner would have been inconceivable prior to the twentieth century. (One may speculate on what might happen to our whole educational system were the conventional textbooks—dry, uninteresting, uninspired as most of them are—to be replaced by others written in the manner of Wells' *Outline* or van Loon's *Story of Mankind.* Think what a composition class might be were a Chesterton or a Christopher Morley, a Stuart P. Sherman or an H. L. Mencken, to write the textbook!)

The value of the lighter essay to the teacher—too frequently not recognized—can be made very great. Students are in English classes primarily to learn how to write. It is trite to say that they will acquire the gift of expression more rapidly if they can be at the same time interested in what they write. Now students—like other human beings (including school teachers)—like best of all to write and talk about themselves. If, then, through the wise comments of the teacher they can be made to realize that such writing will meet the demands of the Department of English for theme work, and if they can be made to realize also, through outside reading in the familiar essay, that such writing on the part of experienced authors is accepted as literature, they will develop both a greater interest in and a deeper respect for what they write. The editor of this collection, for one, is convinced—assuming that the final test of a course in composition is whether the student acquires something of a mastery of expression—that there is nothing in the composition course upon which time may be spent more profitably than upon the familiar essay, and that no form of the student's writing will maintain a higher level of excellence. The novice will learn more about the art of writing because he will have more fun doing it. This is a broad claim to make; but a careful test with a class will demonstrate its soundness.

The object of the present collection has been to bring together representative examples of what is being done to-day in essay-writing on both sides of the Atlantic. In manner of treatment the essays all show a marked tendency towards the familiar essay type, although the subject matter varies from the very light to the more serious.

Two arbitrary limitations have been placed upon the choice of selection: only essays that have appeared in book form and only those by living writers have been included.

The purpose in giving such full information in the bibliographical lists, not only regarding all the volumes of essays that a writer represented in the present collection has written but also regarding all other volumes of essays by present-day writers, has been to lure the user of the text on to a more extensive reading of books of essays. The editor believes that it is only fair, not merely to the authors and their publishers, but also the reader himself, that such information shall include the name and address of the publisher in every case and also the copyright date.

I wish to express my deep appreciation to the following authors and publishers whose generous coöperation in allowing the use of valuable copyrighted material alone has made such a collection possible: William Beebe, Hilaire Belloc, Robert Benchley, Ralph Bergengren, Alexander Black, Margaret Breuning, Charles S. Brooks, Heywood Broun, Gilbert K. Chesterton, Frank Moore Colby, Samuel McChord Crothers, John Galsworthy, Ellwood Hendrick, Oliver Herford, Robert Cortes Holliday, Burges Johnson, Miss Winifred Kirkland, Stephen Leacock, E. V. Lucas, Robert Lynd, John Macy, Don Marquis, Brander Matthews, H. L. Mencken, A. A. Milne, Christopher Morley, George Jean Nathan, A. Edward Newton, Meredith Nicholson, Edmund Lester Pearson, William Lyon Phelps, Miss Agnes Repplier, Stuart

P. Sherman, Logan Pearsall Smith, Simeon Strunsky, Henry van Dyke, Miss Frances Warner, Miss Elisabeth Woodbridge; Henry Holt and Company, Alfred A. Knopf, Inc., George H. Doran Company, Atlantic Monthly Press, Harper & Brothers, Yale University Press, Harcourt, Brace and Company, Dodd Mead and Company, Houghton Mifflin Company, Charles Scribner's Sons, The Macmillan Company, G. P. Putnam's Sons, Boni and Liveright, Doubleday, Page & Company, and E. P. Dutton & Company.

My thanks are due the officials of the Carnegie Library, of Columbus, Ohio, for their many courtesies; likewise they are due my colleague, Assistant Professor Virginia Harlow, and my friend, Mr. William Baxter, for their kindness in reading and correcting proof.

R. W. P.

Greencastle, Indiana
March, 1924

CONTENTS

xiii

ESSAYS BY
PRESENT-DAY WRITERS

ESSAYS BY PRESENT-DAY WRITERS

JUNGLE NIGHT *

By William Beebe

I

WITHIN gun-reach in front of me trudged my little Akawai Indian hunter. He turned his head suddenly, his ears catching some sound which mine had missed, and I saw that his profile was rather like that of Dante. Instantly the thought spread and the simile deepened. Were we two not all alone? and this unearthly hour and light—Then I chuckled softly, but the silence that the chuckle shattered shrank away and made it a loud, coarse sound, so that I involuntarily drew in my breath. But it was really amusing, the thought of Dante setting out on a hunt for kinkajous and giant armadillos. Jeremiah looked at me wonderingly, and we went on in silence. And for the next mile Dante vanished from my thoughts and I mused upon the sturdy little red man. Jeremiah was his civilized name; he would never tell me his real one. It seemed so unsuited to him that I thought up one still less appropriate and called him Nupee—which is the three-toed sloth; and in his quiet way he saw the humor of it, for a more agile human being never lived.

Nupee's face was unclouded, but his position as hunter to

1

our expedition had brought decisions and responsibilities which he had not known before. The simple life,—the unruffled existence in the little open *benab,* with hammock, cassava field, and an occasional hunt,—this was of the past. A wife had come, slipping quietly into his life, Indian-fashion; and now, before the baby arrived, decisions had to be made. Nupee longed for some store shoes and a suit of black clothes. He had owned a big *benab* which he himself had built; but a godmother, like the cowbird in a warbler's nest, had gradually but firmly ousted him and had filled it with diseased relatives, so that it was unpleasant to visit. He now, to my knowledge, owned a single shirt and a pair of short trousers.

The shoes were achieved. I detected in him qualities which I knew that I should find in some one, as I do on every expedition, and I made him perform some unnecessary labor and gave him the shoes. But the clothes would cost five dollars, a month's wages, and he had promised to get married—white-fashion—in another month, and that would consume several times five dollars. I did not offer to help him decide. His Akawai marriage ceremony seemed not without honor, and as for its sincerity—I had seen the two together. But my lips were sealed. I could not tell him that a recementing of the ritual of his own tribe did not seem quite the equal of a five-dollar suit of clothes. That was a matter for individual decision.

But to-night I think that we both had put all our worries and sorrows far away, and I memory as well; and I felt sympathy in the quiet, pliant gait which carried him so swiftly over the sandy trail. I knew Nupee now for what he was—the one for whom I am always on the lookout, the exceptional one, the super-servant, worthy of friendship as an equal. I had seen his uncle and his cousins. They were Indians, nothing more. Nupee had slipped into the place left vacant for a time by Aladdin, and by Satán and Shimosaka, by Drojak and Trujillo—all exceptional, all faithful, all servants first and then friends. I say 'for a time'—for they all hoped, and I think still hope with me, that we shall meet and travel and camp together again, whether in the Cinghalese thorn-bush, or Himalayan dâks, in Dyak canoes or among the camphor groves of Sakarajama.

Nupee and I had not been thrown together closely. This had proved a static expedition, settled in one place, with no dangers to speak of, no real roughing it, and we met only after each hunting trip. But the magic of a full moon had lured me from my laboratory table, and here we were, we two, plodding junglewards, becoming better acquainted in silence than I have often achieved with much talk.

It was nearly midnight. We traversed a broad trail of white sand, between lines of saplings of pale-barked rubber trees, flooded, saturated, with milky-gray light. Not a star appeared in the cloudless sky, which, in contrast to the great silver moon-plaque, was blue-black. These open sandy stretches, so recently etched into what had been primitive jungle, were too glowing with light for most of the nocturnal creatures who, in darkness, flew and ran and hunted about in them. And the lovers of twilight were already come and gone. The stage was vacant save for one actor—the night-hawk of the silvery collar, whose eerie *wheeeo!* or more leisurely and articulate *who-are-you?* was queried from stump and log. There was in it the same liquid tang, the virile ringing of skates on ice, which enriches the cry of the whip-poor-will in our country lanes.

Where the open trail skirted a hillside we came suddenly upon a great gathering of these goat-suckers, engaged in some strange midnight revel. Usually they roost and hunt and call in solitude, but here at least forty were collected on the white sand within an area of a few yards. We stopped and watched. They were dancing—or, rather, popping, as corn pops in a hopper. One after another, or a half dozen at a time, they bounced up a foot or two from the ground and flopped back, at the instant of leaving and returning uttering a sudden, explosive *wop!* This they kept up unceasingly for the five minutes we gave to them, and our passage interrupted them for only a moment. Later we passed single birds which popped and wopped in solitary state; whether practicing, or snobbishly refusing to perform in public, only they could tell. It was a scene not soon forgotten.

Suddenly before us rose the jungle, raw-edged, with border zone of bleached, ashamed trunks and lofty branches white as chalk, of dead and dying trees. For no jungle tree, however hardy, can withstand the blasting of violent sun after the veiling of emerald foliage is torn away. As the diver plunges beneath the waves, so, after one glance backward over the silvered landscape, I passed at a single stride into what seemed by contrast inky blackness, relieved by the trail ahead, which showed as does a ray of light through closed eyelids. As the chirruping rails climbed among the roots of the tall cat-tails out yonder, so we now crept far beneath the level of the moonlit foliage. The silvery landscape had been shifted one hundred, two hundred feet above the earth. We had become lords of creation in name alone, threading our way humbly among the fungi and toad-stools, able only to look aloft and wonder what it was like. And for a long time no voice answered to tell us whether any creature lived and moved in the tree-tops.

The tropical jungle by day is the most wonderful place in the world. At night I am sure it is the most weirdly beautiful of all places outside the world. For it is primarily unearthly, unreal; and at last I came to know why. In the light of the full moon it was rejuvenated. The simile of theatrical scenery was always present to the mind, the illusion lying especially in the completeness of transformation from the jungle by daylight. The theatrical effect was heightened by the sense of being in some vast building. This was due to the complete absence of any breath of air. Not a leaf moved; even the pendulous air-roots reaching down their seventy-foot plummets for the touch of soil did not sway a hair's breadth. The throb of the pulse set the rhythm for one's steps. The silence, for a time, was as perfect as the breathlessness. It was a wonderfully ventilated amphitheatre; the air was as free from any feeling of tropical heat, as it lacked all crispness of the north. It was exactly the temperature of one's skin. Heat and cold were for the moment as unthinkable as wind.

One's body seemed wholly negligible. In soft padding moccasins and easy swinging gait, close behind my Indian hunter, and in such khaki browns that my body was almost invisible to my own downward glance, I was conscious only of the play of my senses: of two at first, sight and smell; later, of hearing. The others did not exist. We two were unattached, impersonal, moving without effort or exertion. It was magic, and I was glad that I had only my Akawai for companion, for it was magic that a word would have shattered. Yet there was this wonderfully satisfying thing about it, that most magic lacks: it exists at present, to-day, perhaps, at least once a month, and I know that I shall experience it again. When I go to the window and look out upon the city night, I find all extraneous light emaciated and shattered by the blare of gas and electricity, but from one upreaching tower I can see reflected a sheen which is not generated in any power-house of earth. Then I know that within the twenty-four hours the *terai* jungles of Garhwal, the treeferns of Pahang, and the mighty *moras* which now surround us, were standing in silvery silence and in the peace which only the wilderness knows.

I soon took the lead and slackened the pace to a slow walk. Every few minutes we stood motionless, listening with mouth as well as ears. For no one who has not listened in such silence can realize how important the mouth is. Like the gill of old which gave it origin, our ear has still an entrance inward as well as outward, and the sweep of breath and throb of the blood are louder than we ever suspect. When at an opera or concert I see some one sitting rapt, listening with open mouth, I do not think of it as ill-bred. I know it for unconscious and sincere absorption based on an excellent physical reason.

It was early spring in the tropics; insect life was still in the gourmand stage, or that of pupal sleep. The final period of pipe and fiddle had not yet arrived, so that there was no hum from the underworld. The flow of sap and the spread of petals were no less silent than the myriad creatures which, I knew, slumbered or hunted on every side. It was as if I had slipped back one dimension in space and walked in a shadow world. But these shadows were not all colorless. Although the light was strained almost barren by the moon mountains, yet the glow from the distant lava and craters still kept something of color, and the green of the leaves, great and small, showed as a rich dark olive. The afternoon's rain had left each one filmed with clear water, and this struck back the light as polished silver. There was no tempered illumination. The trail ahead was either black, or a solid sheet of light. Here and there in the jungle on each side, where a tree had fallen, or a flue of clear space led moon-wards, the effect was of cold electric light seen through trees in city parks. When such a shaft struck down upon us, it surpassed simile. I have seen old paintings in Belgian cathedrals of celestial light which now seems less imaginary.

At last the silence was broken, and like the first breath of the trade-wind which clouds the Mazaruni surface, the mirror of silence was never quite clear again—or so it seemed. My northern mind, stored with sounds of memory, never instinctively accepted a new voice of the jungle for what it was. Each had to go through a reference clearing-house of sorts. It was like the psychological reaction to words or phrases. Any strange wail or scream striking suddenly upon my ear instantly crystallized some vision of the past—some circumstance or adventure fraught with similar sound. Then, appreciably as a second thought, came the keen concentration of

every sense to identify this new sound, to hear it again, to
fix it in mind with its character and its meaning. Perhaps
at some distant place and time, in utterly incongruous surroundings, it may in turn flash into consciousness—a memory-
simile stimulated by some sound of the future.

II

I stood in a patch of moonlight listening to the baying of
a hound—or so I thought: that musical ululation which links
man's companion wolf-wards. Then I thought of the packs
of wild hunting dogs, the dreaded 'warracabra tigers,' and I
turned to the Indian at my elbow, full of hopeful expectation.
With his quiet smile he whispered, 'Kunama,' and I knew I
had heard the giant tree-frog of Guiana—a frog of size and
voice well in keeping with these mighty jungles. I knew
these were powerful *beenas* with the Indians, tokens of good
hunting, and every fortunate *benab* would have its dried
mummy frog hung up with the tail of the giant armadillo
and other charms. Well might these batrachians arouse profound emotions among the Indians, familiar as they are with
the strange beings of the forest. I could imagine the great
goggle-eyed fellow sprawled high near the roof of the jungle,
clutching the leaves with his vacuum-cupped toes. The
moonlight would make him ghostly—a pastel frog; but in
the day he flaunted splashes of azure and green on his scarlet
body.

At a turn in the trail we squatted and waited for what the
jungle might send of sight or sound. And in whispers Nupee
told me of the big frog *kunama,* and its ways. It never came
to the ground, or even descended part way down the trees;
and by some unknown method of distillation it made little
pools of its own in deep hollows, and there lived. And this
water was thick like honey and white like milk, and when
stirred became reddish. Besides which, it was very bitter.

If a man drank of it, forever after he hopped each night and clasped all the trees which he encountered, endlessly endeavoring to ascend them and always failing. And yet, if he could once manage to reach a pool of *kunama* water in an uncut tree and drink, his manhood would return and his mind be healed.

When the Indians desired this *beena,* they marked a tree whence a frog called at night, and in the daytime cut it down. Forming a big circle, they searched and found the frog, and forthwith smoked it and rubbed it on arrows and bow before they went out. I listened gravely and found that it all fitted in with the magic of the night. If an Indian had appeared down the trail, hopping endlessly and gripping the trunks, gazing upward with staring eyes, I should not have thought it more strange than the next thing that really happened.

We had settled on our toes in another squatting-place—a dark aisle with only scattered flecks of light. The silence and breathlessness of the moon-craters could have been no more complete than that which enveloped us. My eye wandered from spot to spot, when suddenly I began to think of that great owl-like goatsucker, the 'poor-me-one.' We had shot one at Kalacoon a month before and no others had called since, and I had not thought of the species again. Quite without reason I began to think of the bird, of its wonderful markings, of the eyes which years ago in Trinidad I had made to glow like iridescent globes in the light of a flash—and then a poor-me-one called behind us, not fifty feet away. Even this did not seem strange among these surroundings. It was an interesting happening, one which I have experienced many times in my life. It may have been just another coincidence. I am quite certain it was not. In any event it was a Dantesque touch, emphasized by the character of the call—the wail of a lost soul being as good a simile as any other. It started as a high, trembling wail, the final cry being lost in the depths of whispered woe:—

Oo————ooh!

oh!

oh!

oh!

oh!

oh!

Nupee never moved; only his lips formed the name by which he knew it—*kalawoe*. Whatever else characterized the sounds of the jungle at night, none became monotonous or common. Five minutes later the great bird called to us from far, far away, as if from another round of purgatory—an eerie lure to enter still deeper into the jungle depths. We never heard it again.

Nature seems to have apportioned the voices of many of her creatures with sensitive regard for their environment. Sombre voices seem fittingly to be associated with subdued light, and joyous notes with the blaze of sunlit twigs and open meadows. A bobolink's bubbling carol is unthinkable in a jungle, and the strain of a `wood pewee on a sunny hillside would be like an organ playing dance-music. This is even more pronounced in the tropics, where, quite aside from any mental association on my part, the voices and calls of the jungle reflect the qualities of that twilight world. The poor-me-one proves too much. He is the very essence of night, his wings edged with velvet silence, his plumage the mingled concentration of moss and lichens and dead wood.

I was about to rise and lead Nupee still farther into the gloom when the jungle showed another mood—a silent whimsy, the humor of which I could not share with the little red man. Close to my face, so near that it startled me for a moment, over the curved length of a long, narrow caladium leaf, there came suddenly two brilliant lights. Steadily they moved onward, coming up into view for all the world like two tiny headlights of a motor-car. They passed, and the broadside view of this great elater was still absurdly like the profile of a miniature tonneau with the top down. I laughingly thought to myself how perfect the illusion would be if a red tail-light should be shown, when to my amazement a rosy red light flashed out behind, and my bewildered eyes all but distinguished a number! Naught but a tropical forest could present such contrasts in such rapid succession as the poor-me-one and this parody of man's invention.

I captured the big beetle and slid him into a vial, where in his disgust he clicked sharply against the glass. The vial went into my pocket and we picked up our guns and crept on. As we traversed a dark patch, dull gleams like heat lightning flashed over the leaves, and, looking down, I saw that my khaki was aglow from the illuminated insect within. This betrayed every motion, so I wrapped the vial in several sheets of paper and rolled it up in my handkerchief. The glow was duller but almost as penetrating. At one time or another I have had to make use of all my garments, from topee to moccasins, in order to confine captives armed with stings, beaks, teeth, or fangs, but now I was at a complete loss. I tried a gun-barrel with a handkerchief stopper, and found that I now carried an excellent, long-handled flashlight. Besides, I might have sudden use for the normal function of the gun. I had nothing sufficiently opaque to quench those flaring headlights, and I had to own myself beaten and release him. He spread his wings and flew swiftly away, his red light glowing derisively; and even in the flood of pure moonlight he moved within an aura which carried far through the jungle. I knew that killing him was of no use, for a week after death from chloroform I have seen the entire interior of a large insect box brilliantly lighted by the glow of these wonderful candles, still burning on the dead shoulders of the same kind of insect.

Twice, deeper in the jungle, we squatted and listened, and twice the silence remained unbroken and the air unmoved. Happening to look up through a lofty, narrow canyon of dark foliage, I was startled as by some sudden sound by seeing a pure white cloud, moon-lit, low down, pass rapidly across.

It was first astounding, then unreal: a bit of exceedingly poor work on the part of the property man, who had mixed the hurricane scenery with that of the dog-days. Even the elements seemed to have been laved with magic. The zone of high wind, with its swift-flying clouds, must have been flowing like a river just above the motionless foliage of the tree-tops.

This piece of ultra-unnaturalism seemed to break part of the spell and the magic silence was lifted. Two frogs boomed again, close at hand, and now all the hound similitude was gone, and in its place another, still more strange, when we think of the goggle-eyed author far up in the trees. The sound now was identical with the short cough or growl of a hungry lion, and though I have heard the frogs many times since that night, this resemblance never changed or weakened. It seemed as if the volume, the roaring outburst, could come only from the throat of some large, full-lunged mammal.

A sudden tearing rush from the trail-side, and ripping of vines and shrubs, was mingled with deep, hoarse snorts, and we knew that we had disturbed one of the big red deer—big only in comparison with the common tiny brown brockets. A few yards farther the leaves rustled high overhead, although no breath of wind had as yet touched the jungle. I began a slow, careful search with my flashlight, and, mingled with the splotches and specks of moonlight high overhead, I seemed to see scores of little eyes peering down. But at last my faint electric beam found its mark and evolved the first bit of real color which the jungle had shown—always excepting the ruby tail-light. Two tiny red globes gleamed down at us, and as they gleamed, moved without a sound, apparently unattached, slowly through the foliage. Then came a voice, as wandering, as impersonal as the eyes—a sharp, incisive *wheeeeeat!* with a cat-like timber; and from the eyes and voice I reconstructed a night monkey—a kinkajou.

Then another notch was slipped and the jungle for a time showed something of the exuberance of its life. A paca leaped from its meal of nuts and bounced away with quick, repeated pats; a beetle with wings tuned to the bass clef droned by; some giant tree-cricket tore the remaining intervals of silence to shreds with unmuted wing-fiddles, *cricks* so shrill and high that they well-nigh passed beyond the upper register of my ear out into silence again. The roar of another frog was comforting to my ear-drum.

Then silence descended again, and hours passed in our search for sound or smell of the animal we wished chiefest to find—the giant armadillo. These rare beings have a distinct odor. Months of work in the open had sharpened my nostrils so that on such a tramp as this they were not much inferior to those of Nupee. This sense gave me as keen pleasure as eye or ear, and furnished quite as much information. The odors of city and civilization seemed very far away: gasolene, paint, smoke, perfumery, leather—all these could hardly be recalled. And how absurd seemed society's unwritten taboo on discussion of this admirable but pitifully degenerate sense! Why may you look at your friend's books, touch his collection of *netsukés,* listen to his music, yet dare sniff at naught but his blossoms!

In the open spaces of the earth, and more than anywhere in this conservatory of unblown odors, we come more and more to appreciate and envy a dog's sensitive muzzle. Here we sniffed as naturally as we turned ear, and were able to recognize many of our nasal impressions, and even to follow a particularly strong scent to its source. Few yards of trail but had their distinguishable scent, whether violent, acrid smell or delectable fragrance. Long after a crab-jackal had passed, we noted the stinging, bitter taint in the air; and now and then the pungent wake of some big jungle-bug struck us like a tangible barrier.

The most tantalizing odors were the wonderfully delicate and penetrating ones from some great burst of blossoms, odors heavy with sweetness, which seeped down from vine or tree high overhead, wholly invisible from below even in broad daylight. These odors remained longest in memory, perhaps because they were so completely the product of a single sense. There were others too, which were unforgettable, because, like the voice of the frog, they stirred the memory a fraction before they excited curiosity. Such I found the powerful musk from the bed of leaves which a fawn had just left. For some reason this brought vividly to mind the fearful compound of smells arising from the decks of Chinese junks.

III

Along the moonlit trail there came wavering whiffs of orchids, ranging from attar of roses and carnations to the pungence of carrion, the latter doubtless distilled from as delicate and as beautiful blossoms as the former. There were, besides, the myriad and bewildering smells of sap, crushed leaves, and decaying wood; acrid, sweet, spicy, and suffocating, some like musty books, others recalling the paint on the Noah's Ark of one's nursery.

But the scent of the giant armadillo eluded us. When we waded through some new, strange odor I looked back at Nupee, hoping for some sign that it was the one we sought. But that night the great armored creatures went their way and we ours, and the two did not cross. Nupee showed me a track at the trail-side made long ago, as wide and deep as the spoor of a dinosaur, and I fingered it reverently as I would have touched the imprint of a recently alighted pterodactyl, taking care not to spoil the outlines of the huge claw-marks. All my search for him had been in vain thus far, though I had been so close upon his trail as to have seen fresh blood. I had made up my mind not to give up, but it seemed as if success must wait for another year.

We watched and called the ghostly kinkajous and held them fascinated with our stream of light; we aroused unnamable creatures which squawked companionably at us and rustled the tree-top leaves; we listened to the whispered rush of passing vampires skimming our faces and were soothed by the hypnotic droning hum which beetles left in their swift wake. Finally we turned and circled through side trails so narrow and so dark that we walked with outstretched arms, feeling for the trunks and lianas, choosing a sloth's gait and the hope of new adventures rather than the glare of my flash on our path.

When we entered Kalacoon trail, we headed toward home. Within sight of the first turn a great black branch of a tree had recently fallen across the trail in a patch of moonlight. Before we reached it, the branch had done something it should not have done—it had straightened slightly. We strained our eyes to the utmost but could not, in this eerie light, tell head from tail end of this great serpent. It moved very slowly, and with a motion which perfectly confounded our perception. Its progress seemed no faster than the hour hand of a watch, but we knew that it moved, yet so close to the white sand that the whole trail seemed to move with it. The eye refused to admit any motion except in sudden shifts, like widely separated films of a motion-picture. For minute after minute it seemed quiescent; then we would blink and realize that it was two feet higher up the bank. One thing we could see—a great thickening near the centre of the snake: it had fed recently and to repletion, and slowly it was making its way to some hidden lair, perhaps to lie motionless until another moon should silver the jungle. Was there any stranger life in the world?

Whether it was a giant bushmaster or a constrictor, we could not tell in the diffused light. I allowed it to go unharmed, for the spell of silence and the jungle night was too strongly woven to be shattered again by the crash of gun or rifle. Nupee had been quite willing to remain behind, and now, as so often with my savage friends, he looked at me wonderingly. He did not understand and I could not explain. We were at one in the enjoyment of direct phenomena; we could have passed months of intimate companionship in the wilds as I had done with his predecessors; but at the touch of abstract things, of letting a deadly creature live for any reason except for lack of a gun—then they looked at me always with that puzzled look, that straining to grasp the something which they knew must be there. And at once always followed instant acceptance, unquestioning, without protest. The transition was smooth, direct, complete: the sahib had had opportunity to shoot; he had not done so; what did the sahib wish to do now—to squat longer or go on?

We waited for many minutes at the edge of a small glade, and the event which seemed most significant to me was in actual spectacle one of the last of the night's happenings. I sat with chin on knees, coolie-fashion—a position which, when once mastered, and with muscles trained to withstand the unusual flexion for hour after hour, is one of the most valuable assets of the wilderness lover and the watcher of wild things. It enables one to spend long periods of time in the lowest of umbrella tents, or to rest on wet ground or sharp stones where actual sitting down would be impossible. Thus is one insulated from *bêtes rouges* and enthusiastic ants whose sole motto is eternal preparedness. Thus too one slips, as it were, under the visual guard of human-shy creatures, whose eyes are on the lookout for their enemy at human height. From such a position, a single upward leap prepares one instantly for advance or retreat, either of which manœuvres is well within instant necessity at times. Then there were always the two positions to which one could change if occasion required—flat-footed, with arm-pits on knees, or on the balls of the feet with elbows on knees. Thus is every muscle shifted and relaxed.

Squatting is one of the many things which a white man may learn from watching his *shikarees* and guides, and which, in the wilderness, he may adopt without losing caste. We are a chair-ridden people, and dare hardly even cross our knees in public. Yet how many of us delight in sitting Buddha-fashion, or as near to it as we can attain, when the ban of society is lifted! A chairless people, however, does not necessarily mean a more simple, primitive type. The Japanese method of sitting is infinitely more difficult and complex than ours. The characters of our weak-thighed, neolithic forbears are as yet too pronounced in our own bodies for us to keep an upright position for long. Witness the admirable admittance of this anthropological fact by the architects of our subway cars, who know that only a tithe of their patrons will be fortunate enough to find room on the cane-baked seats which have come to take the place of the stumps and fallen logs of a hundred thousand years ago. So they have thoughtfully strung the upper reaches of the cars with imitation branches and swaying lianas, to which the last-comers cling jealously, and swing with more or less of the grace of their distant forbears. Their fur, to be sure, is rubbed thinner; nuts and fruits have given place to newspapers and novels, and the roar and odors are not those of the wind among the leaves and blossoms. But the simile is amusing enough to end abruptly, and permit individual imagination to complete it.

When I see an overtired waiter or clerk swaying from foot to foot like a rocking elephant, I sometimes place the blame further back than immediate impatience for the striking of the closing hour. It were more true to blame the gentlemen whose habits were formed before caste, whose activities preceded speech.

We may be certain that chairs will never go out of fashion. We are at the end of bodily evolution in that direction. But to see a white-draped, lanky Hindu, or a red-cloaked lama of the hills, quietly fold up, no matter where he may be, is to witness the perfection of chairless rest. One can read or write or doze comfortably, swaying slightly with a bird's unconscious balance, or, as in my case at present, wholly disarm suspicion on the part of the wild creatures by sinking from the height of a man to that of a jungle deer. And still I had lost nothing of the insulation which my moccasins provided from all the inconveniences of the forest floor. Look-

ing at Nupee after this rush of chaotic thoughts which came
between jungle happenings, I chuckled as I hugged my knees,
for I knew that Nupee had noticed and silently considered
my little accomplishment, and that he approved, and I knew
that I had acquired merit in his sight. Thus may we revel
in the approval of our super-servants, but they must never
know it.

From this eulogy of squatting, my mind returned to the
white light of the glade. I watched the motionless leaves
about me, many of them drooping and rich maroon by daylight, for they were just unbudded. Reaching far into the
dark mystery of the upper jungle stretched the air-roots,
held so straight by gravity, so unheeding of the whirling of
the planet through space. Only one mighty liana—a
monkey-ladder—had revolted against this dominance of the
earth's pull and writhed and looped upon itself in fantastic
whorls, while along its length rippled ever the undulations
which mark this uneasy growth, this crystallized Saint Vitus
plant.

A momentary shiver of leaves drew our eyes to the left,
and we began to destroy the optical images evolved by the
moon-shadows and to seek the small reality which we knew
lived and breathed somewhere on that long branch. Then
a sharp crack like a rifle lost whatever it was to us forever,
and we half leaped to our feet as something swept downward
through the air and crashed length after length among the
plants and fallen logs. The branches overhead rocked to and
fro, and for many minutes, like the aftermath of a volcanic
eruption, came a shower, first of twigs and swirling leaves,
then of finer particles, and lastly of motes which gleamed
like silver dust as they sifted down to the trail. When the
air cleared I saw that the monkey-ladder had vanished and
I knew that its yards upon yards of length lay coiled and
crushed among the ferns and sprouting palms of the jungle
floor. It seemed most fitting that the vegetable kingdom, whose silence and majesty gave to the jungle night

its magic qualities, should have contributed this memorable climax.

Long before the first Spaniard sailed up the neighboring river, the monkey-ladder had thrown its spirals aloft, and through all the centuries, all the years, it had seen no change wrought beneath it. The animal trail was trod now and then by Indian hunters, and lately we had passed several times. The sound of our guns was less than the crashing fall of an occasional forest tree. Now, with not a leaf moved by the air, with only the two of us squatting in the moonlight for audience, the last cell had given way. The sap could no longer fight the decay which had entered its heart; and at the appointed moment, the moment set by the culmination of a greater nexus of forces than our human mind could ever hope to grasp, the last fibre parted and the massive growth fell.

In the last few minutes, as it hung suspended, gracefully spiraled in the moonlight, it had seemed as perfect as the new-sprouted *moras* at my feet. As I slowly walked out of the jungle I saw in this the explanation of the simile of artificial scenery, of all the strange magic which had come to me as I entered. The alchemy of moonlight turned all the jungle to perfect growth, growth at rest. In the silvery light was no trace of gnawing worm, of ravening ant, or corroding fungus. The jungle was rejuvenated and made a place more wonderful than any fairyland of which I have read or which I have conceived. The jungle by day, as I have said—that, too, is wonderful. We may have two friends, quite unlike in character, whom we love each for his own personality, and yet it would be a hideous, an unthinkable thing to see one transformed into the other.

So, with the mist settling down and tarnishing the great plaque of silver, I left the jungle, glad that I could be far away before the first hint of dawn came to mar the magic. Thus in memory I can keep the dawn away until I return.

And sometime in the future, when the lure of the full moon

comes, and I answer, I shall be certain of finding the same
silence, the same wonderful light, and the waiting trees and
the magic. But Nupee may not be there. He will perhaps
have slipped into memory, with Drojak and Aladdin. And
if I find no one as silently friendly as Nupee, I shall have to
watch alone through my jungle night.

THE HUMOUR OF THE PUBLIC *

By Max Beerbohm

THEY often tell me that So-and-so has no sense of humour.
Lack of this sense is everywhere held to be a horrid disgrace,
nullify any number of delightful qualities. Perhaps the most
effective means of disparaging an enemy is to lay stress on his
integrity, his erudition, his courage, the fineness of his head,
the grace of his figure, his strength of purpose, which has
overleaped all obstacles, his goodness to his parents, the kind
word that he has for every one, his musical voice, his freedom
from aught that in human nature is base; and then to say
what a pity it is that he has no sense of humour. Perfection
is not loved in this imperfect world; so that the more highly
you extol any one, the more eagerly will your audience accept
anything you may have to say against him. And what could
match for deadliness the imputation of being without sense
of humour? To convict a man of that lack is to strike him
with one blow to a level with the beasts of the field—to kick
him, once and for all, outside the human pale. What is it
that mainly distinguishes us from the brute creation? That
we walk erect? Some brutes are bipeds. That we do not slay
one another? We do. That we build houses? So do they.
That we remember and reason? So, again, do they. That
we converse? They are chatterboxes, whose lingo we are not
sharp enough to master. On no possible point of superiority
can we preen ourselves, save this: that we can laugh, and
that they, with one notable exception, cannot.

Belief in the general humorousness of the human race is

* From *Yet Again;* published, 1923, by Alfred A. Knopf, Inc.
Reprinted by permission of the publishers.

more deep-rooted for that every man is certain that he himself is not without sense of humour. A man will admit cheerfully that he does not know one tune from another, or that he cannot discriminate the vintages of wines. The blind beggar does not seek to benumb sympathy by telling his patrons how well they are looking. The deaf and dumb do not scruple to converse in signals. 'Have you no sense of beauty?' I said to a friend who in the Academia of Florence suggested that we had stood long enough in front of the 'Primavera.' 'No!' was his simple, straightforward, quite un-answerable answer. But I have never heard a man assert that he had no sense of humour. And I take it that no such assertion ever was made. Moreover, were it made it would be a lie. Every man laughs. Frequently or infrequently, the corners of his mouth are drawn up into his cheeks, and through his parted lips comes his own particular variety, soft or loud, of that noise which is called laughter. Fre-quently or infrequently, every man is amused by something. Every man has a sense of humour, but not every man has the same sense. A may be incapable of smiling at what has convulsed B, and B may stare blankly when he hears what has rolled A off his chair. Jokes are so diverse that no one man can see them all. The very fact that he can see one kind is proof positive that certain other kinds will be invisible to him. And so egoistic in his judgment is the average man that he is apt to suspect of being humourless any one whose sense of humour squares not with his own. But the suspicion is always false, incomparably useful though it is in the form of an accusation.

Having no love for the public, I have often accused that body of having no sense of humour. Conscience pricks me to atonement. Let me withdraw my oft-made imputation, and show its hollowness by examining with you, reader (who are, of course, no more a member of the public than I am), what are the main features of that sense of humour which the public does undoubtedly possess.

The word 'public' must, like all collective words, be used with caution. When we speak of our hair, we should remember not only that the hairs on our head are all numbered, but also that there is a *catalogue raisonné* in which every one of those hairs is shown to be in some respect unique. Similarly, let us not forget that 'public' denotes a collection not of identical units, but of units separable and (under close scrutiny) distinguishable one from another. I have said that not every man has the same sense of humour. I might have said truly that no two men have the same sense of humour, for that no two men have the same brain and heart and experience, by which things the sense of humour is formed and directed. One joke may go round the world tickling myriads, but no two persons will be tickled in precisely the same way, to precisely the same degree. If the vibrations of inward or outward laughter could be (as some day, perhaps, they will be) scientifically registered, differences between them all would be made apparent to us. 'Oh,' is your cry whenever you hear something that especially amuses you. 'I must tell that to' whomever you credit with a sense of humour most akin to your own. And the chances are that you will be disappointed by his reception of the joke. Either he will laugh less loudly than you hoped, or he will say something which reveals to you that it amuses him and you not in quite the same way. Or perhaps he will laugh so long and loudly that you are irritated by the suspicion that you have not yourself gauged the full beauty of it· In one of his books (I do not remember which), though they, too, I suppose, are all numbered) Mr. Andrew Lang tells a story that has always delighted and always will delight me. He was in a railway-carriage, and his travelling-companions were two strangers, two silent ladies, middle-aged. The train stopped at Nuneaton. The two ladies exchanged a glance. One of them sighed, and said, 'Poor Eliza! She had reason to remember Nuneaton!' . . . That is all. But how much! how deli-ciously and memorably much! How infinite a span of conjecture is in those dots which I have just made! And yet, would you believe me? some of my most intimate friends, the people most like to myself, see little or nothing of the loveliness of that pearl of price. Perhaps you *would* believe me. That is the worst of it: one never knows. The most sensitive intelligence cannot predict how will be appraised its any treasure by its how near soever kin.

This sentence, which I admit to be somewhat mannered, has the merit of bringing me straight to the point at which I have been aiming: that, though the public is composed of distinct units, it may roughly be regarded as a single entity. Precisely because you and I have sensitive intelligences, we cannot postulate certainly anything about each other. The higher an animal be in grade, the more numerous and recondite are the points in which its organism differs from that of its peers. The lower the grade, the more numerous and obvious the points of likeness. By 'the public' I mean that vast number of human animals who are in the lowest grade of intelligence. (Of course, this classification is made without reference to social 'classes.' The public is recruited from the upper, the middle, and the lower class. That the recruits come mostly from the lower class is because the lower class is still the least well-educated· That they come in as high proportion from the middle class as from the less well-educated upper class, is because the 'young Barbarians,' reared in a more gracious environment, often acquire a grace of mind which serves them as well as would mental keenness.) Whereas in the highest grade, to which you and I belong, the fact that a thing affects you in one way is no guarantee that it will not affect me in another, a thing which affects one man of the lowest grade in a particular way is likely to affect all the rest very similarly. The public's sense of humour may be regarded roughly as one collective sense.

It would be impossible for any one of *us* to define what are the things that amuse him. For him the wind of humour bloweth where it listeth. He finds his jokes in the unlikeliest places. Indeed, it is only there he finds them at all. A thing that is labelled 'comic' chills his sense of humour instantly—perceptibly lengthens his face. A joke that has not a serious background, or some serious connexion, means nothing to him. Nothing to him, the crude jape of the professional jester. Nothing to him, the jangle of the bells in the wagged cap, the thud of the swung bladder. Nothing, the joke that hits him violently in the eye, or pricks him with a sharp point. The jokes that he loves are those quiet jokes which have no apparent point—the jokes which never can surrender their secret, and so can never pall. His humour is an indistinguishable part of his soul, and the things that stir it are indistinguishable from the world around him. But to the primitive and untutored public, humour is a harshly definite affair. The public can achieve no delicate process of discernment in humour. Unless a joke hits it in the eye, drawing forth a shower of illuminative sparks, all is darkness. Unless a joke be labelled 'Comic! Come! why don't you laugh?' the public is quite silent. Violence and obviousness are thus the essential factors. The surest way of making a thing obvious is to provide it in some special place, at some special time. It is thus that humour is provided for the public, and thus that it is easy for the student to lay his hand on materials for an analysis of the public's sense of humour. The obviously right plan for the student is to visit the music halls from time to time and to buy the comic papers. Neither these halls nor these papers will amuse him directly through their art, but he will instruct himself better from them than from any other source, for they are the authentic sources of the public laughter. Let him hasten to patronise them.

He will find that I have been there before him. The music halls I have known for many years. I mean, of course, the real old-fashioned music halls, not those depressing palaces where you see by grace of a biograph things that you have

seen much better, and without a headache, in the street, and
pitiable animals being forced to do things which Nature has
forbidden them to do—things which we can do so much better
than they, without any trouble. Heaven defend me from those
meaningless palaces! But the little old music halls have
always attracted me by their unpretentious raciness, their
quaint monotony, the reality of the enjoyment on all those
stolidly rapt faces in the audience. Without that monotony
there would not be the same air of general enjoyment, the
same constant guffaws, that monotony is the secret of the success of music halls. It is not enough for the public to know
that everything is meant to be funny, that laughter is craved
for every point in every 'turn.' A new kind of humour,
however obvious and violent, might take the public unawares,
and be received in silence. The public prefers always that
the old well-tested and well-seasoned jokes be cracked for it.
Or rather, not the same old jokes, but jokes on the same old
subjects. The quality of the joke is of slight import in comparison with its subject. It is the matter, rather than the
treatment, that counts, in the art of the music hall. Some
subjects have come to be recognized as funny. Two or three
of them crop up in every song, and before the close of the
evening all of them will have cropped up many times. I speak
with authority, as an earnest student of the music halls. Of
comic papers I know less. They have never allured me. They
are not set to music—an art for whose cheaper and more
primitive forms I have very real sensibility; and I am not, as
I peruse one of them, privy to the public's delight: my copy
cannot be shared with me by hundreds of people whose mirth
is wonderful to see and hear. And the bare contents are not
such as to enchant me· However, for the purposes of this
essay, I did go to a bookstall and buy as many of these papers
as I could see—a terrific number, a terrific burden to stagger
away with.

I have gone steadily through them, one by one. My main
impression is of wonder and horror at the amount of hebdo-

madal labor implicit in them. Who writes for them? Who
does the drawings for them—those thousands of little drawings, week by week, so neatly executed? To think that daily
and nightly, in so many an English home, in a room sacred
to the artist, sits a young man inventing and executing designs for *Chippy Snips!* To think how many a proud mother
must be boasting to her friends: 'Yes, Edward is doing wonderfully well—more than fulfilling the hopes we always had
of him. Did I tell you that the editor of *Natty Tips* has
written asking him to contribute to his paper? I believe I
have the letter on me. Yes, here it is,' etc., etc.! The awful
thing is that many of the drawings in these comic papers are
done with very real skill. Nothing is sadder than to see the
hand of an artist wasted by alliance to a vacant mind, a
common spirit. I look through these drawings, conceived
all so tritely and stupidly, so hopelessly and helplessly, yet
executed—many of them—so very well indeed, and I sigh
over the haphazard way in which mankind is made. However, my concern is not with the tragedy of these draughts-
men, but with the specific forms taken by their humour.
Some of them deal in a broad spirit with the world-comedy,
limiting themselves to no set of funny subjects, finding inspiration in the habits and manners of men and women at
large. 'HE WON HER' is the title appended to a picture of
a young lady and the gentleman seated in a drawing-room,
and the libretto runs thus: *'Mabel:* Last night I dreamt of
a most beautiful woman. *Harold:* Rather a coincidence. I
dreamt of you, too, last night.' I have selected this as a
typical example of the larger style. This style, however,
occupies but a small space in the bulk of the newspapers
that lie before me. As in the music halls, so in these papers,
the entertainment consists almost entirely of variations on
certain ever-recurring themes. I have been at pains to draw
up a list of these themes. I think it is exhaustive. If any
fellow-student detect an omission, let him communicate with
me. Meanwhile, here is my list:—

Mothers-in-law
Hen-pecked husbands
Twins
Old maids
Jews
Frenchmen, Germans, Italians, Negroes (*not Russians, or other foreigners of any denomination*)
Fatness
Thinness
Long hair (*worn by a man*)
Baldness
Sea-sickness
Stuttering
Bad cheese
'*Shooting the moon*' (*slang expression for leaving a lodging-house without paying the bill*).

You might argue that one week's budget of comic papers is no real criterion—that the recurrence of these themes may be fortuitous. My answer to that objection is that this list coincides exactly with a list which (before studying these papers) I had made of the themes commonest, during the past few years, in the music halls. This twin list, which results from separate study of the two chief forms of public entertainment, may be taken as a sure guide to the goal of our inquiry.

Let us try to find some unifying principle, or principles, among the variegated items. Take the first item—*Mothers-in-law*. Why should the public roar, as roar it does, at the mere mention of that relationship? There is nothing intrinsically absurd in the notion of a woman with a married daughter. It is probable that she will sympathise with her daughter in any quarrel that may arise between husband and wife. It is probable, also, that she will, as a mother, demand for her daughter more unselfish devotion than the daughter herself expects. But this does not make her ridiculous. The public laughs not at her, surely. It always respects a tyrant. It laughs at the implied concept of the oppressed son-in-law, who has to wage unequal warfare against two women. It is amused by the notion of his embarrassment. It is amused by suffering. This explanation covers, of course, the second item on my list—*Hen-pecked husbands*. It covers, also, the third and fourth items. The public is amused by the notion of a needy man put to double expense, and of a woman who has had no chance of fulfilling her destiny. The laughter at Jews, too, may be a survival of the old Jew-baiting spirit. Or this laughter may be explained by that fact which alone can explain why the public laughs at *Frenchmen, Germans, Italians, Negroes*. Jews, after all, are foreigners, strangers, and the public has never got used to them. The only apparent reason why it laughs at the notion of *Frenchmen,* etc., is that they are unlike itself. (At the mention of *Russians and other foreigners* it does not laugh, because it has no idea what they are like: it has seen too few samples of them.)

So far, then, we have found two elements in the public's humour: delight in suffering, contempt for the unfamiliar. The former motive is the more potent. It accounts for the popularity of all the other items: *extreme fatness, extreme thinness, baldness, sea-sickness, stuttering,* and (as entailing distress for the landlady) *'shooting the moon.'* The motive of contempt for the unfamiliar accounts for *long hair* (*worn by a man*). Remains one item unexplained. How can mirth possibly be evoked by the notion of *bad cheese?* Having racked my brains for the solution, I can but conjecture that it must be the mere ugliness of the thing. Why any one should be amused by mere ugliness I cannot conceive. Delight in cruelty, contempt for the unfamiliar, I can understand, though I cannot admire them. They are invariable elements in children's sense of humour, and it is natural that the public, as being unsophisticated, should laugh as children laugh. But any nurse will tell you that children are frightened by ugliness. Why, then, is the public amused by it? I know not. The laughter at *bad cheese* I abandon as a mystery. I pitch it among such other insoluble problems as *Why does the public laugh when an actor and actress in a quite serious play kiss each other? Why does it laugh when a meal is eaten on the stage? Why does it laugh when any actor has to say 'damn'?*

If they cannot be solved soon, such problems never will be solved. For Mr. Forster's Act will soon have had time to make apparent its effects; and the public will proudly display a sense of humour as sophisticated as our own.

ON "AND" *

By Hilaire Belloc

Dark eyes adventure bring: the blue, serene,
Do promise Paradise—and yours are green.

THIS little jewel—called "The Lover's Complaint"—is ascribed by some to Herrick. They are wrong. It proceeds from a younger but already faltering pen.

I introduce it only at the head of this to illustrate the singular depth, the weight, the value of the word "and." Even in the English tongue, the noblest vehicle of expression (but in this point weak), the word "and" plays its subtle parts.

We lack the double "and" of antiquity—that subtle repetitive effect in which the classics abound. We have no *"que"* to our *"et"*; we have no τε to our καὶ we have only our plain "and." But even so, our plain "and" has much diversity about it: a versatile, mercurial word: a knight in the chess play of prose.

"How is this?" you say. " 'And' would seem to be but a redundant word to express some addition already apparent."

" 'He was drunk, disorderly !' 'And' would seem to be stuck in between the two affirmations from a sort of laziness of the mind."

You are wrong. It is a great pleasure to me to tell you that you are wrong.

Even if "and" only pursued this function of letting the mind repose it might be welcomed as a bed; but it does much more. It introduces emphasis, as in the poignant sentence: "Their choice was turbot—and boiled." It also has an elevating effect, hooking up something to the level of the rest; as where it is written:

> Nibbity, bibbity, bobbity bo!—
> *And* the little brown bowl—
> We'll drink to the Barley Mow!

The little brown bowl would have come in absurdly: it would have jolted the mind like a bump in the road, were it not for that precious little "and," which catches it neatly up, putting upon one level that which goes before with that which comes after.

"And" is also indicative. Thus a man whom you meet talks glibly upon one subject after another, rapidly, yet more rapidly, tumbling over himself, desiring to avoid your eye. But he must take breath. You seize your moment and you say, "And what about that five pounds?" The "and" makes all the difference. It makes your remark part of the conversation. A gesture, not a blow.

In the same way you can recall an omitted name. When you have praised Tom, Dick, Harry, you add gently, "And Jack, what about Jack?" It is a pleasant, easy reproach or a reminder. Very much nicer than saying, "Why not a word about Jack?"—which would be brutal.

"And" is also what the older grammarians have called stammerative—that is, it fills a chasm in the public speeches of public men, though here it is not so useful as certain other sounds. I have made a study of the sounds common to politicians in distress. I find that out of one hundred occasions "er—er" will come in eighty times; "I—I—I" eleven times; the less graceful "and . . . , and . . . , and" during periods of embarrassment only accounts for five. Moreover, the repeated "and" is hardly ever used in the absolute; by public speakers it is nearly always used with "er."

"And" also has the value of an affix. It comes before a lot of little phrases, where it acts like glue, sticking that little phrase on to the rest—"and" if, "and" even, "and" though; a humble use, but necessary enough, allowing the mind to work in a soft material.

"And" has various rhetorical uses which are to be admired —you can make long lists with it.

So attractive is "and" to the human mind that it will often expand itself, developing like a lot of soap bubbles—"and so," "and moreover," "and also." But the best of all these phrases—the king of them—is "and also, what is more." It is the most familiar of all phrases in the mouths of politicians. Do violence to yourself, force yourself to listen to a politician making speeches in private conversation as is the politician's way. You will hear that phrase repeated. "And also, what is more." It is native to the tub-thumping fraternity. These things give a sentence the advantage of piling up wordy wealth, as it were, very satisfactory to the fatigued or the empty or the hesitant.

Those great men, our fathers, felt about "and" something reverend or peculiar, so that they hardly thought of it as a word, but as a sort of symbol. They put it at the end of the alphabet, calling it "ampersand." It is one of the worst things about our detestable time that this ancient national thing "ampersand" is forgotten. The old refrain used to be: a, b, c, . . . , x, y, z, *ampersand*—that long word "ampersand," that fine ritual title, referred to the symbol "&" which "and" alone of words possesses. You find it in the old horn books. The children of England knew it by heart for centuries. But the modern flood came: it is gone.

The enemies of "and" will have it that a good style in English is to be obtained by cutting out "and." These are the same people who say that a good style is to be obtained by cutting out adjectives. There are no such short cuts.

Also, to be an enemy of "and" is to be an enemy of all good things. It is to fear exuberance, which is the tide of life.

"And" has, again, rhythmical value, as in the ecclesiastical or liturgical line:

And Parson and Clerk and the Devil and all

—with hosts of other lines which dignify the vast storehouse of the English lyric.

Of the modern masterpieces there is one—the best known of all, perhaps—where "and" does an enormous amount of work, which is the poem of *Innisfree*. It gives the rhythm as well as the mystery. I should like to see what the fools who are for cutting out "and" would make of that poem.

But the most sublime use of "and," alas! we have not. It is the "and" disjunctive; on which turned one of the great moments of history.

For you must know that when the second Council of Nicea finally condemned the monstrosities of the Iconoclasts, a saintly bishop from Cyprus wrote his opinion in Greek saying, "I revere, I embrace the sacred images, και I give worship to the Life-giving Trinity"—which is as much as to say, that he would be polite enough to an image, *but* his worship he reserved for the only true object of worship.

Now, this pronouncement was carried to a Council of the West, sitting at Frankfort, where there were bishops of the Pyrenees, of Gaul, of the Rhine Valley, of the Low Countries, of the Burgundian Hills, of the Swiss Mountains—indeed of all parts whatsoever that owed allegiance to Charlemagne.

At that moment Charlemagne was already wishing to be an emperor in the West. Those who served him were only too glad to find the Empire of the East—which claimed to be universal—making a howler. But the swarm of holy and unholy men at Frankfort were abominably ignorant of Greek. They did not understand the disjunctive value of και. They thought it a mere barbaric "and." They translated this

famous phrase "I jumble up in one worship God and images."
They rushed out with some fury against such a doctrine.
They registered their hatred of it. On this point also Gibbon
has (as one might expect) abominably falsified history. . . .
But no matter.

The Bishops of Frankfort said what they had to say. In
vain did those of Rome, who were acquainted with Greek,
tell them that they had taken the sentence exactly upside
down—that it meant "I do *not* worship the images. I distinguish the observance I give them from the worship I offer
to That which alone is worthy of worship." They still clung
to their primitive error. With difficulty were they led back
into the right fold.

What great consequences their ignorance might have had!
We might to-day be deprived of the Bambino. We might
have lost Brou (but not Santiago, I think; for the Spaniards,
and in particular the Galicians, are of a temper which will
stand no nonsense. Though 1462 General Councils had condemned images, the Spaniard would have had them all the
same: in which I praise him. Honour to the Pilar!).

Now, though it does not concern the little word "and," yet
I am reminded (by this mention of the Second Council of
Nicea) of a certain story which, as you may not previously
have heard it, I will now proceed to relate. With that story
I shall conclude; nor will your prayers and entreaties, however loud and passionate, move me to continue. I will tell
you the story; then I will have done.

The story is this. As the Eastern bishops were travelling
to the second Council of Nicea, the more worldly of them
(these were the greater part) were very much disgusted to
meet one particularly good bishop who had been bred a shepherd. He was poor. His manners were bad. He did not
shave regularly. He was badly dressed. He was what they
call in Birmingham "no class."

They jeered at him a little, but more than their jeering
was their fear lest they should lose caste by entering the

Imperial City in such company. So after this saintly man had made himself quite intolerable at dinner, they cast up a plot against him.

He had come with only one deacon, sitting each of them upon a mule, the one a brown mule, the other mottled. The mules were stabled in the great inn of the village where all were assembled. When the saintly, but not smart, bishop had gone to his rest, the smart bishops secretly sent a bravo into the stable to cut off the heads of the two mules. "In this way," said these wicked, worldly bishops, "we shall be spared the humiliating presence of the boor when we enter the imperial town; nor will men ever know that we kept such low company."

Long before it was dawn the poor Bishop's deacon, like a good deacon, a good rustic deacon, shook himself out of sleep. He went down to the stable with a lantern to get ready the beasts against the morning journey. With what horror did he not see there two heads lying upon the ground! The one was of his own mottled mule, the other of his master's brown mule. The mottled head lay severed upon the straw beside the brown head, the headless trunks leaning all collapsed against the stall sides.

The deacon, rushing up to his master, banged at the door, saying, "My Lord! My Lord! Evil men have cut off our mules' heads!" The Right Reverend, only half awake, said, "Sew them on again! When I wake I will attend to it."

The deacon went down to the stable. With many tears he sewed on the two heads of the dead mules. The Bishop, when he had arisen from sleep, said his prayers, came down into the stable, where, he having blessed the two mules, they came to life again in the most natural manner in the world. When he had breakfasted, he rejoined his deacon. Mounting the two beasts, they rode out into the break of the day. But, the light broadening as they approached the city gate, the crowd saw with astonishment a brown mule with a mottled head abreast of a mottled mule with a brown head, for the deacon, confused in the half darkness of the morning, had sewed the wrong heads to the wrong bodies.

Note the effect—as the veracious chronicler gives it. "Thus by that very action whereby these evil men had hoped to bring their companion to shame they did but the rather thrust him into glory; for their cruelty to the dumb beasts did but serve to heighten his holiness, making proof of God's power through him who could bring the dead to life."

Many are the morals of this tale, one of which is that it is silly to take more trouble than is necessary. For if the wicked Bishops had only drugged the mules instead of cutting their heads right off there would have been no miracle, nor glory to their despised colleague. Another is that if a thing is true you must believe it, however astonishing and unlikely it may sound in the ear of the unbeliever. Another is that a bishop has the right to get up rather later than the lower branches of the hierarchy. There are many other morals; but I will end. For if I go on I shall certainly bring "and" into my own sentences, *which up to this point I have managed to avoid.* "And" is not really necessary at all.

A LITTLE DEBIT IN YOUR TONNEAU *

BY ROBERT C. BENCHLEY

MOTORISTS, as a class, are not averse to public discussion of their troubles. In fact, one often wonders how some of them ever get time to operate their cars, so tied up do they seem to be with these little experience-meetings, at which one man tells, with appropriate gestures, how he ran out of gas between Springfield and Worcester, while another gives a perfect bit of character acting to show just how the policeman on the outskirts of Trenton behaved.

But there seems to be one phase of the motorist's trials which he never bares to the public. He will confide to you just how bad the gasoline was that he bought at the country garage; he will make it an open secret that he had four blow-outs on the way home from the country-club; but of one of his most poignant sorrows he never speaks. I refer to the guests who snuggle in his tonneau.

Probably more irritations have arisen from the tonneau than from the tires, day in and day out, and yet you never hear a man say, "Well, I certainly had an unholy crew of camp-followers out with me to-day—friends of my wife." Say what you will, there is an innate delicacy in the average motorist, or such repression could not be.

Consider the types of tonneau guests. They are as generic and fundamental as the spectrum and you will find them in Maine and New Mexico at the same time.

* From *Of All Things!* copyright, 1921, by Henry Holt and Company. Reprinted by permission of the author and the publishers.

There is the first, or major, classification, which may be designated as the Financially Paralyzed. Persons in this class, on stepping into your machine, automatically transfer all their money troubles to you. You become, for the duration of the ride, whether it be to the next corner or to Palm Beach, their financial guardian, and any little purchases which are incidental to the trip (such as three meals a day) belong to your "list of running expenses." There seems to be something about the motion of the automobile that inhibits their ability to reach for their purses, and they become, if you want to be poetical about it, like clay in the hands of the potter. Whither thou goest they will go; thy check-book is their check-book. It is just like the one great, big, jolly family—of which you are the father and backer.

Such people always make a great to-do about starting off on a trip. You call for them and they appear at the window and wave, to signify that they see you, and go through motions to show that just as soon as Clara has put on her leggings they will be down. Soon they appear, swathed in a tremendous quantity of motor wraps and veils (you can usually tell the guests in a car by the number of head-veils they wear) and get halfway down the walk, when Clara remembers her rain-coat and has to swish back upstairs, veils and all. Out again, and just as they get wedged into the tonneau, the elderly guest wonders if there is time for some one to run in again and tell Helma that if the Salvation Army man comes for the old magazines she is to tell him to come again to-morrow. By the time this message is relayed to Helma Garcia one solid half-hour has been dissipated from the cream of the morning. This does not prevent the guests from remarking, as the motor starts, that it certainly is a heavenly day and that it couldn't have been better if it had been ordered. Knowing the type, you can say to yourself that if the day *had* been ordered you know who would have had to give the order and pay the check.

From that time on, you are the moneyed interest behind

the venture. Meals at road-houses, toll charges, evening papers, hot chocolates at the country drug store, hair net for Clara, and, of course, a liberal injection of gasoline on the way home, all of these items and about fourteen others come in your bailiwick. The guests have been asked out for a ride, and "findings is keepings." If you have money enough to run a car, you probably have money enough to support them for a day or so. That's only fair, isn't it?

Under a sub-head (a), in this same category, come the guests who are stricken with *rigor mortis* when there are any repairs to be made about the machine. Male offenders in this line are, of course, the only ones that can be dealt with here; putting on a tire is no job for women and children. But the man who is the life of the party in the tonneau throughout the trip, who thinks nothing of climbing all over the back of the car in imitation of a Roman charioteer, will suddenly become an advocate of the basic eight-hour working day which began just eight hours before, whenever there is a man's work to be done on one of the tires. He will watch you while you work, and always has a good word to say or a quip to snap at you to keep you cheered up, but when it comes to taking off his coat and lending a hand at the jack he is an Oriental incense-holder on the guest-room mantel. He admits in no uncertain tones, that he is a perfect dub when it comes to handling machinery and that he is more apt to be in the way at a time like this than not. And maybe he is right, after all.

We next come to the class of tonneau-freight who are great believers in what Professor Muensterberg called "Auto-Suggestion." These people, although not seated in the driver's seat, have their own ideas on driving and spare no pains to put their theories in the form of suggestions. In justice to the Great Army of the Unemployed known as "guests" it must be admitted that a large percentage of these suggestions emanate from some member of the owner's family and not from outsiders. It is very often Mrs. Wife who is off-side in this play, but as she is usually in the tonneau, she comes under the same classification.

There are various ways of framing suggestions to the driver from the back seat. They are all equally annoying. Among the best are:

"For heaven's sake, George, turn in a little. There is a car behind that wants to pass us."

"Look out where you're going, Stan."

"Henry, if you don't slow down I'm going to get out and take the train back home."

If this is accompanied by a clutching gesture at the driver's arm it is sure to throw him into a good humor for the rest of the trip, so that a good time will be had by all present.

Although guests are not so prone to make suggestions on the running of the car as are those who, through the safety of family connection, may do so without fear of bodily assault from the driver, nevertheless, a guest may, according to the code, lean over the back of the seat and slip little hints as to the route. Especially if one of them be entrusted with a Blue Book does this form of auto-suggestion become chronic.

"It says here that we should have taken that road to the right back there by the Soldiers' Monument," informs the reader over your shoulder. Or—

"Somehow this doesn't seem like the right road. Personally, I think that we ought to turn around and go back to the cross-roads."

If it is Mrs. Wife in the tonneau who has her own ideas on the route, you might as well give in at her first suggestion, for the risk that she is right is too great to run. If she says that she would advise taking the lane that runs around behind that schoolhouse, take it. Then, if it turns out to be a blind alley, you have the satisfaction of saying nothing, very eloquently and effectively. But if you refuse to take her suggestion, and *your* road turns out to be even halfway wrong, you might as well turn the wheel over to your little son and go South for the winter, for you will never hear the ultimate cry of triumph. Your season will practically be ruined. I can quote verbatim from the last affair of this kind:

(Voice from the tonneau) : "Albert, I think we ought to have taken the road at the left."

"No we hadn't."

"I'm sure of it. I saw a sign which said 'Paxton' on it."

"No, you didn't."

"Well, you wait and see."

"I'm waiting."

There is a silence for ten minutes, while the car jounces along a road which gets narrower and rockier.

(Voice from the tonneau) : "I suppose you think this is the way to Paxton?"

"I certainly *do*."

"Oh, you make me sick!"

Silence and jounces.

Sudden stop as the road ends at a silo.

"I beg your pardon [addressed to a rustic], which is the road to Paxton?"

"Paxton?"

"Yes."

"The road to Paxton?"

"Yes."

"Well, you go back over the rud you just come over, about three mile, till you come to a rud turnin' off to the right with a sign which says 'Paxton.' "

(Voice from the tonneau, beginning at this point and continuing all of the way back, all the rest of the day and night and until snow falls) : *"There!* what did I tell you? But, oh no, you know it all. Didn't I tell you"—etc., etc.

On the whole, it would seem that the artists who draw the automobile advertisements make a mistake in drawing the tonneau so roomy and so full of people. There should be no tonneau.

FURNACE AND I *

By Ralph Bergengren

SUMMER is the favorite time to advertise furnaces, for, although a pacifist might argue that being prepared for cold weather encourages frost, the practical persons who make and sell heating plants are firm believers in preparedness. They produce diagrams and pictures, showing how *their* furnace bisects the coal bill, and how easily a pretty child can run it from the front hall.

But my furnace is different. I defy the prettiest child imaginable to run it. Indeed, in a strict sense, I defy anybody to run it; for this furnace has a mind of its own and an odd ambition to behave like a thermometer· On a warm day it goes up, on a cold day it goes down; in zero weather it takes all the time of a determined man to head it off from becoming a large, inconvenient refrigerator. As for bisecting coal bills, the creature *likes coal*. I have even thought that it uttered strange, self-congratulatory, happy noises whenever there occurred a rise in the price of its favorite edible.

Before meeting this furnace I had lived in apartments, and my mental conception of a ton of coal had been as of something enormous, sufficient to heat the average house a month. A furnace was to me a remote mystery operated by a high priest called 'janitor,' whom I vaguely connected with the lines of Smollett,—

* From *The Comforts of Home;* copyright, 1918, by The Atlantic Monthly Press, Inc. Reprinted by permission of the author and the publishers.

Th' Hesperian dragon not more fierce and fell;
Nor the gaunt, growling janitor of Hell.

I took my heat as a matter of course. If I wanted more of it,
I spoke warmly to the janitor through a speaking tube, and—
after a while—there was more heat. If I wanted less, I
spoke to him coldly, in the same distant, godlike way, and
—after a while—there was less heat. In neither case, I
discovered, did an ordinary tone of voice get any result whatever; and, although a fat man himself, he sometimes growled
back through the tube very much like the gaunt specimen
mentioned by Smollett. But I gave little thought to him.
I had what is called an 'intelligent idea' that to produce
more heat he opened a 'draft,' and to reduce heat he closed it,
the effect of a draft on a furnace being just the opposite to
its effect on a janitor. At night he 'shook the furnace down,'
in the morning he 'shook the furnace up.' One gathers such
knowledge casually, without conscious effort or realization.
I had in fact no more curiosity about the furnace than about
the sun, for I seemed as unlikely to run one heater as the
other.

Then, like many another man who has lived in apartments,
I turned suburbanite. I had a furnace, and I had to run it
myself. How well I remember that autumn day when I
started my first furnace fire!

There sat the monster on the floor of the cellar, impassive
as Buddha, and apparently holding up the house with as many
arms as an octopus—hollow arms through which presently
would flow the genial heat. I peeked cautiously through
a little door into his stomach, and marveled at its hollow im-
mensity. I reached in till my arm ached—and my hand
dangled in empty space. But my intelligence told me that
there must be a bottom. Crumbling a newspaper into a great
wad, I dropped it down, down into the monster's gullet,
where it vanished forever. I crumpled and dropped another;
I continued, until at last—oh, triumph of mind and industry

over incalculable depth!—I *saw newspaper,* and had something tangible on which to erect a pyre of kindlings. Where I could reach I laid them crosswise, and where I couldn't I tossed them in at varying angles, gaining skill with practice.

'It is like a great wooden nest!' cried I in astonishment. '*Now* I know why the coal I have bought for my furnace is called "egg." '

I lit the fire and made a grand smoke.

It rose through the kindlings; it piled out through the little door; it hung like great cobwebs to the roof of the cellar. With great presence of mind I hastily closed the little door and ran lightly up the cellar-stairs. The smoke had preceded me; it got there first through the registers; and more was coming.

I met a woman.

'*Is* the house afire?' she asked excitedly.

I calmed her. 'It is *not,*' I replied quietly, in a matter-of-course way. 'When you start a fire for the winter it always smokes a little.'

We opened the windows. We went outside and looked at the house. It leaked smoke through every crevice except, curiously enough, the chimney. Ah-h-h-h-h! I saw what had happened. I groped my way to the cellar and opened the back damper. Now the smoke went gladly up the chimney, and the view through the little door was at once beautiful and awful: it was like looking into the heart of an angry volcano. Evidently it was time to lay the eggs on the nest.

I shoveled the abyss full of coal, and the volcano became extinct. Presently, instead of a furnace full of fire, I had a furnace full of egg coal. I began taking it out, egg by egg, at first with my fingers and then with the tongs from the dining-room fireplace. And when the woman idly questioned me as to what I was going to do down cellar with the tongs, I bit my lips.

To the man who runs it (an absurd term as applied to a thing that has no legs and weighs several tons) the furnace is his first thought in the morning and his last thought at night. His calendar has but two seasons—winter, when the furnace is going, and summer, when the furnace is out. But in summer his thoughts are naturally more philosophical. He sees how profoundly this recent invention (which he is not at the time running) has changed man's attitude toward nature.

I am, of course, not referring to those furnaces which are endowed with more than the average human intelligence; those superfurnaces which are met with in the advertisements, which shake themselves down, shovel their own coal, carry and sift their own ashes, regulate their own draughts, and, if they do not actually order and pay for their own coal, at least consume it as carefully as if they did.

With a furnace like mine a man experiences all the emotions of which he is capable. He loves, he hates, he admires, he despises, he grieves, he exults. There have been times when I have felt like patting my furnace; and again, times when I have slammed his little door and spoken words to him far, far hotter than the fire that smouldered and refused to burn in his bowels. I judge from what I have read that taming a wild animal must be a good deal like taming a furnace, with one important exception: the wild-animal-tamer never loses his temper or the beast would kill him; but a furnace, fortunately for suburban mortality, cannot kill its tamer.

When his furnace happens to be good-natured, however, a man will often find the bedtime hour with it pleasant and even enjoyable. He descends, humming or whistling, to the cellar; and the subsequent shaking and shoveling is, after all, no more than a healthy exercise which he would not otherwise take and which will make him sleep better. He is friendly with this rotund, coal-eating giant; he regards it almost like a big baby which he is putting to bed—or, at least, he *might* so regard it if putting a baby to bed was one of his recognized pleasures.

But, oh, what a difference in the morning! He awakes in

the dark, startled perhaps from some pleasant dream by the wild alarm-m-m-m of a clock under his pillow; and outside the snug island of warmth on which he lies, the Universe stretches away in every direction, above, below, and on every side of him, cold, dreary, and unfit for human habitation, to and beyond the remotest star. In that cold Universe how small he is!—how warm and how weak! Instantly he thinks of the furnace, and the remotest star seems near by comparison. The thought of getting up and going down cellar seems as unreal as the thought of getting up and going to meet the sun at that pale streak which, through his easterly window, heralds the reluctant coming of another day. Yet he knows that he *must,* and that eventually he *will,* get up. In vain he tells himself how splendid, how invigorating will be the plunge *from his warm bed* right into the fresh, brisk, hygienic morning air.

The fresh, brisk, hygienic morning air does not appeal to him. Unwillingly he recalls a line in the superfurnace advertisement,—'Get up warm and cosy,'—and helplessly wishes that *he* had such a furnace. 'Like Andrew Carnegie!' he adds bitterly. At that moment he would anarchistically assassinate Andrew, provided he could do it without getting up. Nevertheless—he gets up! He puts on—'Curse it, *where* is that sleeve?'—the bath-robe and slippers that have been all night cooling for him, and starts on his lonely journey through the tomblike silence. Now, if ever, is the time to hum, but there is not a hum in him: down, down, down he goes to the cellar and peeks with dull hope through the familiar little door. 'Good morning, Fire.' He shakes, he shovels, he opens drafts and manipulates dampers. And the Furnace, impassive, like a Buddha holding up the house with as many arms as an octopus, seems to be watching him with a grave yet idle interest. Which is all the more horrible because it has no face.

THE TRUTH ABOUT WOMEN *

By Alexander Black

"When I have one foot in the grave," said Tolstoy to Maxim Gorky, "I will tell the truth about women. I shall tell it, jump into my coffin, pull the lid over me, and say, 'Do what you like now.'" That the threat was not merely whimsical is more than suggested by Gorky's comment: "The look he gave us was so wild, so terrifying, that we all fell silent for a time."

Gorky, who, on his own account, seldom gives us occasion to suspect him of being a postponing commentator, makes it plain enough in the narration of his talks with the awesome compatriot that Tolstoy was usually ready with the ultimate word, that he was willing to call a spade something just as bad. Yet in this matter of the truth about women there is the effect of pause before the unspeakable. We are, indeed, left with a feeling that, after saying so much about women in one way or another, Tolstoy, impatient of codes, excoriatingly contemptuous of trimmed opinion, tolerated the pressure of one reserve—that one complex was to be last to die.

Any theory that his deferred analysis was simply something ungentlemanly is, of course, scarcely tenable, since he had been unquotably candid on many an occasion which seemed to establish clearly enough a fact of no reserve whatever. If he had been a devout feminist all his life, the last-moment declaration might have been, for example, a simple recanta-

* From *The Latest Thing and Other Things;* copyright, 1922, by Harper & Brothers. Reprinted by permission of the author and the publishers.

tion, a leering or passionate confession of hatred long concealed, a defiance of all cowardly conveniences. Having
published his disenchantment, having grinned at the puerili-
ties of romance, having stripped sex of its glamour, having
rivaled St. Chrysostom in scathing description of the female,
what could remain to be spilled at the brink of the grave?
Certainly that "terrifying" look could not promise anything
sensationally sweet·

Aside from the foolishness of planning for a one-foot-in-
the-grave crisis, it is to be noted that even a Tolstoy would,
with the best or worst of intentions, or the keenest of expectations, find himself to be Tolstoy to the end. And being
Tolstoy to the end, Tolstoy habits were likely to hold.

A marked Tolstoy habit was that of promising to be more
violent if not more conclusive. Probably this habit is always
likely to be present in those whose business is ·expression.
The best that may be said will leave art in debt to the thought
and the emotion. Only one ·who is greater than anything
he does is ever likely to do anything great. Thus margins
of the unexpressed are inevitable. And what is true of the
artist is doubtless true, in some degree, of all of us. Indeed,
it is quite evident that it was not the artist side of Tolstoy
that recognized, or lamented, or threatened as to things
unspoken. The grizzled seer who raged before Gorky was
starkly human in his ways, and was never more male than
after he had long accustomed himself to maleness as a remi-
niscence, and to femaleness as a spectacle. Old age, even of
the mellow kind, seldom fails to secrete some acrid distillation. A theory, a prejudice, a rebellion, can acquire in the
fermentation of years a bitterness of savor that is often shockingly in contrast to perhaps conspicuous urbanities which
accompany them.

Amid all such survivals sex hostilities present a sharp effect.
Perhaps the effect is accentuated by fading signs of sex. We
do not need the support of Mr. Freud to believe, for instance,
that old maids of both sexes (for I speak of a state of mind)

are often the most acrimonious critics of the drama of sex. Simple old age, whatever its history, naturally recruits the non-participating gallery, and we often have occasion to suspect the making of common cause between those who have always been aloof from the drama and those who are aloof at last—between irritated nonparticipants and disenchanted survivors. Naturally, too, a Tolstoy, confessing a history, would claim to speak with special authority. A participant is always the more dogmatic. If he has seen the folly of a thing, he feels superior in authority to one who has only guessed it, or reasoned it, or has lacked the enterprise to reach the limits of folly.

In this matter Tolstoy would have admitted or insisted that he knew what he was talking about· His disciples unite in revealing his definitive style of speech. Coleridge wished that he might be as sure of anything as Tom Macaulay was of everything. Gorky and the rest found that it was better to let Tolstoy keep the floor when he chose to take it. Johan Bojer said to me of a certain eminent British literary man he had met: "I wondered why he was so *angry* about things." Evidently one never wondered about Tolstoy. His angers had a sublimity. He could be Messianic, and he could slash like a Hebrew prophet. His denunciations were appalling. They were more likely to make his hearers "silent for a time" than to loosen contradictory talk; so that Gorky was following the practice in leaving as it fell this mystery of a promised last cry. Yet it would have been appropriate, I am sure, for some one to suggest that Tolstoy write the tremendous thing and leave it with his codicils, marked, "The Truth About Women."

Men have always exhibited an anxiety as to this matter of the truth about women. Sometimes the anxiety has shown in an eagerness to tell it themselves. Again it has appeared in the tone of their welcome to some one else's disclosure. The great thing, we might gather, was recognized as having the truth told somehow, this with the implication that the truth had hitherto been withheld, or perhaps merely mislaid. The very young or the very old have been most conspicuous in the field of revelation. Male creatures of, say, seventeen, have been known to acquire a sudden and absolutely conclusive insight into all womenkind. Beginning without bias, perhaps (and quite usually), with a special disposition of favor, these very young investigators have been known to emerge with a conviction of having been grossly deceived. No later sureness can hope quite to equal this first sureness. In its passion of resentment, in its squirming humiliation at being fooled, in its bitter betrayal, as at the altar of all hope, adolescent conviction can reach a suicidal intensity. The soured adoration of a boy does not say, "You know how women are." In the midst of the cataclysm a boy believes that no one hitherto has known how women are. He is the appointed Columbus on the sea of sex.

Where the young cynic is indignant, the old cynic is progressively contemptuous. He perhaps recovered from that first indignation, and passed through a long mid-period of mature and judicial investigation. Then he knew. He has not merely a belief. He has a knowledge. In the presence of a cross section of feminine psychology, with all of its revolting revelatory detail, he intrenches himself at last in a settled exasperation or in a complacent disillusionment capable of sitting up, under challenge, to be witheringly final. The old cynic may have preferred, or may think he has preferred, the meek, "womanly" type. He may, on the other hand, have had a dream of a woman who would be not only easily inflammable, but gorgeously explosive, and of himself as carrying the only flame. He may have looked for violet eyes, or for some one named Iseult; for a woman superbly stupid or for one as sophisticated as a blonde stenographer. It does not matter, once he has reached the stage of well-ripened disappointment. He acquires a rich store of citations. He backs contemporary testimony with classical examples. He points to a history reeking with evidences of the awful truth about women. He is ready to indorse the report of the Preacher, who found one sought-for man among a thousand, "but a woman among all those have I not found."

Possibly there was a time, in the youth of the world, when the truth about women was less a discovery, less something flashed in an apocalyptic moment, and more a brazen fact of common understanding. Yet this seems doubtful. Some truths are essentially of the hiding kind. It may be that men have intuitively aided the hiding of this one. They have claimed as much. They have seemed to drape woman with what they have wished her to be, then exulted in tearing off the covering. They have set her up like a graven image, then hurled missiles at her because she did not answer their prayers.

Literature is rich in anthologies of disenchantment. As a subject, woman has been as necessary to pessimism as to romance. She has been the goddess, and she has been the goat. *Cherchez la femme.* Something has always been wrong with the world. Nothing could be clearer in the records than that it has been convenient to find woman as the explanation. If any era gets ready to decline and fall, track down the odor of musk. When a man or a civilization is "successful" there is a rush to woman. When there is failure, it is toward woman that the accusing finger is pointed. The Bible begins with the sad story of woman's culpability, and it ends with a scathing allegory that sets the image of her erring body in a high and horrible prominence. The devil is male, as befits his large functions, but no literature conceals his chief weapon. The sacrifice of the anchorite is an escape from women. The mind hates abstractions. Even the male mind, that alone is supposed to be capable of abstractions, has preferred to personify. Having decided that angels are male, it fixed the images of Life and Death. For Temptation it made a digression. Woman is Temptation, *vide* Genesis and all the epics. Having envisaged Woman as Temptation, it has been easy, under the spell of antithesis, to envisage

Man as the eternal St. Anthony, with the supreme preoccupation of not succumbing. He is the searcher for the Holy Grail. She is the vampire. He is pictured as persistently aspiring, she as persistently vamping.

The truth about her, then, would be assumed to point toward unmasking some secret whose betrayal would destroy her power, or at least, and at last, fortify men against the danger. Man has felt compelled to go on marrying her and, by the promptings of a dogged optimism, even to go on pretending that she is what she ought to be. But he has always found something pleasurable in confessing the pretense at the right moment; and he has never ceased to hope that the coming of the truth, something more than the superficial truth with which everybody is familiar—the penetrating, ultimate truth—might do its great work. In a large literature of exasperation there are countless signs of a feeling that illusion should be dispelled for good and all; that, as in the matter of some dog ordinance, women should be tied up, muzzled, or otherwise subjected to a safe restraint, and that the sex hitherto victimized should be educated to a new caution, a new severity, and especially to a new sense of custodian responsibility.

This sense of a custodian responsibility doubtless explains much that has happened and much that has been said. A ruling that women shall not smoke in some place where men are freely permitted to smoke, is no more indicative of this sense of custodianship than ten thousand acts and opinions which have gone before. The past is littered with eloquent indications of man's intention to take care of women. His peculiar methods of taking care of them are often hard to read at a distance, but these methods have been steadfastly maintained. The need to take care of them was predicated upon theories which he was at some trouble to invent. And he was continually forced to do fresh inventing, for new considerations came up. His ingenuity never waned. Even when social rearrangements introduced extraordinary compli-

cations, he was ready. He still worked on a basic premise.
He was in charge.

I knew a man who had not done any real work for twenty
years. His wife was the wage earner. He let her add to this
the cooking and the mending of his clothes. But he remained
the head of the house, took her money, and made a tight
allowance to her for lunches and carfare. He was not original or peculiar. He had the basic philosophy to go on. He
was a perfect example of a tenacious tradition. Once the
world had its formulas beautifully arranged.

There came a time, however, when the basic philosophy
began to look frayed. The whole theory of taking care of
woman involved her occupying a "place," so that one who
played the part of a showman exhibiting the world might be
free to say that over there, in a cage, were the women. But the
women broke out of the cage. They roved over the whole
picture. This made it exceedingly difficult to go on thinking
about taking care of them. And conditions that made it
difficult to take care of them made it not less difficult to know
the truth about them. The first condition of taking care
of children, for example, is knowing just where they are.
When women stopped knowing that their proper place is in
the kitchen the trouble began.

Then some one announced that there was a sex war. A sex
war, like any other war, must have an original lie back of it.
The original lie back of a sex war would be that the sexes are
essentially antagonistic. There are people who believe that.
Such a belief can breed a state of mind in which there arises
a yearning to tell the truth about women. Some people have
a passion for discovering antagonisms. They would like to
build an inverted monism that revealed the universe as an
extension of the Kilkenny cats. To tell them that the an-
tagonism was not in sex but in interests growing out of sex,
that these interests had been affected greatly by a one-sided
pressure, and that they were subject to change with world
change, would be to take away a certain comfortable misery.

Moreover, it would to an awkward extent interfere with, or, at all events, take some of the zest from the attainment of that great ideal of revealing the truth about women.

The tendency to believe that there is a special and sinister "truth" about women, in whatever types of mind it may appear, and at whichever stage of age or youth it may manifest itself, was nourished by conditions that quite plainly have begun to disappear. No supplanting conditions can be quite so favorable to a successful attitude of male supervision or privileged male analysis. Womankind will never again be an incidental element of mankind. As civilization advances it will grow harder to indicate women as representing one of the minor appointments, harder to think of them as a creature group. They have smashed the tradition of "place." They have overrun the forbidden industries and professions. They are doing all the things they are unfitted for. They occupy judgeships. They sit in legislatures. They have accepted fusion in the melting pot of world effort.

This ought to prove, I suppose, that the truth about women must now be much more complicated than it used to be. It ought to prove that a vision of the truth about women must become a vastly more subtle matter. It might turn out to be a more annoying truth than it ever was before. Yet there is a better hope. If maleness can no longer be put on one side of the picture, and femaleness on the other, where each group may glare at and accuse the other; if the blending of effort in affairs means anything; if there is any wisdom in saying that there is no sex in science or in art; if religion may revise its bisecting dogmas; if women themselves may join the preachers and prophets, the obliterations must do something to traditions of antipathy, must at some point begin to suggest, even to stodgy or senile minds, the oneness of mankind.

A new Tolstoy who should threaten that, when he had one foot in the grave, he would tell the truth about humanity, would not be credited with a superior impudence. He would be credited with an inferior humor. The notion of a separable truth about women will begin to wear the same complexion. The real truth about women will be known when the real truth about men is known. To have read one will be to have read the other. The aspiration to do the reading will always be praiseworthy. Such an aspiration is indeed inevitable. It has always existed. It has always been defeated. But it would be a misfortune if frustration enfeebled the wish. This supreme curiosity is indicative of mankind's desire to be a participating creator. So long as man wants to know, his power will increase. If he ever really knows, he may be awed. He may indeed find the truth terrifying. Yet he will by then have lost some of his fears, perhaps even his fear of women and of words.

HE TRIES A CAFETERIA *

By Margaret Breuning

"Let's try one of those cafeteria places to-night," I suggested to Charles. When we took Cousin Caroline's apartment for a few weeks she asked us not to use the electric range, "experiment" with it, was her way of putting it, but I didn't repeat that to Charles, so we had to take our meals out. "Cafeteria?" asked Charles. "What's that? One of those places where everything is automatic?" But I told him that it was a place where you wait on yourself and I had never noticed anything like that getting automatic with him.

"I'd just as soon eat one place as another," he said, "but I would like to know why they call it such a name: it sounds like a vine or a patent medicine—wistaria, castoria, cafeteria—" and he would have gone on that way till he finished up the dictionary, but I got him started before the crowded time. I didn't know just how Charles and a cafeteria would make out together, but I knew all I wanted about Charles and a crowd.

It was a little discouraging at the start, for we had to get in line, and when we were at the food place we found that we should have taken trays at the start, so we had to go back and get in line all over again, and I felt that Charles was a little restive. When we reached the food counter the second time he began to read the schedule of prices over very slowly out loud and comment on each item. Of

56

course, this kept the line back and didn't make him exactly popular with the people who had to wait.

"Why is bean soup more than pea soup?" he asked. "One bean," called out the girl. "I didn't ask for bean soup," he shouted; "I only asked why it cost more. It's no more nourishing and certainly beans don't cost—" A determined-looking woman with a net bag full of knobby bundles wedged in and got by Charles. "If this man is going to lecture on dietetics, he ought to have a platform and hire some one to listen to him," she said. "Fish cakes and beans" —this was to the girl behind the counter; and before she got her order, Charles was past her again and gave her net bag such a bump that things jingled in it, and when I saw her later something sticky had run all over it as though a bottle had broken. I was sorry, but I could have told her not to excite Charles: he is nothing if not temperamental. He got his food all picked out after a while and found a table for us, and then I went for a glass of water (I never shall believe that any one knows which are the clean and which the used glasses), and when I got back to our table Charles wasn't there, and as I looked around I saw him at another, eating away, while his tray was right by me. Before I had time to reach him and tell him he was at the wrong table up came a tiny little woman, who started to sit down; then when she saw Charles, she jumped up again and looked around; then she looked down at the tray.

"Well, of all the impertinent things," she called out so loud that every one heard. "My good man, if you are in need of a meal I will gladly give you—" "Are you addressing me?" asked Charles, in what I knew he thought was a majestic manner, but he was eating corn on the cob, and you can't be very majestic while you are doing that. "Because, if you are, you would better talk to some one else. This is my dinner. I selected it, and I paid for it, and if it comes to giving food away you'd better try some one else, as I said. I had too hard a time to find this to let a crumb of it go." He took to gnawing away on the corn cob again. The woman seemed speechless and then she went away and got some one called a checker. I always thought it was a game but it seems it can be a woman who adds up food, and this chess woman said that wasn't Charles's tray at all. "You didn't have any custard pie, sir," she said.

"Well, I should think not," said Charles—he was pretty well through the corn by this time; "I never eat it; why should I buy it?" "Well, I eat it," interrupted the little woman, pouncing down on him, "and there it is on my tray, and you can get me another right away, taking people's trays and eating their meals." By this time I had a chance to tell Charles he had made a mistake. "Oh, yes, mistake; that's a nice way to put it: beating your meals I call it," snorted the little woman. But I can't say I blame her much. We had it all fixed up and started in again at our own table, but Charles was furious, and furious with me. "What can you expect if you come to such a place?" he asked. "No system, no privacy, everybody eating around on any table they happen to come to. It's no sort of a way. I knew that anything called a cafeteria wouldn't be any good, but you always want to try something new. Well, I hope you're satisfied with this experiment and won't want to do it again." I didn't; I was sure of that.

IN PRAISE OF A LAWN-MOWER *

By Charles S. Brooks

I do not recall that anyone has written the praises of a lawn-mower. I seem to sow in virgin soil. One could hardly expect a poet to lift up his voice on such a homely theme. By instinct he prefers the more rhythmic scythe. Nor, on the other hand, will mechanical folk pay a full respect to a barren engine without cylinders and motive power. But to me it is just intricate enough to engage the interest. I can trace the relation of its wheels and knives, and see how the lesser spinning starts the greater. In a printing press, on the contrary, I hear only the general rattle. Before a gas-engine, also, I am dumb. Its sixteen processes to an explosion baffle me. I could as easily digest a machine for setting type. I nod blankly, as if a god explained the motion of the stars. Even when I select a motor I take it merely on reputation and by bouncing on the cushions to test its comfort.

It has been a great many years since I was last intimate with a lawn-mower. My acquaintance began in the days when a dirty face was a badge of freedom. One early Saturday morning I was hard at work before breakfast. Mother called down through the upstairs shutters, at the first clicking of the knives, to ask if I wore my rubbers in the dew. With the money earned by noon, I went to Conrad's shop. The season for tops and marbles had gone by. But in the

* From *Hints to Pilgrims;* copyright, 1921, by Yale University Press. Reprinted by permission of the author and the publishers.

window there was a peerless baseball with a rubber core, known as a *cock-of-the-walk*. By indecision, even by starting for the door, I bought it a nickel off because it was specked by flies.

It did not occur to me last week, at first, that I could cut the grass. I talked with an Irishman who keeps the lawn next door. He leaned on his rake, took his pipe from his mouth and told me that his time was full. If he had as many hands as a centipede—so he expressed himself—he could not do all the work that was asked of him. The whole street clamored for his service. Then I talked with an Italian on the other side, who comes to work on a motor-cycle with his lawn-mower across his shoulder. His time was worth a dollar an hour, and he could squeeze me in after supper and before breakfast. But how can I consistently write upstairs—I am puttering with a novel—with so expensive a din sounding in my ears? My expected royalties shrink beside such swollen pay. So I have become my own yard-man.

Last week I had the lawn-mower sharpened, but it came home without adjustment. It went down the lawn without clipping a blade. What a struggle I had as a child getting the knives to touch along their entire length! I remember it as yesterday. What an ugly path was left when they cut on one side only! My bicycle chain, the front wheel that wobbled, the ball-bearings in the gear, none of these things were so perplexing. Last week I got out my screwdriver with somewhat of my old feeling of impotence. I sat down on the grass with discouragement in contemplation. One set of screws had to be loosened while another set was tightened, and success lay in the delicacy of my advance. What was my amazement to discover that on a second trial my mower cut to its entire width! Even when I first wired a base-plug and found that the table lamp would really light, I was not more astonished.

This success with the lawn-mower has given me hope.

I am not, as I am accused, all thumbs. I may yet become a handy man around the house. Is the swirl of furnace pipes inside my intellect? Perhaps I can fix the leaky packing in the laundry tubs, and henceforth look on the plumber as an equal brother. My dormant brain cells at last are wakened. But I must curb myself. I must not be too useful. There is no rest for a handy man. It is ignorance that permits a vacant holiday. At most I shall admit a familiarity with base-plugs and picture-wire and rubber washers—perhaps even with canvas awnings, which smack pleasantly of the sea—but I shall commit myself no further.

Once in a while I rather enjoy cleaning the garage—raking down the cobwebs from the walls and windows with a stream from the hose—puddling the dirt into the central drain. I am ruthless with old oil cans and with the discarded clothing of the chauffeur we had last month. Why is an old pair of pants stuffed so regularly in the tool drawer? There is a barrel at the alley fence—but I shall spare the details. It was the river Alpheus that Hercules turned through the Augean stables. They had held three thousand oxen and had not been cleaned for thirty years. Dear me! I know oxen. I rank this labor ahead of the killing of the Hydra, or fetching the golden apples of the Hesperides. Our garage can be sweetened with a hose.

But I really like outside work. Last week I pulled up a quantity of dock and dandelions that were strangling the grass. And I raked in seed. This morning, when I went out for the daily paper, I saw a bit of tender green. The Reds, as I noticed in the headline of the paper, were advancing on Warsaw. France and England were consulting for the defense of Poland, but I ignored these great events and stood transfixed in admiration before this shimmer of new grass.

Our yard, fore and aft, is about an afternoon's work. And now that I have cut it once I have signed up for the summer. It requires just the right amount of intelligence. I would

not trust myself to pull weeds in the garden.   M—— has the
necessary skill for this.   I might pull up the Canterbury
bells which, out of season, I consider unsightly stalks.   And
I do not enjoy clipping the grass along the walks.   It is a
kind of barber's job.   But I like the long straightaways, and
I could wish that our grass plot stretched for another hundred feet.

And I like the sound of a lawn-mower.   It is such a busy
click and whirr.   It seems to work so willingly.   Not even
a sewing-machine has quite so brisk a tempo.   And when a
lawn-mower strikes a twig, it stops suddenly on its haunches
with such impatience to be off again.   "Bend over, won't
you," it seems to say, "and pull out that stick.   These trees
are a pesky nuisance.   They keep dropping branches all the
while.   Now then!   Are we ready?   Whee!   What's an
apple?   I can cut an apple all to flinders.   You whistle and
I'll whirr.   Let's run down that slope together!"

HOLDING A BABY *

By Heywood Broun

When Adam delved and Eve span, the fiction that man is incapable of housework was first established. It would be interesting to figure out just how many foot-pounds of energy men have saved themselves, since the creation of the world, by keeping up the pretense that a special knack is required for washing dishes and for dusting, and that the knack is wholly feminine. The pretense of incapacity is impudent in its audacity, and yet it works.

Men build bridges and throw railroads across deserts, and yet they contend successfully that the job of sewing on a button is beyond them. Accordingly, they don't have to sew buttons.

It might be said, of course, that the safety of suspension bridges is so much more important than that of suspenders that the division of labor is only fair, but there are many of us who have never thrown a railroad in our lives, and yet swagger in all the glory of masculine achievement without undertaking any of the drudgery of odd jobs.

Probably men alone could never have maintained the fallacy of masculine incapacity without the aid of women. As soon as that rather limited sphere, once known as woman's place, was established, women began to glorify and exaggerate its importance, by the pretense that it was all so special and difficult that no other sex could possibly begin to accomplish the tasks entailed. To this declaration men gave immediate and eager assent and they have kept it up. The most casual examination will reveal the fact that all the jokes about the horrible results of masculine cooking and sewing are written by men. It is all part of a great scheme of sex propaganda.

Naturally there are other factors. Biology has been unscrupulous enough to discriminate markedly against women, and men have seized upon this advantage to press the belief that, since the bearing of children is exclusively the province of women, it must be that all the caring for them belongs properly to the same sex. Yet how ridiculous this is.

Most things which have to be done for children are of the simplest sort. They should tax the intelligence of no one. Men profess a total lack of ability to wash baby's face simply because they believe there's no great fun in the business, at either end of the sponge. Protectively, man must go the whole distance and pretend that there is not one single thing which he can do for baby. He must even maintain that he doesn't know how to hold one. From this pretense has grown the shockingly transparent fallacy that holding a baby correctly is one of the fine arts; or, perhaps even more fearsome than that, a wonderful intuition, which has come down after centuries of effort to women only.

"The thing that surprised Richard most," says a recent woman novelist, "was the ease and the efficiency with which Eleanor handled Annabel. . . . She seemed to know by instinct, things that Richard could not understand and that he could not understand how she came by. If she reached out her hands to take Annabel, her fingers seemed, of themselves, to curve into the places where they would fit the spineless bundle and give it support."

At this point, interruption is inevitable. Places indeed! There are one hundred and fifty-two distinctly different ways of holding a baby—and all are right! At least all will do. There is no need of seeking out special places for the hands.

A baby is so soft that anybody with a firm grip can make places for an effective hold wherever he chooses. But to return to our quotation: "If Richard tried to take up the bundle, his fingers fell away like the legs of the brittle crab and the bundle collapsed, incalculable and helpless. 'How do you do it?' he would say. And he would right Annabel and try to still her protests. And Eleanor would only smile gently and send him on some masculine errand, while she soothed Annabel's feelings in the proper way."

You may depend upon it that Richard also smiled as soon as he was safely out of the house and embarked upon some masculine errand, such as playing eighteen holes of golf. Probably, by the time he reached the tenth green, he was too intent upon his game to remember how guile had won him freedom. Otherwise, he would have laughed again, when he holed a twenty-foot putt over a rolling green and recollected that he had escaped an afternoon of carrying Annabel because he was too awkward. I once knew the wife of the greatest billiard player in the world, and she informed me with much pride that her husband was incapable of carrying the baby. "He doesn't seem to have the proper touch," she explained.

As a matter of fact, even if men in general were as awkward as they pretend to be at home, there would still be small reason for their shirking the task of carrying a baby. Except that right side up is best, there is not much to learn. As I ventured to suggest before, almost any firm grip will do. Of course the child may cry, but that is simply because he has become over-particular through too much coddling. Nature herself is cavalier. Young rabbits don't even whimper when picked up by the ears, and kittens are quite contented to be lifted by the scruff of the neck.

This same Nature has been used as the principal argument for woman's exclusive ability to take care of the young. It is pretty generally held that all a woman needs to do to know all about children is to have some. This wisdom is attributed to instinct. Again and again we have been told by rapturous grandmothers that: "It isn't something which can be read in a book or taught in a school. Nature is the great teacher." This simply isn't true. There are many mothers in America who have learned far more from the manuals of Dr. Holt than instinct ever taught them—and Dr. Holt is a man. I have seen mothers give beer and spaghetti and Neapolitan ice-cream to children in arms, and, if they got that from instinct, the only conclusion possible is that instinct did not know what it was talking about. Instinct is not what it used to be.

I have no feeling of being a traitor to my sex, when I say that I believe in at least a rough equality of parenthood. In shirking all the business of caring for children we have escaped much hard labor. It has been convenient. Perhaps it has been too convenient. If we have avoided arduous tasks, we have also missed much fun of a very special kind. Like children in a toy shop, we have chosen to live with the most amusing of talking-and-walking dolls, without ever attempting to tear down the sign which says, "Do not touch." In fact we have helped to set it in place. That is a pity.

Children mean nothing at long range. For our own sake we ought to throw off the pretense of incapacity and ask that we be given a half share in them. I hope that this can be done without its being necessary for us to share the responsibility of dishes also. I don't think there are any concealed joys in washing dishes. Washing children is quite a different matter. After you have washed somebody else's face you feel that you know him better. This may be the reason why so many trained nurses marry their patients—but that is another story. A dish is an unresponsive thing. It gives back nothing. A child's face offers competitive possibilities. It is interesting to see just how high a polish can be achieved without making it cry.

There is also a distinct sense of elation in doing trifling practical things for children. They are so small and so helpless that they contribute vastly to a comforting glow in the ego of the grown-up. When you have completed the rather difficult task of preparing a child for bed and actually getting him there, you have a sense of importance almost divine in its extent. This is to feel at one with Fate, to be the master of another's destiny, of his waking and his sleeping and his going out into the world. It is a brand-new world for the child. He is a veritable Adam and you loom up in his life as more than mortal. Golf is well enough for a Sunday sport, but it is a trifling thing beside the privilege of taking a small son to the zoo and letting him see his first lion, his first tiger and, best of all, his first elephant. Probably he will think that they are part of your own handiwork turned out for his pleasure.

To a child, at least, even the meanest of us may seem glamorous with magic and wisdom. It seems a pity not to take the fullest advantage of this chance before the opportunity is lost. There must come a day when even the most nimble-witted father has to reply, "I don't know." On that day the child comes out of Eden and you are only a man again. Cortes on his lonely peak in Darien was a pigmy discoverer beside the child eating his first spoonful of ice-cream. There is the immediate frightened and angry rebellion against the coldness of it, and then the amazing sensation as the strange substance melts into magic of pleasant sweetness. The child will go on to high adventure, but I doubt whether the world holds for any one more soul-stirring surprise than the first adventure with ice-cream. No, there is nothing dull in feeding a child.

There is less to be said for dressing a child, from the point of view of recreation. This seems to us laborious and rather tiresome, both for father and child. Still I knew one man who managed to make an adventure of it. He boasted that he had broken all the records of the world for changing all or any part of a child's clothing. He was a skilled automobile mechanic, much in demand in races, where tires are whisked on and off. He brought his technic into the home. I saw several of his demonstrations. He was a silent man who habitually carried a mouthful of safety pins. Once the required youngster had been pointed out, he wasted no time in preliminary wheedlings but tossed her on the floor without more ado. Even before her head had bumped, he would be hard at work. With him the thrill lay in the inspiration of the competitive spirit. He endeavored always to have his task completed before the child could begin to cry. He never lost. Often the child cried afterward, but by that time my friend felt that his part of the job was completed—and would turn the youngster over to her mother.

A CHINESE NIGHT (LIMEHOUSE) *

By Thomas Burke

AT LIMEHOUSE

Yellow man, yellow man, where have you been?
Down the Pacific, where wonders are seen.
Up the Pacific, so glamorous and gay,
Where night is of blue, and of silver the day.

Yellow man, yellow man, what did you there?
I loved twenty maids who were loving and fair.
Their cheeks were of velvet, their kisses were fire,
I looked at them boldly and had my desire.

Yellow man, yellow man, what do you know?
That living is lovely wherever I go;
And lovelier, I say, since when soft winds have passed
The tides will race over my bosom at last.

Yellow man, yellow man, why do you sigh?
For flowers that are sweet, and for flowers that die.
For days in fair waters and nights in strange lands,
For faces forgotten and little lost hands.

It was eight o'clock. We had dined in Soho, and conversed amiably with Italian waiters and French wine-men. There were now many slack hours before us, and nothing wherewith to tighten them. We stood in the low-lit gaiety of Old Compton Street, and wondered. We were tired of halls and revues; the theatres had started work; there was nothing

* From *Nights in London;* published, 1918, by Henry Holt and Company. Reprinted by permission of the publishers.

left but to sit in beer-cellars and listen to dreary bands playing ragtimes and bilious waltzes.

Now it is a good tip when tired of the West, and, as the phrase goes, at a loose end, to go East, young man, go East. You will spot a winner every time, if it is entertainment you seek, by mounting the first Eastbound omnibus that passes. For the East is eternally fresh, because it is alive. The West, like all things of fashion, is but a corpse electrified. They are so tired, these lily-clad ladies and white-fronted gentlemen, of their bloodless, wine-whipped frivolities. They want to enjoy themselves very badly, but they do not know how to do it. They know that enjoyment only means eating the same dinner at a different restaurant, and afterwards meeting the same tired people, or seeing the same show, the same songs, jests, dances at different houses. But Eastward . . . there, large and full, blossoms Life—a rather repellent Life, perhaps, for Life is always that. Hatred, filth, love, battle, and death—all elemental things are here, undisguised; and if elemental things repel you, my lamb, then you have no business to be on this planet. Night, in the particular spots of the East to which these pages take you, shows you Life in the raw, stripped of its silken wrappings; and it is of passionate interest to those for whom humanity is the only Book. In the West pleasure is a business; in the East it is recreation. In the East it may be a thinner, poorer body, but it is alive. The people are sick, perhaps, with toil; but below that sickness there is a lust for enjoyment that lights up every little moment of their evening, as I shall show you later, when we come to Bethnal Green, Hoxton, and the athletic saloons. You may listen to Glazounoff's "L'Automne Bacchanale" at the Palace Theatre, danced by Pavlova, but I should not look in Shaftesbury Avenue or Piccadilly for its true spirit. Rather, I should go to Kingsland Road, Tunnel Gardens, Jamaica Road; to the trafficked highways, rent with naphthas, that rush about East India Dock. There, when the lamps are lighted, and bead the night with tears, and the sweet girls go by, and throw their little laughter to the boys—there you have your true Bacchanales.

So, leaving the fixed grin of decay in Coventry Street, we mounted a motor-'bus, and dashed gaily through streets of rose and silver—it was October—and dropped off by the Poplar Hippodrome, whose harsh signs lit the night to sudden beauty.

To turn from East India Dock Road to West India Dock Road is to turn, contradictorily, from West to East, from a fury of lights and noise and faces into a stillness almost chaste. At least, chaste is the first word you think of. In a few seconds you feel that it is the wrong epithet. Something . . . something there is in this dusky, throttled byway that seems to be crawling into your blood. The road seems to slink before you; and you know that, once in, you can only get out by retracing your steps or crossing into the lost Isle of Dogs. Against the wrath of October cloud, little low shops peer at you. In the sharp shadows their lights fall like swords across your path. The shuttered gloom of the eastern side shows strangely menacing. Each whispering house seems an abode of dread things. Each window seems filled with frightful eyes. Each corner, half-lit by a timid gas-jet, seems to harbour unholy features. A black man, with Oriental features, brushes against you. You collide with a creeping yellow man. He says something—it might be Chinese or Japanese or Philippinese jargon. A huge Hindoo shuffles, cat-like, against the shops. A fried-fish bar, its windows covered with Scandinavian phrases, flings a burst of melodious light for which you are grateful.

No; chaste was certainly not the right word. Say, rather, furtive, sinister. You are in Limehouse. The peacefulness seems to be that attendant upon underhand designs, and the twilight is that of people who love it because their deeds are evil.

But now we come to Pennyfields, to the thunderous shadows

of the great Dock, and to that low-lit Causeway that carries such subtle tales of flowered islands, white towns, green bays, and sunlight like wine. At the mouth of Pennyfields is a cluster of Chinks. You may see at once that they dislike you.

But my friend Sam Tai Ling will give us better welcome, I think; so we slip into the Causeway, with its lousy shop-fronts decorated with Chinese signs, among them the Sign of the Foreign Drug Open Lamp. At every doorway stand groups of the gallant fellows, eyeing appreciatively such white girls as pass that way. You taste the curious flavour of the place—its mixture of camaraderie and brutality, of cruelty and pity and tears; of precocious children and wrecked men—and you smell its perfume, the week before last. But here is the home of Tai Ling, one of the most genial souls to be met in a world of cynicism and dyspepsia: a lovable character, radiating sweetness and a tolerably naughty good-ness in this narrow street. Not immoral, for to be immoral you must first subscribe to some conventional morality. Tai Ling does not. You cannot do wrong until you have first done right. Tai Ling has not. He is just non-moral; and right and wrong are words he does not understand. He is in love with life and song and wine and the beauty of women. The world to him is a pause on a journey, where one may take one's idle pleasure while others strew the path with mirth and roses. He knows only two divisions of people: the gay and the stupid. He never turns aside from pleasure, or resists an invitation to the feast. In fact, by our stand-ards a complete rogue, yet the most joyous I have known. Were you to visit him and make his acquaintance, you would thank me for the introduction to so charming a character. I never knew a man with so seductive a smile. Many a time it has driven the virtuously indignant heart out of me. An Oriental smile, you know, is not an affair of a swift moment. It has a birth and a beginning. It awakens, hesitates, grows, and at last from the sad chrysalis emerges the butterfly. A Chinese smile at the full is one of the subtlest expressions of which the human face is capable.

Mr. Sam Tai Ling keeps a restaurant, and, some years ago, when my ways were cast about West India Dock Road, I knew him well. He was an old man then; he is an old man now: the same age, I fancy. Supper with him is something to remember—I use the phrase carefully. You will find, after supper, that soda-mints and potass-water are more than grateful and comforting.

When we entered he came forward at once, and such was his Celestial courtesy that, although we had recently dined, to refuse supper was impossible. He supped with us himself in the little upper room, lit by gas, and decorated with bead curtains and English Christmas-number supplements. A few oily seamen were manipulating the chop-sticks and thrusting food to their mouths with a noise that, on a clear night, I should think, could be heard as far as Shadwell. When honourable guests were seated, honourable guests were served by Mr. Tai Ling. There were noodles, shark's fins, chop suey, and very much fish and duck, and lychee fruits. The first dish consisted of something that resembled a Cornish pasty— chopped fish and onion and strange meats mixed together and heavily spiced, encased in a light flour-paste. Then followed a plate of noodle, some bitter lemon, and finally a pot of China tea prepared on the table: real China tea, remember, all-same Shan-tung; not the backwash of the name which is served in Piccadilly tea-shops. The tea is carefully prepared by one who evidently loves his work, and is served in little cups, without milk or sugar, but flavoured with chrysanthemum buds.

As our meal progressed, the café began to fill; and the air bubbled with the rush of labial talk from the Celestial company. We were the only white things there. All the company was yellow, with one or two tan-skinned girls.

But we were out for amusement, so, after the table hospitality, Sam took us into the Causeway. Out of the coloured darkness of Pennyfields came the muffled wail of reed instruments, the heart-cry of the Orient; noise of traffic; bits of honeyed talk. On every side were following feet: the firm, clear step of the sailor; the loud, bullying boots of the tough; the joyful steps that trickle from "The Green Man"; and, through all this chorus, most insistently, the stealthy, stuttering steps of the satyr. For your Chink takes his pleasure where he finds it; not, perhaps, the pleasure that you would approve, for probably you are not of that gracious temperament that accords pity and the soft hand to the habits of your fellows. Yet so many are the victims of the flesh, and for so little while are we here, that one can but smile and be kind. Besides, these yellow birds come from an Eastern country, where they do not read English law or bother about such trifles as the age of consent.

Every window, as always, was closely shuttered, but between the joints shot jets of slim light, and sometimes you could catch the chanting of a little sweet song last sung in Rangoon or Swatow. One of these songs was once translated for me. I should take great delight in printing it here, but, alas! this, too, comes from a land where purity crusades are unknown. I dare not conjecture what Bayswater would do to me if I reproduced it.

We passed through Pennyfields, through clusters of gladly coloured men. Vaguely we remembered leaving Henrietta Street, London, and dining in Old Compton Street, Paris, a few hours ago. And now—was this Paris or London or Tuan-tsen or Taiping? Pin-points of light pricked the mist in every direction. A tom-tom moaned somewhere in the far-away.

It was now half-past ten. The public-house at the extreme end was becoming more obvious and raucous. But, at a sudden black door, Sam stopped. Like a figure of a shadowgraph he slid through its opening, and we followed. Stairs led straight from the street to a basement chamber—candle-lit, with two exits. I had been there before, but to my companions it was new. We were in luck. A Dai Nippon had berthed a few hours previously, and here was its crew, flinging their wages fast over the fan-tan tables, or letting it go at Chausa-Bazee or Pachassee.

It was a well-kept establishment where agreeable fellows might play a game or so, take a shot of opium, or find other varieties of Oriental delight. The far glooms were struck by low-toned lanterns. Couches lay about the walls; strange men decorated them and three young girls in socks, idiotically drunk. Small tables were everywhere, each table obscured in a fog of yellow faces and greasy hair. The huge scorbutic proprietor, Ho Ling, swam noiselessly from table to table. A lank figure in brown shirting, its fingers curled about the stem of a spent pipe, sprawled in another corner. The atmosphere churned. The dirt of years, tobacco of many growings, opium, betel-nut, bhang, and moist flesh allied themselves in one grand assault on the nostrils. Perhaps you wonder how they manage to keep these places clean. That may be answered in two words: they don't.

On a table beneath one of the lanterns squatted a musician with a reed, blinking upon the company like a sly cat, and making his melody of six repeated notes.

Suddenly, at one of the tables was a slight commotion. A wee slip of a fellow had apparently done well at fan-tan, for he slid from his corner, and essayed a song—I fancy it was meant to be "Robert E. Lee"—in his seaman's pidgin. At least, his gestures were those of a ragtime comedian, and the tune bore some faint resemblance. Or is it that the ragtime kings have gone to the antiquities of the Orient for their melodies? But he had not gone far before Ho Ling, with the dignity of a mandarin, removed him. And the smell being a little too strong for us, we followed, and strolled to the Asiatics' Home.

The smell—yes. There is nothing in the world like the smell of a Chinatown in a Western City. It is a grand battle between a variety of odours, but opium prevails. The mouth of West India Dock Road is foul with it. For you might as well take away a navvy's half-pint of beer as deprive a Chink of his shot of dope and his gambling-table. Opium is forbidden under the L.C.C. regulations, and therefore the Chink sleeps at a licensed lodging-house and goes elsewhere for his fun. Every other house in this quarter is a seamen's lodging-house. These hotels have no lifts, and no electric light, and no wine-lists. You pay threepence a night, and you get the accommodation you pay for. But then, they are not for silk-clad ossifications such as you and me. They are for the lusty coloured lads who work the world with steam and sail: men whose lives lie literally in their great hands, who go down to the sea in ships and sometimes have questionable business in great waters.

These India Docks are like no other docks in the world. About their gates you find the scum of the world's worst countries; all the peoples of the delirious Pacific of whom you have read and dreamed—Arab, Hindoo, Malayan, Chink, Jap, South Sea Islander—a mere catalogue of the names is a romance. Here are pace and high adventure; the tang of the East; fusion of blood and race and creed. A degenerate dross it is, but, do you know, I cannot say that I don't prefer it to the well-spun gold that is flung from the Empire on boat-race nights. Place these fellows against our blunt backgrounds, under the awful mystery of the City's night, and they present the finest spectacle that London affords.

You may see them in their glory at the Asiatics' Home, to which we now came. A delightful place, this home for destitute Orientals; for it has a veranda and a compound, stone beds and caged cubicles, no baths and a billiard-table; and extraordinary precautions are taken against indulgence of the wicked tastes of its guests. Grouped about the giant stove are Asiatics of every country in wonderful toilet creations. A mild-eyed Hindoo, lacking a turban, has appropriated a bath-towel. A Malay appears in white cotton trou-

sers, frock-coat, brown boots, and straw hat; and a stranded
Burmese cuts no end of a figure in under-vest, steward's
jacket, yellow trousers and squash hat. All carry a knife
or a kress, and all are quite pleasant people, who will accept
your Salaam and your cigarette. Rules and regulations for
impossibly good conduct hang on the walls in Hindustani,
Japanese, Swahili, Urdu, and Malayan. All food is prepared
and cooked by themselves, and the slaughter of an animal
for the table must be witnessed and prayed upon by those
of their own faith. Out in the compound is a skittle-alley,
where the boys stroll and play; and costumes, people, and
settings have all the appearance of the *ensemble* of a cheap
revue.

I suppose one dare not write on Limehouse without mentioning opium-rooms. Well, if one must, one must, though
I have nothing of the expected to tell you. I have known
Limehouse for many years, and have smiled many times at the
articles that appear perennially on the wickedness of the
place. Its name evokes evil tradition in the public mind.
There are ingenuous people who regard it as dangerous. I
have already mentioned its sinister atmosphere; but there
is an end of it. There is nothing substantial. These are the
people who will tell you of the lurking perils of certain quarters of London—how that there are streets down which,
even in broad daylight, the very police do not venture unac-
companied. You may believe that, if you choose; it is
simply a tale for the soft-minded with a turn for the melo-
dramatic. There is no such thing as a dangerous street in
London. I have loafed and wandered in every part of London, slums, foreign quarters, underground, and docksides,
and if you must have adventure in London, then you will
have to make your own. The two fiercest streets of the me-
tropolis—Dorset Street and Hoxton Street—are as safe for
the wayfarer as Oxford Street; for women, safer. And the
manners of Limehouse are certainly a lesson to Streatham
Hill.

But we are talking of opium. We left Mr. Tai Ling on the steps of the Asiatics' Home, and from there we wandered to High Street, Poplar, to the house of a gracious gentleman from Pi-chi-li, not for opium but for a chat with him. For my companions had not smoked before, and I did not want two helpless invalids on my hands at midnight. Those amazingly thrilling and amazingly ludicrous stories of East End opium-rooms are mainly, I may say, the work of journalistic specials. A journalistic special is a man who writes thrillingly on old-fashioned topics on which he is ill-informed. The moment he knows something about his subject he is not allowed to write; he ceases to be a special. Also, of course, if a man, on sociological investigation, puts an initial pipe of opium on top of a brandy or so—well, one can understand that even the interior of the Bayswater omnibus may be a haunt of terror and wonder. Taking a jolt of "chandu" in a Limehouse room is about as exciting as taking a mixed vermuth at the Leicester Lounge.

The gracious gentleman received us affably. Through a curtained recess was the small common room, where yellow and black men reclined, in a purple dusk, beaded with the lights of little lamps. The odour was sickly, the air dry. The gentleman wondered whether we would have a room. No, we wouldn't; but I bought cigarettes, and we went upstairs to the little dirty bedrooms. The bed is but a mattress with a pillow. There, if you are a dope-fiend, you may have your pipe and lamp, very cosy, and you may lock the door, and the room is yours until you have finished. One has read, in periodicals, of the well-to-do people from the western end, who hire rooms here and come down, from time to time for an orgy. That is another story for the nursery. White people do visit the rooms, of course, but they are chiefly the white seamen of the locality; and, in case you may ever feel tempted to visit any of the establishments displaying the Sign of the Open Lamp, I may tell you that your first experiment will result in violent nausea, something akin to the effect of the cigar you smoked when you were twelve, but heightened to the *n*th power. Opium does nasty things to the yellow man; it does nastier things to the white man. Not only does it wreck the body, but it engenders and inflames those curious vices to which allusion has been made elsewhere. If you do not believe me, then you may accept the wisdom of an unknown Formosan, who, three hundred years ago, published a tract, telling of the effects of the Open Lamp on the white man. They are, in a word, parallel with the effects of whisky on the Asiatic. Listen:

The opium is boiled in a copper pan. The pipe is in appearance like a short club. Depraved young men, without any fixed occupation, meet together by night and smoke; and it soon becomes a habit. Fruit and sweetmeats are provided for the sailors, and no charge is made for the first time, in order to tempt them. After a while they cannot stay away, and will forfeit all their property so as to buy the drug. Soon they find themselves beyond cure. If they omit smoking for a day, their faces become shrivelled, their lips stand open, and they seem ready to die. Another smoke restores vitality, but in three years they all die.

So now you know. The philanthropic foreigner published his warning in 1622. In 1915 . . . well, walk down Pennyfields and exercise your nose, and calculate how much opium is being smoked in London to-day.

Nobody troubles very much about Chinatown, except the authorities, and their interference is but perfunctory. The yellow men, after all, are, as Prologue to "Pagliacci" observers, but men like you, for joy or sorrow, the same broad heaven above them, the same wide world before them. They are but men like you, though the sanitary officials may doubt it. They *will* sleep six and seven in one dirty bed, and no law of London can change their ways. Anyway, they are peaceful, agreeable people, who ask nothing but to be allowed to go about their business and to be happy in their own way.

They are shy birds, and detest being looked at, or talked to, or photographed, or written about. They don't want white men in their restaurants, or nosing about their places. They carry this love of secrecy to strange lengths. Not so long ago a press photographer set out boldly to get pictures of Chinatown. He marched to the mouth of Limehouse Causeway, through which, in the customary light of grey and rose, many amiable creatures were gliding, levelled his nice new Kodak, and got—an excellent picture of the Causeway after the earthquake. The entire street in his plate was deserted.

Certain impressionable people—Cook's tourists and Civil Servants—return from the East mumbling vague catchwords —mystic, elusive, subtle, haunting, alluring. These London Chinese are neither subtle nor mystic. They are mostly materialist and straightforward; and, once you can gain their confidence, you will find yourself wonderfully at home. But it has to be gained, for, as I have said, they are shy, and were you to try to join a game of cards on a short acquaintance . . . well, it would be easier to drop in for a cigarette with King George. To get into a Grosvenor Square mansion on a ball night is a comparatively easy matter: swank and an evening suit will do it; nothing very exclusive about those people. But the people of Limehouse, and, indeed, of any slum or foreign quarter, are exclusive; and to get into a Poplar dope-house on bargain night demands the exercise of more Oriental ingenuity than most of us possess.

Only at the mid-January festival do they forget themselves and come out of their shells. Then things happen. The West India Dock Road is whipped to life. The windows shake with flowers, the roofs with flags. Lanterns are looped from house to house, and the slow frenzy of Oriental carnival begins. In the morning there is solemn procession, with joss-sticks, to the cemetery, where prayers are held over the graves of departed compatriots, and lamentations are carried out in native fashion, with sweet cakes, whisky, and song and gesture. In the evening—ah!—dancing in the

halls with the white girls. Glamorous January evening . . .
yellow men with much money to spend . . . beribboned girls,
gay, flaunting, and fond of curious kisses . . . lighted lanterns swinging lithely on their strings . . . noise, bustle, and
laughter of the cafés . . . all these things light this little bit
of London with an alluring Eastern flame.

There was a time, years ago, when the East End was the
East End—a land apart, with laws and customs of its own,
cut off from civilization, and having no common ground with
Piccadilly. But the motor-'bus has changed all that. It has
so linked things and places that all individual character has
been swamped in a universal chaos, and there is now neither
East nor West. All lost nooks of London have been dug out
and forced into the traffic line, and boundaries are things
which exist to-day only in the mind of the borough council-
lor. Hyde Park stretches to Shadwell, Hampstead to Albert
Docks. Soho is *vieux jeu*. Little Italy is exploded. The
Russian and Jewish quarters are growing stale and commercial, and the London Docks are a region whose chief features are Cockney warehouse clerks. This corner of Limehouse alone remains defiantly its Oriental self, no part of
London; and I trust that it may never become popular, for
then there will be no spot to which one may escape from
the banalities of the daily day.

But as we stood in the little bedroom of the gentleman
from Pi-chi-li the clock above Millwall Docks shot twelve
crashing notes along the night. The gentleman thrust a
moon face through the dusky doorway to inquire if I had
changed my mind. Would myself and honourable companions smoke, after all? We declined, but he assured me that
we should meet again at Tai-Ling's café, and perhaps hospitality . . .

So we tumbled down the crazy stairs, through the room
from which the Chinks were fast melting, and into the midnight glitter of the endless East India Dock Road. We
passed through streets of dark melancholy, through laby-

rinthine passages where the gas-jets spluttered asthmatically, under weeping railway arches, and at last were free of the quarter where the cold fatalism of the East combats the wistful dubiety of the West. But the atmosphere, physical and moral, remained with us. Not that the yellow men are to blame for this atmosphere. The evil of the place is rather that of Londoners, and the bitter nightmare spirit of the place is rather of them than of Asia. I said that there was little wickedness in Chinatown, but one wickedness there is, which is never spoken of in published articles; opium seems the only point that strangers can fasten on. Even if this wickedness were known, I doubt if it would be mentioned. It concerns ... But I had better not.

We looked back at Barking Road, where it dips and rises with a sweep as lovely as a flying bird's, and on the bashful little streets, whose lights chime on the darkness like the rounding of a verse. Strange streets they are, where beauty is unknown and love but a grisly phantom; streets peopled, at this hour, with loose-lipped and uncomely girls—mostly the fruit of a yellow-and-white union—and with other things not good to be talked of. I was philosophizing to my friend about these things, and he was rhapsodizing to me about the stretch of lamplights, when a late 'bus for the Bank swept along. We took a flying mount that shook the reek of Limehouse from our clothes and its nastiness from our minds, and twenty minutes later we were taking a final coffee at the "Monico."

ON LYING IN BED *

By Gilbert K. Chesterton

LYING in bed would be an altogether perfect and supreme experience if only one had a coloured pencil long enough to draw on the ceiling. This, however, is not generally a part of the domestic apparatus on the premises. I think myself that the thing might be managed with several pails of Aspinall and a broom. Only if one worked in a really sweeping and masterly way, and laid on the colour in great washes, it might drip down again on one's face in floods of rich and mingled colour like some strange fairy rain; and that would have its disadvantages. I am afraid it would be necessary to stick to black and white in this form of artistic composition. To that purpose, indeed, the white ceiling would be of the greatest possible use; in fact it is the only use I think of a white ceiling being put to.

But for the beautiful experiment of lying in bed I might never have discovered it. For years I have been looking for some blank spaces in a modern house to draw on. Paper is much too small for any really allegorical design; as Cyrano de Bergerac says: "Il me faut des géants." But when I tried to find these fine clear spaces in the modern rooms such as we all live in I was continually disappointed. I found an endless pattern and complication of small objects hung like a curtain of fine links between me and my desire. I examined the walls; I found them to my surprise to be already covered with wall-paper, and I found the wall-paper to be already covered with very uninteresting images, all bearing a ridiculous resemblance to each other. I could not understand why one arbitrary symbol (a symbol apparently entirely devoid of any religious or philosophical significance) should thus be sprinkled all over my nice walls like a sort of small-pox. The Bible must be referring to wall-papers, I think, when it says "Use not vain repetitions, as the Gentiles do." I found the Turkey carpet a mass of unmeaning colours, rather like the Turkish Empire, or like the sweetmeat called Turkish delight. I do not exactly know what Turkish delight really is; but I suppose it is Macedonian Massacres. Everywhere that I went forlornly, with my pencil or my paint brush, I found that others had unaccountably been before me, spoiling the walls, the curtains, and the furniture with their childish and barbaric designs.

.   .   .   .   .   .

Nowhere did I find a really clear place for sketching until this occasion when I prolonged beyond the proper limit the process of lying on my back in bed. Then the light of that white heaven broke upon my vision, that breadth of mere white which is indeed almost the definition of Paradise, since it means purity and also means freedom. But alas! like all heavens, now that it is seen it is found to be unattainable; it looks more austere and more distant than the blue sky outside the window. For my proposal to paint on it with the bristly end of a broom has been discouraged— never mind by whom; by a person debarred from all political rights—and even my minor proposal to put the other end of the broom into the kitchen fire and turn it into charcoal has not been conceded. Yet I am certain that it was from persons in my position that all the original inspiration came for covering the ceilings of palaces and cathedrals with a riot of fallen angels or victorious gods. I am sure that it was only because Michael Angelo was engaged in the ancient and honourable occupation of lying in bed that he ever realised how the roof of the Sistine Chapel might be made into an awful imitation of a divine drama that could be enacted in the heavens.

The tone now commonly taken towards the practice of lying in bed is hypocritical and unhealthy. Of all the marks of modernity that seem to mean a kind of decadence, there is none more menacing and dangerous than the exultation of very small and secondary matters of conduct at the expense of very great and primary ones, at the expense of eternal public and tragic human morality. If there is one thing worse than the modern weakening of major morals it is the modern strengthening of minor morals. Thus it is considered more withering to accuse a man of bad taste than of bad ethics. Cleanliness is not next to godliness nowadays, for cleanliness is made an essential and godliness is regarded as an offence. A playwright can attack the institution of marriage so long as he does not misrepresent the manners of society, and I have met Ibsenite pessimists who thought it wrong to take beer but right to take prussic acid. Especially this is so in matters of hygiene; notably such matters as lying in bed. Instead of being regarded, as it ought to be, as a matter of personal convenience and adjustment, it has come to be regarded by many as if it were a part of essential morals to get up early in the morning. It is upon the whole part of practical wisdom; but there is nothing good about it or bad about its opposite.

. . . .

Misers get up early in the morning; and burglars, I am informed, get up the night before. It is the great peril of our society that all its mechanism may grow more fixed while its spirit grows more fickle. A man's minor actions and arrangements ought to be free, flexible, creative; the things that should be unchangeable are his principles, his ideals. But with us the reverse is true; our views change constantly; but our lunch does not change. Now, I should like men to have strong and rooted conceptions, but as for their lunch, let them have it sometimes in the garden, sometimes in bed, sometimes on the roof, sometimes in the top of a tree. Let them argue from the same first principles, but let them do it in a bed, or a boat, or a balloon. This alarming growth of good habits really means a too great emphasis on those virtues which mere custom can misuse, it means too little emphasis on those virtues which custom can never quite ensure, sudden and splendid virtues of inspired pity or of inspired candour. If ever that abrupt appeal is made to us we may fail. A man can get used to getting up at five o'clock in the morning. A man cannot very well get used to being burnt for his opinions; the first experiment is commonly fatal. Let us pay a little more attention to these possibilities of the heroic and the unexpected. I daresay that when I get out of this bed I shall do some deed of an almost terrible virtue.

For those who study the great art of lying in bed there is one emphatic caution to be added. Even for those who can do their work in bed (like journalists), still more for those whose work cannot be done in bed (as, for example, the professional harpooner of whales), it is obvious that the indulgence must be very occasional. But that is not the caution I mean. The caution is this: if you do lie in bed, be sure you do it without any reason or justification at all. I do not speak, of course, of the seriously sick. But if a healthy man lies in bed, let him do it without a rag of excuse; then he will get up a healthy man. If he does it for some secondary hygienic reason, if he has some scientific explanation, he may get up a hypochondriac.

PLEASURES OF ANXIETY *

By Frank Moore Colby

WHAT with the tango and the slit skirt, eugenics and the
pest of women's thinking, the growing impudence of·the poor,
the incorrect conversion of certain negro tribes, and the sudden appearance of a rather strong article on feminism, civilization in this country, and perhaps everywhere, was drawing
to its close in many a serious magazine article, some years
ago. I made rather a conscientious survey of the matter at
that time, and I recall to this day some of the shocking particulars. Down goes the dike, said one; and it seems to
have been the only dike that could have prevented "our
civilization from being engulfed in an overwhelming flood
of riches, and from sinking in an orgy of brutality." Now
that religion has gone, said another, "the old-fashioned
principles of right and wrong have also largely disappeared."
Turning a few pages, I found the "ulcer in our new morality";
a few more, and I saw the "canker at the root of education."
Then I learned how low this nation was rated by a connois-
seur of all the nations of the globe. "Of all the countries I
have ever met," said he, as his mind reverted along the
parallels of latitude to the thirty-seven populations he had
intimately known, "this country, to speak candidly is the least
desirable"; and so he cast off the country as one who throws
away a bad cigar.

And consider society's danger from astrologers. Abolish

* From *The Margin of Hesitation;* copyright, 1921, by Dodd, Mead
and Company. Reprinted by permission of the author and the
publishers.

astrologers at once, said another contributor, and also spirit-
ualists and quacks and prophets; for if we do not, all clean
culture will soon rot and vanish, killed by the germs from this
"cultural underworld." There were dozens of bodings just
as dark as these in other numbers. But there was always a
consolation.

When perils came out in the new numbers, it quieted one
to turn to the old perils in the bound volumes of the file—
yellow perils, black, white, brown, and red ones, horrors of
house-flies and suffragettes, and all the evil kind of micrococ-
cus, back to imperialism and the bicycle skirt of fifteen years
before, and to read, say, of Carrie Nation ravaging Kansas,
and the California lady who used to hurl college professors
through the windows, thus destroying academic liberty, and
McKinley "blood-guilty" and sitting on a "throne," and
Thanksgiving day changed to Shame day or the Devil's own
day by some Boston contributors, and the Stars and Stripes
painted black and "replaced by the skull and cross-bones,"
and bloodshed in fiction, and hazing at West Point, and the
United States government "shaking Porto Rico over hell."
And every time saved by a miracle—the same old family
miracle!

I could not deny that civilization was then in danger,
but it did seem to me that in any serious magazine it always
must be in danger. And it so happened at that time that
every writer was spared all anxiety about any actual danger.
The one thing not noticed on any of the quaking pages I
have mentioned was the shadow of the great war, which was
then approaching.

The contributor of a peril to a magazine is not, as a rule,
an unhappy person. On the contrary, he is often a large,
calm man, with a good appetite, and more cheerful in his
mind than we. If one could feel toward any menace to
humanity as one used to feel toward tales of Jack the Giant
Killer, just believing enough for a little goose-flesh, there
would be more fun in it. Any man who is about half con-

vinced that he and a few others are the sole remaining friends
of civilization finds some dramatic zest in life. It is a mistake to assume that men who earn their living by anxiety
are at all anxious in their private lives.

And it is the same way with all great political despairs
in private conversation. The most depressing talkers
you ever meet are not themselves personally at all depressed. On the contrary, they are, at bottom, rather
gay persons. The hopelessness of the situation really adds,
for the purposes of conversation, to its charm, by absolv-
ing from the need of any personal effort other than the
presumably agreeable one of talking. In middle aged conversation there is always a certain cosiness in political
despair, and the thought of a large general disaster coming
on has, at any rate, one bright side in the way it warms
up elderly conversers. I do not mean to deny that the
disaster may exist even when it is talked about. I merely
mean that if a disaster did not exist it would be necessary to
invent it.

For some time past in common with certain other fellow-
beings, I have read the more or less radical journals with
greater interest than the other kind. What is worse, I enjoy
various eccentric and perhaps fanatical or one-idea'd periodicals more than I do those of sober cast and steady habits
and institutional point of view. I confess a strong distaste,
probably a vulgar one, for all that class of periodicals which
no gentleman's library used to be without. In America I
have found more pleasure in periodicals, which would be reck-
oned by the safe person as unsafe, than I have in the daily
journalism of broadly based opinion on the one hand or the
monthly journalism of no opinion at all on the other hand.
I mean literally pleasure, for in this preference I have not
primarily my country's good in mind, or the future of civilization, or my own or anybody else's moral safety. I suppose I
share these peculiar and ill-regulated tastes with about six
million persons in the English-speaking world. We are con-

sidered a small band, and dangerous, for some reason, though the thing that most often strikes me is how numerous we are and how mild.

Nevertheless it is a minority and most people that I know, for my acquaintances are mainly among the majority, do not find pleasure in this type of journalism, and they too profess to regard it as dangerous. In this for the most part I believe they are hypocrites—not of course in their expression of a lack of pleasure but in the reasons they give for it.

I deny that their dislike is born of any sense of civic danger. It is the product of ennui. People will run, and always have run, grave risks to existing institutions so long as they are amused. When they are not amused they express alarm for the safety of the institutions. It is simply their emphatic way of saying that they are not amused. Thus you will often hear a man say of a certain periodical that it ought to be suppressed, its editor hanged, all its contributors tarred and feathered, and the premises fumigated by the health board, and then add casually that he has picked it up from time to time and simply could not read a word of it. Or you will see an elderly club member so incensed by some article on birth control (hard enough, Heaven knows, for any one to keep his mind on, but not remarkable in any other way) as to be hardly capable of coherent speech, and find him five minutes later with all the pornographic French weeklies on his lap, soothed again and beaming, as if reassured after all in regard to the bloom of innocence that he had almost feared was passing from the world. Not that I pretend to know which is the better for him—the awful Anglo-Saxon solemnity of the article on birth control or the unconquerable hilariousness of certain French minds on subjects more or less akin to it. But neither does he know and he simply does not care. For the rule here applies as it does to a large part of current criticism that distaste sounds more emphatic when expressed as moral disapproval. With most of us the moral counterblast is nothing more than the angry rendering of a yawn.

For one person who is repelled by the views of the sort of periodicals I have mentioned there are a hundred persons repelled by the manner of presenting them, and their objections to that manner, so far as I have heard them expressed, seem to boil down to two main grievances: In the first place an apparent desire on the part of the writers to conceal their thoughts, and in the second place, and what is more important, a degree and continuity of seriousness, unattainable, even on the assumption that its attainment is desirable, by any person in the outside world.

I believe there is a basis for both charges. Concealment of thought, however,—vindictive though it often seems—is, as a rule, involuntary. Social studies are commonly the cause of this defect,—or courses taken during impressionable years at American schools of political science where any lucid way of putting things is always hated, if it is known at all.

As the sort of seriousness of which readers complain I confess I sometimes cannot see the excuse for it. The radical mind seems never to permit itself an instant's respite from its cares. At least I have never happened to meet one of them in print when it was taking it. Pen in hand there seems only one of two things for it to do: Either to tell people how they ought to act or blame them for not doing so.

It is invariably harassed by the cares of a sort of gigantic paternity, and it slumbers not nor sleeps. If it did its watching only over Israel it might lead, comparatively speaking, rather a jolly life; but take its duty to Asia for example. Asia is, to you or me, for comfortable intervals at least, only a distant continent on the map. Asia is never for a moment anything of the sort to a man of these responsibilities. Asia to him is as a little child constantly running some hairbreadth escape. Russia, says he, is not only the acid test of diplomacy; it is the acid test of intelligence. Now of course that is perfectly true, but if you follow him carefully and far enough you will observe that Africa also is an acid test and so is South America. You will observe also that sex, woman, Bolshevism, Shantung, war babies, North Dakota, feeble-mindedness of peace commissioners, Ireland's wrongs, syndicalism, the railway bill, Poland, classicism, ultra-realism, or anything else he may have thought about, supplies the acid test of what to think; and that, as the months pass by, he has gradually narrowed the area of permissible thinking, that is to say the zone of opinion conforming to his own, first to a strip, then to a long line, zigzag and perilous, so narrow that two can scarcely walk abreast on it, and then if they should chance to fall to quarreling one would inevitably be lost.

Now if you will turn back six months on the track of this serious person—a thing that apparently the serious person never does—you will find half a dozen questions reported as about to flame, which, somehow, never flamed at all; and you will find a score of problems which if not solved at that particular instant were to have brought us to the verge of the abyss but which have not been solved since then and seem to have been forgotten even by the writer—along with the abyss. In short, a six months' retrospect of him seems to reveal something seriously amiss with his seriousness. It would seem, after all, that some of the responsibilities were needlessly incurred, or that there were well earned intervals of moral repose of which he might have taken advantage.

A special and temporary reason for it in this country may have been a too close relation with the universities. There has often been an interlocking of college and editorial faculties to an extent most discouraging to an adult general reader who prefers not to continue to be taught—or at least not taught as in a university from which he was probably glad to escape. College and editorial chairs have often got so mixed up that a writer forgot which he was sitting in; hence, floods of didacticism were poured upon the public that were really intended for Sociology B. And as to chairs of English litera-

ture they were notoriously wheeled chairs, all of them, and
likely to turn up at any time in serious journalism, for when
a man once firmly settled down in one of them, he never got
out, and even after resignation would be rolled about in it
all through life, rolled generally into some editorial office.

But any one at all familiar with pen-habits of Americans
ought to know that the sort of persons he thinks he is meeting in these serious pages do not exist. He will not mistake
the heavy hand for the heavy heart and he will not imagine
that those anxieties, running all the way from babies' milk
to the state of Europe in the twenty-fifth century, are really
felt. He will realize the tradition of serious journalism which
demands as a matter of course that a man shall conceal any
tremor of indecision in regard to any subject that comes
along, no matter how tremendous. And he will not confound
a human attitude with a simple matter of conventional
technique.

EVERY MAN'S NATURAL DESIRE TO BE SOMEBODY ELSE *

By Samuel McChord Crothers

Several years ago a young man came to my study with a manuscript which he wished me to criticize.

"It is only a little bit of my work," he said modestly, "and it will not take you long to look it over. In fact it is only the first chapter, in which I explain the Universe."

I suppose that we have all had moments of sudden illumination when it occurred to us that we had explained the Universe, and it was so easy for us that we wondered why we had not done it before. Some thought drifted into our mind and filled us with vague forebodings of omniscience. It was not an ordinary thought, that explained only a fragment of existence. It explained everything. It proved one thing and it proved the opposite just as well. It explained why things are as they are, and if it should turn out that they are not that way at all, it would prove that fact also. In the light of our great thought chaos seemed rational.

Such thoughts usually occur about four o'clock in the morning. Having explained the Universe, we relapse into satisfied slumber. When, a few hours later, we rise, we wonder what the explanation was.

Now and then, however, one of these highly explanatory ideas remains to comfort us in our waking hours. Such a thought is that which I here throw out, and which has doubt-less at some early hour occurred to most of my readers. It is that every man has a natural desire to be somebody else.

This does not explain the Universe, but it explains that perplexing part of it which we call Human Nature. It ex-plains why so many intelligent people, who deal skillfully with matters of fact, make such a mess of it when they deal with their fellow creatures. It explains why we get on as well as we do with strangers, and why we do not get on better with our friends. It explains why people are so often offended when we say nice things about them, and why it is that, when we say harsh things about them, they take it as a compliment. It explains why people marry their opposites and why they live happily ever afterwards. It also explains why some people don't. It explains the meaning of tact and its opposite.

The tactless person treats a person according to a scientific method as if he were a thing. Now, in dealing with a thing, you must first find out what it is, and then act accordingly. But with a person, you much first find out what he is and then carefully conceal from him the fact that you have made the discovery. The tactless person can never be made to understand this. He prides himself on taking people as they are without being aware that that is not the way they want to be taken.

He has a keen eye for the obvious, and calls attention to it. Age, sex, color, nationality, previous condition of servi-tude, and all the facts that are interesting to the census-taker, are apparent to him and are made the basis of his conversa-tion. When he meets one who is older than he, he is con-scious of the fact, and emphasizes by every polite attention the disparity in years. He has an idea that at a certain period in life the highest tribute of respect is to be urged to rise out of one chair and take another that is presumably more comfortable. It does not occur to him that there may remain any tastes that are not sedentary. On the other hand, he sees a callow youth and addresses himself to the obvious callowness, and thereby makes himself thoroughly disliked. For, strange to say, the youth prefers to be addressed as a person of precocious maturity.

The literalist, observing that most people talk shop, takes it for granted that they like to talk shop. This is a mistake. They do it because it is the easiest thing to do, but they resent having attention called to their limitations. A man's profession does not necessarily coincide with his natural aptitude or with his predominant desire. When you meet a member of the Supreme Court you may assume that he is gifted with a judicial mind. But it does not follow that that is the only quality of mind he has; nor that when, out of court, he gives you a piece of his mind, it will be a piece of his judicial mind that he gives.

My acquaintance with royalty is limited to photographs of royal groups, which exhibit a high degree of domesticity. It would seem that the business of royalty when pursued as a steady job becomes tiresome, and that when they have their pictures taken they endeavor to look as much like ordinary folks as possible—and they usually succeed.

The member of one profession is always flattered by being taken for a skilled practitioner of another. Try it on your minister. Instead of saying, "That was an excellent sermon of yours this morning," say, "As I listened to your cogent argument, I thought what a successful lawyer you would have made." Then he will say, "I did think of taking to the law."

If you had belonged to the court of Frederick the Great you would have proved a poor courtier indeed if you had praised His Majesty's campaigns. Frederick knew that he was a Prussian general, but he wanted to be a French literary man. If you wished to gain his favor you should have told him that in your opinion he excelled Voltaire.

We do not like to have too much attention drawn to our present circumstances. They may be well enough in their

way, but we can think of something which would be more
fitting for us. We have either seen better days or we expect
them.

Suppose you had visited Napoleon in Elba and had sought
to ingratiate yourself with him.

"Sire," you would have said, "this is a beautiful little empire of yours, so snug and cozy and quiet. It is just such a
domain as is suited to a man in your condition. The climate
is excellent. Everything is peaceful. It must be delightful
to rule where everything is arranged for you and the details
are taken care of by others. As I came to your dominion I
saw a line of British frigates guarding your shores. The
evidences of such thoughtfulness are everywhere."

Your praise of his present condition would not have en-
deared you to Napoleon. You were addressing him as the
Emperor of Elba. In his own eyes he was Emperor, though in
Elba.

It is such a misapprehension which irritates any mature
human being when his environment is taken as the measure
of his personality.

The man with a literal mind moves in a perpetual comedy
of errors. It is not a question of two Dromios. There are
half a dozen Dromios under one hat.

How casually introductions are made, as if it were the
easiest thing in the world to make two human beings acquainted! Your friend says "I want you to know Mr. Stifflekin," and you say that you are happy to know him. But does
either of you know the enigma that goes under the name of
Stifflekin? You may know what he looks like and where he
resides and what he does for a living. But that is all in the
present tense. To really know him you must not only know
what he is but what he used to be; what he used to think he
was; what he used to think he ought to be and might be if
he worked hard enough. You must know what he might
have been if certain things had happened otherwise, and you
must know what might have happened otherwise if he had

been otherwise. All these complexities are a part of his own dim apprehension of himself. They are what make him so much more interesting to himself than he is to any one else.

It is this consciousness of the inadequacy of our knowledge which makes us so embarrassed when we offer any service to another. Will he take it in the spirit in which it is given?

That was an awkward moment when Stanley, after all his hardships in his search for Dr. Livingstone, at last found the Doctor by a lake in Central Africa. Stanley held out his hand and said stiffly, "Dr. Livingstone, I presume?" Stanley had heroically plunged through the equatorial forests to find Livingstone and to bring him back to civilization. But Livingstone was not particularly anxious to be found, and had a decided objection to being brought back to civilization. What he wanted was a new adventure. Stanley did not find the real Livingstone till he discovered that the old man was as young at heart as himself. The two men became acquainted only when they began to plan a new expedition to find the source of the Nile.

The natural desire of every man to be somebody else explains many of the minor irritations of life. It prevents that perfect organization of society in which every one should know his place and keep it. The desire to be somebody else leads us to practice on work that does not strictly belong to us. We all have aptitudes and talents that overflow the narrow bounds of our trade or profession. Every man feels that he is bigger than his job, and he is all the time doing what theologians called "works of supererogation."

The serious-minded housemaid is not content to do what she is told to do. She has an unexpended balance of energy. She wants to be a general household reformer. So she goes to the desk of the titular master of the house and gives it a thorough reformation. She arranges the papers according to her idea of neatness. When the poor gentleman returns and finds his familiar chaos transformed into a hateful order, he becomes a reactionary.

The serious manager of a street railway company is not content with the simple duty of transporting passengers cheaply and comfortably. He wants to exercise the functions of a lecturer in an ethical culture society. While the transported victim is swaying precariously from the end of a strap he reads a notice urging him to practice Christian courtesy and not to push. While the poor wretch pores over this counsel of perfection, he feels like answering as did Junius to the Duke of Grafton, "My Lord, injuries may be atoned for and forgiven, but insults admit of no compensation."

A man enters a barber shop with the simple desire of being shaved. But he meets with the more ambitious desires of the barber. The serious barber is not content with any slight contribution to human welfare. He insists that his client shall be shampooed, manicured, massaged, steamed beneath boiling towels, cooled off by electric fans, and, while all this is going on, that he shall have his boots blacked.

Have you never marveled at the patience of people in having so many things done to them that they don't want, just to avoid hurting the feelings of professional people who want to do more than is expected of them? You watch the stoical countenance of the passenger in a Pullman car as he stands up to be brushed. The chances are that he doesn't want to be brushed. He would prefer to leave the dust on his coat rather than to be compelled to swallow it. But he knows what is expected of him. It is a part of the solemn ritual of traveling. It precedes the offering.

The fact that every man desires to be somebody else explains many of the aberrations of artists and literary men. The painters, dramatists, musicians, poets, and novelists are just as human as housemaids and railway managers and porters. They want to do "all the good they can to all the people they can in all the ways they can." They get tired of the ways they are used to and like to try new combinations.

So they are continually mixing things. The practitioner of one art tries to produce effects that are proper to another art.

A musician wants to be a painter and use his violin as if it were a brush. He would have us see the sunset glories that he is painting for us. A painter wants to be a musician and paint symphonies, and he is grieved because the uninstructed cannot hear his pictures, although the colors do swear at each other. Another painter wants to be an architect and build up his picture as if it were made of cubes of brick. It looks like brick-work, but to the natural eye it doesn't look like a picture. A prose-writer gets tired of writing prose, and wants to be a poet. So he begins every line with a capital letter, and keeps on writing prose.

You go to the theater with the simple-minded Shakespearean idea that the play's the thing. But the playwright wants to be a pathologist. So you discover that you have dropped into a gruesome clinic. You sought innocent relaxation, but you are one of the non-elect and have gone to the place prepared for you. You must see the thing through. The fact that you have troubles of your own is not a sufficient claim for exemption.

Or you take up a novel expecting it to be a work of fiction. But the novelist has other views. He wants to be your spiritual adviser. He must do something to your mind, he must rearrange your fundamental ideas, he must massage your soul, and generally brush you off. All this in spite of the fact that you don't want to be brushed off and set to rights. You don't want him to do anything to your mind. It's the only mind you have and you need it in your own business.

But if the desire of every man to be somebody else accounts for many whimsicalities of human conduct and for many aberrations in the arts, it cannot be lightly dismissed as belonging only to the realm of comedy. It has its origin in the nature of things. The reason why every man wants to be somebody else is that he can remember the time when he was somebody else. What we call personal identity is a very changeable thing, as all of us realize when we look over old photographs and read old letters.

The oldest man now living is but a few years removed from the undifferentiated germ-plasm, which might have developed into almost anything. In the beginning he was a bundle of possibilities. Every actuality that is developed means a decrease in the rich variety of possibilities. In becoming one thing it becomes impossible to be something else.

The delight in being a boy lies in the fact that the possibilities are still manifold. The boy feels that he can be anything that he desires. He is conscious that he has capacities that would make him a successful banker. On the other hand, there are attractions in a life of adventure in the South Seas. It would be pleasant to lie under a bread-fruit tree and let the fruit drop into his mouth, to the admiration of the gentle savages who would gather about him. Or he might be a saint—not a commonplace modern saint who does chores and attends tiresome committee meetings, but a saint such as one reads about, who gives away his rich robes and his purse of gold to the first beggar he meets, and then goes on his carefree way through the forest to convert interesting robbers. He feels that he might practice that kind of unscientific charity, if his father would furnish him with the money to give away.

But by and by he learns that making a success in the banking business is not consistent with excursions to the South Seas or with the more picturesque and unusual forms of saintliness. If he is to be in a bank he must do as the bankers do.

Parents and teachers conspire together to make a man of him, which means making a particular kind of man of him. All mental processes which are not useful must be suppressed. The sum of their admonitions is that he must pay attention. That is precisely what he is doing. He is paying attention to a variety of things that escape the adult mind. As he wriggles on the bench in the schoolroom, he pays attention to all that is going on. He attends to what is going on out-of-doors; he sees the weak points of his fellow pupils, against whom he is planning punitive expeditions; and he is delightfully conscious of the idiosyncrasies of the teacher. Moreover, he is a youthful artist and his sketches from life give acute joy to his contemporaries when they are furtively passed around.

But the schoolmaster says sternly, "My boy, you must learn to pay attention; that is to say, you must not pay attention to so many things, but you must pay attention to one thing, namely the second declension."

Now the second declension is the least interesting thing in the room, but unless he confines his attention to it he will never learn it. Education demands narrowing of attention in the interest of efficiency.

A man may, by dint of application to a particular subject, become a successful merchant or real-estate man or chemist or overseer of the poor. But he cannot be all these things at the same time. He must make his choice. Having in the presence of witnesses taken himself for better for worse, he must, forsaking all others, cleave to that alone. The consequence is that, by the time he is forty, he has become one kind of a man, and is able to do one kind of work. He has acquired a stock of ideas true enough for his purposes, but not so transcendentally true as to interfere with his business. His neighbors know where to find him, and they do not need to take a spiritual elevator. He does business on the ground floor. He has gained in practicality, but has lost in the quality of interestingness.

The old prophet declared that the young men dream dreams and the old men see visions, but he did not say anything about the middle-aged men. *They* have to look after the business end.

But has the man whose working hours are so full of responsibilities changed so much as he seems to have done? When he is talking shop is he "all there"? I think not. There are elusive personalities that are in hiding. As the rambling

mansions of the old Catholic families had secret panels opening into the "priest's hole," to which the family resorted for
spiritual comfort, so in the mind of the most successful man
there are secret chambers where are hidden his unsuccessful
ventures, his romantic ambitions, his unfulfilled promises.
All that he dreamed of as possible is somewhere concealed in
the man's heart. He would not for the world have the public
know how much he cares for the selves that have not had a
fair chance to come into the light of day. You do not know
a man until you know his lost Atlantis, and his Utopia for
which he still hopes to set sail.

When Dogberry asserted that he was "as pretty a piece of
flesh as any is in Messina" and "one that hath two gowns
and everything handsome about him," he was pointing out
what he deemed to be quite obvious. It was in a more intimate
tone that he boasted, "and a fellow that hath had losses."

When Julius Cæsar rode through the streets of Rome in his
chariot, his laurel crown seemed to the populace a symbol
of his present greatness. But gossip has it that Cæsar at
that time desired to be younger than he was, and that before
appearing in public he carefully arranged his laurel wreath
so as to conceal the fact that he had *had* losses.

Much that passes for pride in the behavior of the great
comes from the fear of the betrayal of emotions that belong
to a simpler manner of life. When the sons of Jacob saw
the great Egyptian officer to whom they appealed turn away
from them, they little knew what was going on. "And Joseph
made haste, for his bowels did yearn upon his brother: and
he sought where to weep; and he entered into his chamber,
and wept there. And he washed his face, and went out, and
refrained himself." Joseph didn't want to be a great man.
He wanted to be human. It was hard to refrain himself.

What of the lost arts of childhood, the lost audacities and
ambitions and romantic admirations of adolescence? What
becomes of the sympathies which make us feel our kinship

to all sorts of people? What becomes of the early curiosity in regard to things which were none of our business? We ask as Saint Paul asked of the Galatians, "Ye began well; who did hinder you?"

The answer is not wholly to our discredit. We do not develop all parts of our nature because we are not allowed to do so. Walt Whitman might exult over the Spontaneous Me. But nobody is paid for being spontaneous. A spontaneous switchman on the railway would be a menace to the traveling public. We prefer some one less temperamental.

As civilization advances and work becomes more specialized, it becomes impossible for any one to find free and full development for all his natural powers in any recognized occupation. What then becomes of the other selves? The answer must be that playgrounds must be provided for them outside the confines of daily business. As work becomes more engrossing and narrowing the need is more urgent for recognized and carefully guarded periods of leisure.

The old Hebrew sage declared, "Wisdom cometh from the opportunity of leisure." It does not mean that a wise man must belong to what we call the leisure classes. It means that if one has only a little free time at his disposal, he must use that time for the refreshment of his hidden selves. If he cannot have a sabbath rest of twenty-four hours, he must learn to sanctify little sabbaths, it may be of ten minutes' length. In them he shall do no manner of work. It is not enough that the self that works and receives wages shall be recognized and protected; the world must be made safe for our other selves. Does not the Declaration of Independence say that every man has an inalienable right to the pursuit of happiness?

To realize that men are not satisfied with themselves requires imagination, and we have had a terrible example of what misfortunes come from the lack of imagination. The Prussian militarists had a painstaking knowledge of facts, but they had a contempt for human nature. Their tactlessness was almost beyond belief. They treated persons as if they were things. They treated facts with deadly seriousness, but had no regard for feelings. They had spies all over the world to report all that could be seen, but they took no account of what could not be seen. So, while they were dealing scientifically with the obvious facts and forces, all the hidden powers of the human soul were being turned against them. Prussianism insisted on highly specialized men who have no sympathies to interfere with their efficiency. Having adopted a standard, all variation must be suppressed. It was against this effort to suppress the human variations that the world fought. We did not want all men to be reduced to one pattern. And against the effort to produce a monotonous uniformity we must keep on fighting. It was of little use to dethrone the Kaiser if we submit to other tyrants of our own making.

QUALITY *

By John Galsworthy

I KNEW him from the days of my extreme youth, because
he made my father's boots; inhabiting with his elder brother
two little shops let into one, in a small by-street—now no
more, but then most fashionably placed in the West End.

That tenement had a certain quiet distinction; there was
no sign upon its face that he made for any of the Royal
Family—merely his own German name of Gessler Brothers;
and in the window a few pairs of boots. I remember that
it always troubled me to account for those unvarying boots
in the window, for he made only what was ordered, reaching
nothing down, and it seemed so inconceivable that what he
made could ever have failed to fit. Had he bought them to
put there? That, too, seemed inconceivable. He would
never have tolerated in his house leather on which he had
not worked himself. Besides, they were too beautiful—the
pair of pumps, so inexpressibly slim, the patent leathers with
cloth tops, making water come into one's mouth, the tall
brown riding boots with marvellous sooty glow, as if, though
new, they had been worn a hundred years. Those pairs
could only have been made by one who saw before him the
Soul of Boot—so truly were they prototypes incarnating the
very spirit of all foot-gear. These thoughts, of course, came
to me later, though even when I was promoted to him, at the
age of perhaps fourteen, some inkling haunted me of the
dignity of himself and brother. For to make boots—such

* From *The Inn of Tranquillity;* copyright, 1912, by Charles Scribner's Sons. Reprinted by permission of the author and the publishers.

boots as he made—seemed to me then, and still seems to me, mysterious and wonderful.

I remember well my shy remark, one day, while stretching out to him my youthful foot:

"Isn't it awfully hard to do, Mr. Gessler?"

And his answer, given with a sudden smile from out of the sardonic redness of his beard: "Id is an Ardt!"

Himself, he was a little as if made from leather, with his yellow crinkly face, and crinkly reddish hair and beard, and neat folds slanting down his cheeks to the corners of his mouth, and his guttural and one-toned voice; for leather is a sardonic substance, and stiff and slow of purpose. And that was the character of his face, save that his eyes, which were gray-blue, had in them the simple gravity of one secretly possessed by the Ideal. His elder brother was so very like him—though watery, paler in every way, with a great industry—that sometimes in early days I was not quite sure of him until the interview was over. Then I knew that it was he, if the words, "I will ask my brudder," had not been spoken; and, that, if they had, it was his elder brother.

When one grew old and wild and ran up bills, one somehow never ran them up with Gessler Brothers. It would not have seemed becoming to go in there and stretch out one's foot to that blue iron-spectacled glance, owing him for more than—say—two pairs, just the comfortable reassurance that one was still his client.

For it was not possible to go to him very often—his boots lasted terribly, having something beyond the temporary— some, as it were, essence of boot stitched into them.

One went in, not as into most shops, in the mood of: "Please serve me, and let me go!" but restfully, as one enters a church; and, sitting on the single wooden chair, waited— for there was never anybody there. Soon, over the top edge of that sort of well—rather dark, and smelling soothingly of leather—which formed the shop, there would be seen his face, or that of his elder brother, peering down. A guttural sound, and the tip-tap of bast slippers beating the narrow wooden stairs, and he would stand before one without coat, a little bent, in leather apron, with sleeves turned back, blinking—as if awakened from some dream of boots, or like an owl surprised in daylight and annoyed at this interruption.

And I would say: "How do you do, Mr. Gessler? Could you make me a pair of Russia leather boots?"

Without a word he would leave me, retiring whence he came, or into the other portion of the shop, and I would continue to rest in the wooden chair, inhaling the incense of his trade. Soon he would come back, holding in his thin, veined hand a piece of gold-brown leather. With eyes fixed on it, he would remark: "What a beaudiful biece!" When I, too, had admired it, he would speak again. "When do you wand dem?" And I would answer: "Oh! As soon as you conveniently can." And he would say: "To-morrow fordnighd?" Or if he were his elder brother: "I will ask my brudder!"

Then I would murmur: "Thank you! Good-morning, Mr. Gessler." "Goot-morning!" he would reply, still looking at the leather in his hand. And as I moved to the door, I would hear the tip-tap of his bast slippers restoring him, up the stairs, to his dream of boots. But if it were some new kind of foot-gear that he had not yet made me, then indeed he would observe ceremony—divesting me of my boot and holding it long in his hand, looking at it with eyes at once critical and loving, as if recalling the glow with which he had created it, and rebuking the way in which one had disorganized this masterpiece. Then, placing my foot on a piece of paper, he would two or three times tickle the outer edges with a pencil and pass his nervous fingers over my toes, feeling himself into the heart of my requirements.

I cannot forget that day on which I had occasion to say to him: "Mr. Gessler, that last pair of town walking-boots creaked, you know."

He looked at me for a time without replying, as if expecting me to withdraw or qualify the statement, then said:

"Id shouldn'd 'ave greaked."

"It did, I'm afraid."

"You goddem wed before dey found demselves?"

"I don't think so."

At that he lowered his eyes, as if hunting for memory of those boots, and I felt sorry I had mentioned this grave thing.

"Zend dem back!" he said; "I will look at dem."

A feeling of compassion for my creaking boots surged up in me, so well could I imagine the sorrowful long curiosity of regard which he would bend on them.

"Zome boods," he said slowly, "are bad from birdt. If I can do noding wid dem, I dake dem off your bill."

Once (once only) I went absent-mindedly into his shop in a pair of boots bought in an emergency at some large firm's. He took my order without showing me any leather, and I could feel his eyes penetrating the inferior integument of my foot. At last he said:

"Dose are nod my boods."

The tone was not one of anger, nor of sorrow, not even of contempt, but there was in it something quiet that froze the blood. He put his hand down and pressed a finger on the place where the left boot, endeavoring to be fashionable, was not quite comfortable.

"Id 'urds you dere," he said. "Dose big virms 'ave no self-respect. Drash!" And then, as if something had given way within him, he spoke long and bitterly. It was the only time I ever heard him discuss the conditions and hardships of his trade.

"Dey get id all," he said, "dey get id by adverdisement, nod by work. Dey dake it away from us, who lofe our boods. Id gomes to this—bresently I haf no work. Every year id gets less—you will see." And looking at his lined face I saw things I had never noticed before, bitter things and bitter struggle—and what a lot of gray hairs there seemed suddenly in his red beard!

As best I could, I explained the circumstances of the purchase of those ill-omened boots. But his face and voice made so deep impression that during the next few minutes I ordered many pairs. Nemesis fell! They lasted more terribly than ever. And I was not able conscientiously to go to him for nearly two years.

When at last I went I was surprised to find that outside one of the two little windows of his shop another name was painted, also that of a bootmaker—making, of course, for the Royal Family. The old familiar boots, no longer in dignified isolation, were huddled in the single window. Inside, the now contracted well of the one little shop was more scented and darker than ever. And it was longer than usual, too, before a face peered down, and the tip-tap of the bast slippers began. At last he stood before me, and, gazing through those rusty iron spectacles, said:

"Mr. ——, isn'd it?"

"Ah! Mr. Gessler," I stammered, "but your boots are really *too* good, you know! See, these are quite decent still!" And I stretched out to him my foot. He looked at it.

"Yes," he said, "beople do nod wand good boods, id seems."

To get away from his reproachful eyes and voice I hastily remarked: "What have you done to your shop?"

He answered quietly: "Id was too exbensif. Do you wand some boods?"

I ordered three pairs, though I had only wanted two, and quickly left. I had, I do not know quite what feeling of being part, in his mind, of a conspiracy against him; or not perhaps so much against him as against his idea of boot. One does not, I suppose, care to feel like that; for it was again many months before my next visit to his shop, paid, I remember, with the feeling: "Oh! well, I can't leave the old boy—so here goes! Perhaps it'll be his elder brother!"

For his elder brother, I knew, had not character enough to reproach me, even dumbly.

And, to my relief, in the shop there did appear to be his elder brother, handling a piece of leather.

"Well, Mr. Gessler," I said, "how are you?"

He came close, and peered at me.

"I am breddy well," he said slowly; "but my elder brudder is dead."

And I saw that it was indeed himself—but how aged and wan! And never before had I heard him mention his brother. Much shocked, I murmured: "Oh! I am sorry!"

"Yes," he answered, "he was a good man, he made a good bood; but he is dead." And he touched the top of his head, where the hair had suddenly gone as thin as it had been on that of his poor brother, to indicate, I suppose, the cause of death. "He could nod ged over losing de oder shop. Do you wand any boods?" And he held up the leather in his hand: "Id's a beaudiful biece."

I ordered several pairs. It was very long before they came —but they were better than ever. One simply could not wear them out. And soon after that I went abroad.

It was over a year before I was again in London. And the first shop I went to was my old friend's. I had left a man of sixty, I came back to one of seventy-five, pinched and worn and tremulous, who genuinely, this time, did not at first know me.

"Oh! Mr. Gessler," I said, sick at heart; "how splendid your boots are! See, I've been wearing this pair nearly all the time I've been abroad; and they're not half worn out, are they?"

He looked long at my boots—a pair of Russia leather, and his face seemed to regain steadiness. Putting his hand on my instep, he said:

"Do dey vid you here? I 'ad drouble wid dat bair, I remember."

I assured him that they had fitted beautifully.

"Do you wand any boods?" he said. "I can make dem quickly; id is a slack dime."

I answered: "Please, please! I want boots all round—every kind!"

"I will make a vresh model. Your food must be bigger." And with utter slowness, he traced round my foot, and felt my toes, only once looking up to say:

"Did I dell you my brudder was dead?"

To watch him was painful, so feeble had he grown; I was glad to get away.

I had given those boots up, when one evening they came. Opening the parcel, I set the four pairs out in a row. Then one by one I tried them on. There was no doubt about it. In shape and fit, in finish and quality of leather, they were the best he had ever made me. And in the mouth of one of the town walking-boots I found his bill. The amount was the same as usual, but it gave me quite a shock. He had never before sent it in till quarter day. I flew down-stairs, and wrote a check, and posted it at once with my own hand. A week later, passing the little street, I thought I would go in and tell him how splendidly the new boots fitted. But when I came to where his shop had been, his name was gone. Still there, in the window, were the slim pumps, the patent leathers with cloth tops, the sooty riding boots.

I went in, very much disturbed. In the two little shops —again made into one—was a young man with an English face.

"Mr. Gessler in?" I said.

He gave me a strange, ingratiating look.

"No, sir," he said, "no. But we can attend to anything with pleasure. We've taken the shop over. You've seen our name, no doubt, next door. We make for some very good people."

"Yes, yes," I said; "but Mr. Gessler?"

"Oh!" he answered; "dead."

"Dead! But I only received these boots from him last Wednesday week."

"Ah!" he said; "a shockin' go. Poor old man starved 'imself."

"Good God!"

"Slow starvation, the doctor called it! You see he went to work in such a way! Would keep the shop on; wouldn't have a soul touch his boots except himself. When he got an order, it took him such a time. People won't wait. He lost everybody. And there he'd sit, goin' on and on—I will say that for him—not a man in London made a better boot! But look at the competition! He never advertised! Would 'ave the best leather, too, and do it all 'imself. Well, there it is. What could you expect with his ideas?"

"But starvation——!"

"That may be a bit flowery, as the sayin' is—but I know myself he was sittin' over his boots day and night, to the very last. You see I used to watch him. Never gave 'imself time to eat; never had a penny in the house. All went in rent and leather. How he lived so long I don't know. He regular let his fire go out. He was a character. But he made good boots."

"Yes," I said, "he made good boots."

And I turned and went out quickly, for I did not want that youth to know that I could hardly see.

ADVENTURES IN PHILOSOPHY *

By Ellwood Hendrick

I

A LITTLE HOMILY ON THE TRUTH

WE sorely need a clearer conception of the truth. We need it in the business of living; especially as a means of avoiding misunderstandings. If we have an abstract idea of what the truth is we are less likely to err in the belief that we are right before we know the truth. In adventuring upon a theory which for the past few years has seemed to me to hold we shall hardly be charged with applying new meanings to old words if we say that facts and the truth are not the same. Facts are parts of the truth, just as wheels, rods, levers, and the like are parts of a machine. If we say "the whole truth" every time we refer to the truth, it might make the idea more clear, but let us agree to consider it so, without the need of saying two words where one will do.

If you strike me, that becomes a fact as soon as you have done it. Whether you have struck me or not is a question of fact and not a question of truth. The truth may be that you struck me to call my attention to impending danger, or you may have struck me in anger, or the blow may be an unimportant episode in a long fight between us.

The truth, as I conceive it, is all the facts in their right or correct relation, the relation which they must bear to one

* From *Percolator Papers;* copyright, 1919, by Harper & Brothers. Reprinted by permission of the author and the publishers.

114

another when the truth is attained. Thus the truth becomes an abstract thing, because we know *what* it is, although we may not know *it*. Rarely, indeed, are we able to gather all the facts in relation to a subject, on the one hand, or to correlate them, on the other; nevertheless, we must do this if we would know the truth.

If this definition is unfamiliar, if we are not accustomed to consider the truth in this sense, I think it will do us no harm to bear it in mind. In courts of law, according to current practice, it might not hold, but we are, fortunately, under no obligation to order our thinking according to processes of law.

If we exalt the truth and reverence it, the glib and hysterical brothers and sisters who, grasping a single fact, proceed to preach that and that only as the truth, will cause less annoyance. We may acknowledge their facts as facts, which is all they can ask of us. If we still remain unconvinced of the truth of their preachments we shall be contradicting no one. The truth is very great, very large, and when Lessing prayed that to him be given the privilege to seek the truth rather than to know it, because to know it he was not worthy, he spoke as one of the wisest of men. To seek it, to get nearer to it, sometimes perhaps to get a glimpse of it, is all that we may hope for; it is the best that we can do.

Suppose you and I look at a tree on a hillside. We see only the leaves, and we observe that the tree is green. The tree *is* green; that is a fact. Let us make a note of it. Then suppose we go a distance away and look at it again. The tree is blue. It is idle for us to say, "It seems blue, but it really is green," because our very organs which gave the reaction of green a while ago now give the reaction of blue. By the same token that the tree was green when we saw it near by it is blue when we see it from afar. So let us make a second note: the tree is blue. Here we have two contradictory statements of fact, neither false, and yet neither the whole truth. The truth about the color of the tree involves a great range of subjects, including the physics of light, the anatomy and physiology of the human eye, photochemistry—in short, a vast store of learning and understanding.

Many facts which seem irreconcilable become harmonious parts of the truth when all the facts are arranged in their right order. So the truth should make us humble and patient with one another. None of us has faculties of universal co-ordination, and our blind spots, instead of being little delinquencies of perception, are in reality vast areas. The most we can claim is that we have a few sighted spots. To see all the facts in their right relation is what we might call the Olympian Vision.

II

THE GREEN TREE

The first time I visited Charlotte, North Carolina, I had some business to transact with a charming, soft-spoken old gentleman who wore a broad-brimmed felt hat. When our business was completed for the day we walked leisurely about the town. "Charlotte," said the gentleman of the sombrero, "is all to' up over a dispute which is ragin' among our people."

"What is the cause of it?" I asked.

"Free grace and fo'ordination," he answered.

I was delighted, and wrote a long letter home about it that night. Charlotte seemed so very archaic! This was many years ago, and since then Charlotte has grown to be a great manufacturing town with a grand hotel and clubs and all the things that modern industry and wealth bring about. In those days there were the Presbyterians and Baptists on the one side and the Methodists and Lutherans on the other, and the adherents of the little Episcopal Church, who were divided on the question. These included substantially the whole white population. Now, unless I am sorely mistaken, Charlotte has ceased to worry over "free grace and fo'ordination"; she is modern and up-to-date. But if my surmise be correct, she has gone backward intellectually; she only thinks herself modern; she has become commercial and has ceased to participate in the intellectual life of the day. For the old question whereby Charlotte was "all to' up" abides in philosophy. Turn whichever way we will, we meet that same old nagging problem, teasing us, on the one hand, with what seems to be proof that we have no free will at all, and insisting, on the other, that a very good reason why we have free will is because we know we have it.

Many of us have ceased to be Presbyterians or Baptists or Methodists or Episcopalians, but as soon as we venture into biology we find ourselves urged to join either the Mechanist or the Vitalist denomination, and there we find the same old dispute raging again among our biological people.

This is, indeed, the comedy domain of philosophy. The Greeks used to dispute over it. St. Paul appeared to have the problem solved, and so did St. Augustine. Pelagius differed from them, and so did his followers—with some warmth. The harmony between Luther and John Calvin over the matter was not striking; Servetus had an opinion which went up in smoke; the savants of Charlotte, North Carolina, talked themselves out over it—and now behold the biologists in battle array! If it were given to us to live to a prodigious number of years and to observe the earth from afar, we should see the philosophers in dispute over this problem throughout the ages, never agreeing and never persuading one another. It is a very enduring subject.

But is not this dispute over the question whether we have free will or not very like a dispute that we might engage in over the color of a tree—whether it be green or blue? It hardly seems worth while to boast or to grow angry in protesting that we have absolute free will, when a little surgical operation of one sort or another, or a shock, or a blow upon the head, may change our nature entirely. Why not proceed along the mechanistic way seeking the mechanical, physical, and chemical causes of every act, and thus gather as many facts as we can? If every act seems to be a response to a stimulus, why deny it? We shall not have achieved the truth when we have learned the exact process of every act, but we shall be much wiser than we are now. We shall advance toward the truth when we learn the relation to one another of those processes of which we are now so ignorant. And if from the study of the facts at hand we reach the conclusion that we have no free will at all, but are mere automata, with no power of choice or selection throughout our lives, is it not time to pause and admit that we may not have all the facts yet? Also that such as we have may not be in their right order before our vision?

There are some verses by John Godfrey Saxe, called "The Blind Men and the Elephant," which are very instructive. According to Saxe, six wise men of Indostan, all of them very wise, but all of them blind, went to see the elephant. One examined its side and declared the elephant was very like a wall; another, feeling its trunk, was sure the elephant was very like a snake; another concluded from its leg that it was very like a tree; another, examining one of its tusks, knew that the elephant was very like a spear; the expert who examined its ear found it to resemble a fan, and the authority who grasped its tail was equally certain that the elephant was very like a rope. According to the legend, they are still disputing over it.

Now the truth is bigger than an elephant, and our vision of it is narrower than the observations of each of the blind men. And we should bear in mind that they were right, every one of them. Each had a fact; none knew the truth. None had a theory of the truth; each knew what he knew, and that was enough for him. We can well imagine one of them saying, "If a thing is so, it's so, and you can't get around it; my senses bear me witness; the elephant is very like a snake."

If we have a good working method of dealing with facts it is a good thing to hold to it just as we do well to hold fast to the fact that the tree is green when we look at it near by. It seems to be a part of the truth. And the mechanistic theory, which will have nothing to do with spooks or ghosts or with vital sparks with qualities that are not material, is helpful, wholesome, and illuminating. It makes for clean thinking. It will not countenance the Pickwickian point of view, which is very popular and current in our day. It provides that facts be gathered by observation and the study of cause and effect. It also seems to lead to the conclusion that every act is the only one possible under conditions as they exist. Now if this reasoning appears sound, let us, instead of frothing at the mouth and denouncing the sincere men who have reached these conclusions, admit it— as a part of the truth.

If through another chain of reasoning, or through consciousness, or by any other means, we come to a conclusion opposed to this, there is no occasion to boast that the first conclusion is disproved. If we reach both conclusions, we may know that we have not yet achieved the truth, but, for aught we know, both may be right. That we have free will and that we have not free will may be, both of them, parts of the truth, just as the opposed statements that the tree is green and that it is blue are parts of the truth.

We may say that the whole organization of human conduct is based upon the free will of the individual; but the organization of human conduct, like many another good thing, is based in large part upon fancy. When we consider acts from anear we might as well admit that free will seems to play very little, if any, part in them. Here is the human machine with its equipment, the consciousness including a part of that group of records and nerve centers which are "connected up," the connecting up occurring automatically along the line of least resistance; and then, given the stimulus, the one and only reaction which can occur does occur. There would need to be a difference in the equipment or the stimulus to bring about a different reaction. The conclusion, you observe, is precisely the same as that reached by the late and occasionally lamented John Calvin, except that he maintained that every current through the colloidal content of every nerve was a special, volitional act of the Deity, "for His own glory."

This view, that every act is automatic if considered by itself, has great merit. If we consider it to be a part of the truth, we are likely to have far more abundant charity for one another. By it we enlarge our sympathy. For instance, we may say that everybody always does his best at the time he acts. If he does evil, there is a reason for it, a structural reason. His sympathetic equipment may be atrophied. Or he may be angry. In either case we are dealing with facts close at hand and our business is with his condition. The cause of it may be due to his grandfather, or to a false leading in his early childhood. We should diagnose his case and determine what part of his equipment is atrophied or what part so congested that his way was the path of crime. And if he is angry we should regard him as a nervous invalid until his attack is over and the anger bodies are eliminated from his system or until his injured brain cells are restored.

There is an illuminating book by Doctor Crile, of Cleveland, on *The Origin and Nature of the Emotions,* that is very enlightening about anger. He postulates that by evolution we have developed what he calls "nociceptors," which give the warning of pain in the presence of danger, and that these warnings are given according to the experience of the race. The equipment provides against such external injuries as the goring and tearing by an animal's teeth in far greater measure than against the more modern devices of swift-moving bullets and very sharp instruments, because the experience of the race against teeth is so much greater than with bullets and swords. It is imaginable that if a sword were sharp enough and thin enough and swung with sufficient speed, the old Chinese legend of the master headsman might almost escape fiction. In this, it may be recalled, the executioner graciously gave a pinch of snuff to each of his victims, who remained comfortably unaware that his head had been severed from his body. By the sneezes which followed the perfect swordsmanship was revealed; the heads rolled off, and the surprised offenders proceeded to die with all haste and propriety.

Another interesting warning is found in the fact that we are ticklish in our ears and nostrils and on the soles of our feet, where buzzing insects are likely to sting.

Now in danger these warnings elicit the response either of flight or of turning and facing it, and so we become either afraid or angry. Doctor Crile notes two features in connection with these emotions which are interesting in regard to what we are discussing: he finds that during the processes of anger and fear we suffer inhibitions of all other faculties than those which are of value in fighting or running away. We are useless, inefficient, incompetent, in every other respect. When we are angry we have not our normal equipment because the greater part is blocked off, and we are no more our complete selves than when, if ever, we are very drunk. The second observation is that under anger or fear there occurs a destruction of brain cells that are but slowly repaired, and, under stress of severe and prolonged emotion, the brain is permanently injured. These notes have been vastly illuminating to me in regard to the dreadful war which now rages, and I think we may well pause to consider how difficult the recovery will be after it is over, when so many minds that are crippled by passion must attempt the work that calls for entire men.

The Man of Wrath with a great lust to kill ceases to inspire us. We know that he is of value in hand-to-hand combats, but he is a nuisance, and even worse, in a fight where cool heads and steady hands are needed for machine-guns. He is potential in instigating war, but he is incompetent to end it. He is a drum-major of anarchy.

We also learn that the emotional hurrah of the man in high authority is evidence that he is unfit for his job, because under emotion his qualities of judgment are paralyzed and his sense of co-ordination is atrophied.

While confining ourselves to the mechanistic point of view we may describe judgment as the operation of selecting the best thing available to do at the time—just as the tree reaches out toward the light—and we may regard it as mechanical. As in a Jacquard loom the woof is run through those openings that are before it, so the judgment, the determining bobbin, as we might call it, passes through those channels of the mind that are open to it, and determines the act which we mechanically perform.

We may regard impulse as something different from reason if we want to, but to me the difference seems to be in name rather than in fact. If judgment is automatic it may operate so rapidly that it skips consciousness, but that is no ground for calling it a thing apart. Under impulse we act rapidly, so that consciousness is often skipped in the process, and usually there is an emotional drive to it. An impulse seems to me to be a quick, emotional leading or drive to an act, and as much of an automatic response to stimulus as to eat when we are hungry or to drink when we are thirsty. In doing many things we skip consciousness after we are used to doing them, although at first, when we are learning how, they involve great effort.

There are also automatic vanities which we have discussed elsewhere, of which a notable example is our disposition to justify ourselves, any time and all the time. We are apt to think that we thought, when we were acting so rapidly that the act skipped consciousness. And in explaining afterward, our sense of veracity is under the greatest strain. We fool ourselves into the belief that we deliberated over every possibility, when in fact we were following blindly the drive within us to do that which was the only possible thing that we could do under existing conditions.

III

THE BLUE TREE

Free will is a long way from our acts, yet we have a constructive faculty. Although often within a very narrow range, we have the ordering of our lives in our hands. This constructive faculty is in use when we are conjuring up our ideals. We can of our own volition say, "I will plan my life to do this thing." We can of our own will select a picture in our minds and hold it in our consciousness as a stimulus. More likely than not we get the idea from some one else; but such ideas, as they are given to us, become our property, to do with as we will, to adopt as ideals or to reject. Many things influence us in this; we are not as free as we think we are; we generate our own energy, and some of us are equipped with very low-power dynamos; but the process of selecting those purposes and ways of life which we project into our consciousness by our own will is the occasion of our greatest freedom.

As we grow older we become either more firm of purpose or more obedient to any stimulus; what we have made of our lives becomes more fixed; but at no time are we complete. We may change our whole nature at fifty as well as at thirty or fifteen—but we are less likely to. This business of combining impressions and setting them up as ideals is the substance of our free will. We may fall short of our ideals, we may be entirely different from what we meant to be, and yet be following them as nearly as we can. The question of responsibility is: With what earnestness do we select our ideals, and with what effort do we project them into our consciousness?

The difference between achieving an ideal and performing an act is rather hazy, I'll admit; but I imagine the one to be the little push we give of our own desire and choice when a picture comes into consciousness that we want to have represent us. "That is mine!" we say, and we proceed to conform to the picture, to drive it into consciousness, to recall it, to urge it upon ourselves until in the end we act that way, and this because we want to. The picture is the stimulus, but the process of selection seems supermechanical. Although I cannot imagine how we can think without our thinking-machines, it seems that somewhere in the process freedom has entered in and we thus become, let us say, the navigating officers of our lives. On the other hand, the direct performance of an act seems an automatic response to the strongest stimulus in the mind at the time.

This may seem like arguing in a circle, because the mechanism that we employ when we are selecting our ideals is substantially the same as that which we use when we perform an act. But the stimulus comes from within. Responsibility is a quality that we recognize, and to consider it a fiction seems premature—as though we had not yet a clear vision of the truth of the matter.

In the late Christian Herter's remarkable and, in many respects, illuminating book called *Biologic Aspects of Human Problems* he develops consciousness as an "awareness of self" that arises in a certain complexity of organism under certain conditions. This awareness of self becomes more abundant as what we might call the harmonious complexity of the organism increases. Now, responsibility, or the capacity to choose of our own accord, like consciousness, is a quality that seems to be present in us. It would be futile to deny consciousness because we do not understand just how and where it begins. And it seems equally idle to deny responsibility. It seems to me to be a late accompaniment of this awareness of self which we know we have, and to my way of thinking it functions when we order our lives.

So we may conceive these two statements as being parts of the truth—that whatever any one does, it seems the best that he can do at the time, and also that whatever any one does is qualified by the manner in which he has ordered his life. This idealizing ego, then, is as much a part of ourselves as are our fingers and toes. It is also selective. Now, if it appears that we have no free will when we commit an act, but have free will when we order our lives, we surely have not the whole truth in hand, but the theory may lead us nearer to it.

IV

THE GOD IN THE MACHINE

Here I respectfully ask your pardon. Despite my protestations I have already burdened you with a definition of the truth that is not in the dictionaries, and now I am about to ask you to consider religion from a point of view that does not seem to be current. I admit frankly that it is not only distressing to the reader, but also that it makes for confusion, to frame new definitions for old words as one proceeds; but, *"Gott hilf mir; ich kann nicht anders!"*

It seems to me that, so far as our civilization is concerned, the concept of religion *per se* is modern. There is no Germanic word for it; in English, German, Dutch, and Scandinavian, the Latin word has been imported and substituted for faith, belief, and even for dogma and theology. In the sense in which I want to use the word there is no plural. Christianity, Buddhism, Brahminism, Judaism, Mohammedanism are not so many religions (although I must admit that the Latins, who gave us the word, would have used it in this sense) ; they are, let us say, faiths or beliefs or confessions. At all events, if we agree to call them such, it will leave us free to use the word religion without thinking of the minister, the Sunday-school, or the choir in which we used to sing. Of course, the minister and the Sunday-school and the church choir may have functioned as parts of religion, but to think of them as the substance of it might get them out of their right relation to the idea which I am trying to express.

In the chapter called "The Blue Tree" we considered how we may, of our own free will, select impressions or ideas, and by making ideals of them drive them into consciousness so that they shall serve both as stimuli and inhibitions to our actions. We called this the ordering of life. In the process we are open to impressions, although we determine within ourselves, subject, of course, to our limitations, which of these impressions we shall select. Now, the function of providing ideals and offering them and teaching them, so that we may order our lives aright and thus approach the truth, seems to me to be the great province of religion. We may practise religion either with or without dogma. The man of faith may have great religious value, and again he may have no religious value at all. There are, for example, religious Christians, and, on the other hand, Christians of great piety who are not religious. The anchorite who whips and distresses himself to save his own soul is not practising religion; he is exercising his faith. The Samaritan who picks up the fallen wanderer by the wayside and by his act also enlarges the vision of the man he helps, so that the stimulus of sympathy enters into him, is doing a religious act. Faith may be a stimulus to religious acts, and we know that it often is; but since often it is not, we may as well address ourselves to that aspect of religion which we can understand, regarding it as having to do with the ordering of our lives, and not as related to dogma or faith save as dogma or faith may induce it. Then we find that everybody has the religious equipment, just as he has a sympathetic equipment, although both may be greatly atrophied. With his mind, although we cannot fail to recognize a conflict between science and the Bible and science and dogma, there is no conflict between science and religion.

This view of religion takes the subject out of the domain of metaphysics and mysteries and recognizes it as a specific department of human life. By it we reach the conclusion that it is a necessary function, in which we are all interested. The truly religious man is he who helps you and me to be of positive value to the world in which we live and, in one way or another, to approach the truth. Whether he be a Christian or a Jew or anything else is his affair—his faith, his profession. His religion is in his ideals and his use of them.

We must have ideals. We can do nothing without them. And this essay is written in the sincere belief that as we approach the truth with understanding, one human problem after another will be solved. Only, we must order our lives aright or else we cannot approach the truth. We cannot, otherwise, get the facts into focus. So all the world needs religion—to-day, it would seem, more than ever before. Dogmas that we cannot believe will not answer the purpose. Apologetics often offend more than they aid. Religion is bigger than any church or any creed or any faith, and its business is the development of a wiser and a better humanity.

V

INTO THE UNKNOWN

We have discussed the problem of free will and found it not very free, and yet I have tried to develop the idea that we have the ordering of our lives in our own hands. Now let us adventure farther, and this time into the unknown, with analogy as our guide.

We have seen how facts are parts of the truth and that we reap confusion if we consider them as substitutes for it. We might postulate a law of arrangement, a law of order, that holds good in regard to the truth and applies also to animate and inanimate things. We see this ordering of the composite parts into their right relation in the formation of a crystal. We need not question now why the molecules join according to a mathematical scale to form a symmetrical body; suffice it for the present to observe that they do. The molecules are individual, but they group themselves into something that is not a molecule—into a crystal. We may compare a crystal to the truth, and the molecules to the facts which constitute it. Until the molecules are in their right order there is no crystal. Until the facts are in their right order there is no truth.

We, as men and women, are composed of innumerable particles of many different kinds. Their good condition and orderly arrangement are necessary to our being. Let us consider, for example, our white blood corpuscles or leucocytes. They work with what almost appears to be intelligence in overcoming disease. They are not simple little things by any means; they are marvelously complex. They respond to a stimulus and go to work, just as we do. Sometimes they are weak, inefficient, and sick; and then we languish or die because they do not do their work. They are mechanical entities, and are subject to physical and chemical laws.

Now we are mechanical entities and we constitute something greater than ourselves. We group ourselves artificially into nations which a congress has power to change by moving a boundary line from one side of us to the other. We divide humanity into other groups, as into families, because of immediate consanguinity, and into races, based on what appears to be a remoter consanguinity. We divide ourselves again into long-headed and broad-headed classes. The facts upon which these groupings are based do not accord with one another, nor do they tell us much about what humanity means. They are desirable facts and, in a way, it is worth knowing that some of us are of one nation and some of another; some long-headed and some broad; some one thing and others something else; but a new and greater meaning might be applied to us by a master mind, the greater anthropologist who could explain the human family as it has not been explained before.

The news of battles does not tell us what is really happening to us all; and there are problems ahead even graver and more important than who shall win. Is not victory itself a curse to the winner who lacks the character to meet his obligations? Some day, let us hope, a wiser generation will follow that will refuse to accept the wrath and hate that we cherish, and will work diligently to repair the havoc of this war. Then perhaps the greater anthropologist will come.

Collective humanity is, indeed, a strange phenomenon. Constantly destroying itself, it is at war with half of nature and cultivates as richly as it can the other half. It has a marvelous faculty for helping itself, and then, when a part of it has achieved a high order of living and gathered in those things of the earth which it desires, there is usually a great fall, and as the years roll on, the dull, stupid toiler guides his plow over the land that once was Carthage and Nineveh. What is it that makes collective humanity sick? What was the disease of Babylon and of the forgotten city that underlies it? After all the analyses, what was the sickness of Rome? Why did Europe go to sleep for a thousand years, and what was it that killed the intellect of the Saracens? Why did Persia die?

Collective humanity is a thing, a being that grows well and is strong and becomes godlike, and then again sickens and becomes foolish, and the spirit of it fades away until slavery under a benign master would be an advantage. Collective humanity as we see it is a great jumble of parts, related, unrelated, and in dire confusion. What is it doing? Not one of us can tell.

Now let us imagine leucocytes to have consciousness and vision, and let us consider a single one of them. Its abode is in the blood of somebody—of you, let us say; and its life is very exciting for it because it never knows what its path will be. Sometimes it is driven into one of your fingers, again into one of your toes; it may be busy on a little scratch well covered up, or it may suddenly have to do battle with a tetanus bacillus. Ask a leucocyte what it knows of life, and it might well answer that it is a continuous problem; it would tell you all sorts of interesting things about your interior— which is its whole world—but it could not tell anything about you. Even so simple a detail as that, for instance, you do not like parsnips, could not occur to this leucocyte, because you do not eat them, and so it has no experience with parsnips. Really, the leucocytes with consciousness, which I am imagining, are very like us; they are in their world and we in ours. And we may be very like them—parts of a Great Intelligence as much beyond us as we are beyond the leucocytes which form parts of us.

Humanity has always been speculating about this Greater Intelligence, and yet speculation has always been discouraged on the ground that the matter is all settled. This conservatism is what gives us such amazing dicta as the Westminster Shorter Catechism and the Thirty-nine Articles. The usual human concept of the Greater Intelligence is as of one apart from us and appearing in all manifestations of power. It has been proposed that we may come into sight and communication with it after death; and the fear of it, described as the beginning of wisdom, has also been used to make us do strange things in accordance with traditions and myths older than history.

Even analogy will only help us occasionally here, and otherwise we have nothing to guide us in these vaster regions but the imagination. And yet, if we can imagine some relation between human beings and a possible Greater Intelligence, a relation which does not seem false or impossible, we may be taking steps in advance. If we imagine this and imagine that and then something else, it may be that some day somebody will imagine a working hypothesis which does not seem to offend against the truth.

Now suppose the working hypothesis should involve the conception of human beings as minute particles of the Greater Intelligence, citing the analogy of the leucocytes or any other swarm of microscopic units. We need not then restrict ourselves to their reactions in the human body. We are different, are differently constructed, and this remarkable quality of consciousness is, at all events, far greater in the human being than it is, for instance, in a leucocyte. Without doubt it reaches farther. Nor need we restrict the Greater Intelligence to our own limitations. We are not conscious of our blood corpuscles, but that is no reason why the Greater Intelligence may not be conscious of us. We know, as we have said, that if our white blood corpuscles are weak, inefficient, or sick, we languish, and that our welfare requires that they be in health. So, if we consider collective humanity and observe that it advances in knowledge, in understanding, in order, and in righteousness, we may then feel that it is well with the Greater Intelligence of which we are a part. But if we live in idleness and waste and hatred and cruelty and malice, and cause misery and degradation, it would seem that we are offending and injuring the Greater Intelligence, the God of all of us. This makes the Greater Intelligence in a way dependent upon us, so that it loses health and welfare and power when we undermine the health and welfare of one another.

Sometime when we know more than we do now, there may be available a working hypothesis along these lines and in accord with familiar facts. It is interesting to speculate upon what the results may be. Hebrew poetry has given us a tradition and a conception of a deity apart from ourselves and pregnant with the greatest conceivable measure of power. The Christian, Jewish, and Mohammedan peoples worship an Almighty Divinity that rules the stars and the uttermost heavens, the nebulæ as well as the sun and its planets, including the earth. The thought of any other is condemned. Beginning with a tribal master of its fate inspired by selfishness, lust, and wrath, humanity has magnified its conception of its god until it has exalted him beyond the earth and projected him through the ether into a million other worlds. It may be that we shall be guided back again to a God of all men and women, exercising vast powers of the spirit when in health and when His component particles are doing their work as they should, but losing power to lead or guide if mankind is wayward and corrupt.

CONCERNING REVOLVING DOORS *

By Oliver Herford

THERE has been some discussion of late as to the etiquette of the revolving door. When a man accompanied by a woman is about to be revolved in it, which should go first? Some think the man should precede the woman, furnishing the motive power, while she follows idly in the next compartment. Others hold that the rule "Ladies first" can have no exception, therefore the man must stand aside and let the female of the species do the rough work of starting the door's revolution while the man, coming after, keeps it going and stops it at the right moment.

"Starting something" is perhaps of all pastimes in the world the one most popular with the sex we are accustomed to call the gentle sex; one might almost say that "starting something" is Woman's prerogative; on the other hand there is nothing on earth so abhorrent to that same gentle sex as the thing that is called Consistency; and though she may be perfectly charmed to start a revolution in South America, or in silk pajamas, or suffrage, or the rearing of children, it does not follow that she will take kindly to the idea of starting the revolution of a revolving door.

As for the rule "Ladies first," its application to the etiquette of doors in general (as distinguished from the revolving variety) is purely a matter of geography. In some European countries it is the custom, when entering a room, for the man

* From *Neither Here Nor There;* copyright, 1922, by George H. Doran Company. Reprinted by permission of the author and the publishers.

to precede the woman, and if it be a closed street or office door, the man will open it and following the door inward, hold the door open while she passes in. If the door opens outward the woman naturally enters first, since her companion must remain outside to hold the door open.

The American rule compelling the woman to precede her escort when entering a room or building doubtless originated with our ancestor the cave man.

On returning to his Apartment with his wife after a hunting expedition Mr. Hairy K. Stoneaxe would say with persuasive Neolithic smile (and gentle shove) "After you my dear," being rewarded for his politeness by advance information as to whether there were Megatheriums or Loxolophodons or an ambuscade of jealous rivals lurking in the darkness of his stone-upholstered sitting-room.

By all means let the lady go first; by so doing we pay the homage that is due to her sex and even though there are no Megatheriums or Loxolophodons in these days—there *may* be burglars! Only in the case of a door that must be opened inwards would I suggest an amendment. What more lamentable sight than that of a gentle lady squeezing precariously through a half-opened door while her escort, determined that though they both perish in the attempt, she shall go first, reaches awkwardly past her shoulder in the frantic endeavor to push back the heavy self-closing door while at the same time contorting the rest of his person into the smallest possible compass that she may have room to pass without disaster to her ninety-dollar hat, not to speak of her elbows and shins.

How much happier—and happiness is the mainspring of etiquette—they would be, this same pair, if (with a possible "allow me" to calm her fears) the escort should push boldly the door to its widest openness and holding it thus with one hand behind his back, with the other press his already removed hat against his heart as the lady grateful and unruffled sweeps majestically by.

ON WEARING A HAT *

By Robert Cortes Holliday

THERE is a good deal to be said about wearing a hat. And yet this humorous custom, this rich topic, of wearing a hat has been sadly neglected, as far as I can make out, by scholars, scientists, poets, composers, and other "smart" people.

Man has been variously defined, as the religious animal, and so on; but also, to the best of my knowledge and belief, he is the only animal that wears a hat. He has become so accustomed to the habit of wearing his hat that he does not feel that he is himself out of doors without it. Mr. Howells (I think it was) has told us in one of his novels of a young man who had determined upon suicide. With this intent he made a mad dash for the sea. But on his way there a sudden gust of wind blew off his hat; instinctively he turned to recover it, and this action broke the current of his ideas. With his hat he recovered his reason, and went home as alive as usual. His hat has come to mean for man much more than a protection for his head. It is for him a symbol of his manhood. You cannot more greatly insult a man than by knocking off his hat. As a sign of his reverence, his esteem, his respect, a man bares his head. Though, indeed, the contentious Mr. Chesterton somewhere argues that there is no more reason for a man's removing his hat in the presence of ladies than for his taking off his coat and waistcoat.

In the more complex social organisms of Europe the custom of lifting the hat to other men whom one thus acknowledges

* From *Walking-Stick Papers;* copyright, 1918, by George H. Doran Company. Reprinted by permission of the author and the publishers.

as superiors is much more prevalent than in our democratic country. Though in America we remove our hats in elevators upon the entrance of ladies, a practice which is not followed in England. It was Mrs. Nickleby who indicated the extreme politeness of the noble gentlemen who showed her to her carriage by the celebrated remark that they took their hats "completely off." We express great joy by casting our hats into the air. If I wish to show my contempt for you I will wear my hat in your house; if I wish you to clear out of my house I say: "Here's your hat"; if I am moved to admiration for you I say: "I take off my hat to you." I greatly enjoy seeing you run after your hat in the street, because you are thereby made excessively ridiculous. The comic Irishman of the vaudeville stage makes his character unmistakable to all by carrying his clay pipe in his hat band. The English painter, Thomas Gainsborough, gave his name to a hat. The seasoned newspaper man displays his cynical nature and complete disillusionment by wearing his hat at his desk. A hat worn tilted well back on the head indicates an open nature and a hail-fellow-well-met disposition; while a hat decidedly tilted over one eye is the sign of a hard character, and one not to be trifled with. In the literature of alcoholism it is written that a common hallucination of the inebriate is that a voice cries after him: "Where did you get that white hat?" Upon assuming office the cardinal is said to "take the hat." When a man is conspicuously active in American political life "his hat is in the ring." Whistler topped off his press-agent eccentricity with a funny hat. The most idiosyncratic hat at present in America is that which decorates the peak of Mr. Bliss Carman. The hat-stands in our swagger hotels make a great deal of money; I know a gentleman who affirmed that a hat which had originally cost him three dollars had cost him eighteen dollars to be got back from hat-checking stands. Cheap people evade the hat-boy.

When the present enthusiast for the splendid subject of

hats was a small boy it was the ambition of every small boy of his acquaintance to be regarded as of sufficient age to possess what we termed a "dice hat," what is commonly called a "derby," what in England they call a "darby," what Dickens aptly referred to as a "pot-hat," what, in one highly diverting form, is sometimes referred to on the other side as a "billy-cock." That singular structure for the human head, the derby hat, one time well-nigh universally worn, has now gone somewhat out of fashion and been superseded by the soft hat of smart design, though there are indications, I fear, that the derby is coming in again. When we were young the soft hat was most commonly worn by veterans of the Civil War, in a pattern called a "slouch hat" or "Grand Army hat." Though, indeed, such romantic beings as cowboys in popular ten cent literature and the late Buffalo Bill wore sombreros, and the picturesque Mexican a high peaked affair.

Our grandfathers wore "stove-pipe hats"; and the hats of politicians were one time frequently called "plug hats." This male head-dress even more extraordinary than the derby, books of etiquette sometimes say you should not call a "silk hat" but a "high hat." In London but a few years ago no man ever went into the City with other than a top-hat, or "topper" as they say there. It is said that the going out of general favour of the silk hat has been occasioned in a considerable degree by the popularity of raincoats in preference to umbrellas. If you observe any great crowd in England to-day you will find in it few hats of any kind; it is in the main a sea of caps. The American "dude" and the anti-bellum British "knut" always wore silk hats. Gentlemen at the British race courses and fine old clubmen of Pall Mall affect a white or grey top hat, of the sort which was so becoming an ornament to the late King Edward. The opera hat is said to have startled many persons who had not seen it before. Intoxicated gentlemen in funny pictures have always smashed their silk hats. Some men have worn a silk hat only on the occasion of their marriage. High hats are worn by small boys in England. The most useful occupation to-day is that which envolves the wearing of a "tin hat."

The day in the autumn fixed by popular mandate when the straw hat is to be discarded for the season is hilariously celebrated in Wall Street by the destruction by the affronted populace of the straw hats of those who have had the temerity or the thoughtlessness to wear them. Coloured men in livery stables, however, sometimes wear straw hats the year round. To the habit generally of wearing a hat baldness is attributed by some. And the luxuriant hair of Indians and of the cave-man is pointed to as illustrating the beneficent result of not wearing a hat. And now and then somebody turns up with the idea in his head that he doesn't need a hat on it. There is a white garbed gentleman of Grecian mould who parades Broadway every day without a hat.

It is indisputable that the hats women wear to-day are more beautiful than they have been for generations, perhaps centuries. Yet this fact has met with little expression of appreciation. This present excellence is because women's hats now are the product of intellectual design. In the '80's the idea was entertained that decoration of a woman's hat was increased by attaching to it something in the way of beads or feathers wherever there was a space free. A fashionable woman's hat to-day may be as simple and, in its way, as effective an art as a Whistler symphony; a single splotch of colour, it may be, acting as a foil against a rich mass. Or the hat is a replica, as it were, of the celebrated design of a period in history. But the erudite subject of women's hats should not be touched upon without a salute to that racy model which crowns the far-famed 'Arriet, whose Bank-holiday attire was so delightedly caressed by the pencil of the late Phil May. None could forget his tenderly human drawing of the lady with the bedraggled feather over one eye who has just been ejected by the bar-man, and who turns to him to say: "Well, the next time I goes into a public house, I goes where I'm *respected!*"

A hat is distinguished from a cap or bonnet by the possession of a brim. The modern hat can be traced back to the
petasus worn by the ancient Romans when on a journey; and
hats were also thus used by the earlier Greeks. Not until
after the Norman conquest did the use of hats begin in
England. A "hatte of biever" was worn by one of the "nobels
of the lande, mett at Clarendom" about the middle of the
12th century; and Froissart describes hats that were worn at
Edward's court in 1340, when the Garter order was instituted.
The use of the scarlet hat which distinguishes cardinals was
sanctioned in the 13th century by Pope Innocent IV. The
merchant in Chaucer's Canterbury Tales had

"On his head a Flaundrish bever hat";

and from this period onwards frequent mention is made of
"felt hattes," "beever hattes," and other like names. Throughout mediæval times the wearing of a hat was regarded as a
mark of rank and distinction. During the reign of Elizabeth
the caprices of fashion in hats were many and various.

The Puritans affected a steeple crown and broad brimmed
hat, while the Cavaliers adopted a lower crown and a broader
brim ornamented with feathers. In the time of Charles II.
still greater breadth of brim and a profusion of feathers were
fashionable features of hats, and the gradual expansion of
brim led to the device of looping or tying up that portion.
Hence arose various fashionable "cocks" in hats; and ulti-
mately, by the looping up equally of three sides of the low-
crowned hat, the cocked hat which prevailed throughout the
18th century was elaborated. The Quaker hat, plain, low in
crown, and broad in brim, originated with the sect in the
middle of the 17th century. The silk hat is an article of
recent introduction. Though it was known in Florence
about a century ago, its manufacture was not introduced into
France till about 1825, and its development has taken place
entirely since that period. In all kinds of hat-making the

French excel; in the United Kingdom the felt hat trade is principally centred in the neighbourhood of Manchester; and in the United States the States of New York and New Jersey enjoy the greater part of the industry.

So much for hats.

*"Don't burn any of the old books. A man craves a certain
amount of nonsense. Some of the most unmitigated nonsense
I know was originally written down as sense, and I was
made to study it."*

—EPHRAIM STEBBINS.

A CHAIR OF NONSENSE *

BY BURGES JOHNSON

IT is easy to talk sense! As babies we link up words into
sentences that express reasonable ideas. It is true that the
human animal in his primitive days, before he has come into
his lingual heritage, often babbles in words of his own creation; or for a year or two shapes old words into strange unin-
herited phrases. "My dear, the child is talking nonsense!"
Sometimes he croons his nonsense to tunes—nonsense tunes—
of his own making. But all this is an art that he soon
forgets and too often never regains.

Yes, it is easy for grown-ups to talk sense; quite as easy as
for you now to retort, "Well then, why don't you do it?" Man's
more obvious thoughts have all been formulated so many
times that they have taken unto themselves fixed forms of
expression which our tongues can instantly utter in response
to the slightest impulse. "How do you do?" "Many happy
returns of the day," "Trust in an overruling Providence,"
"Truth is stranger than fiction," "It's all for the best."
These are easy to say and easy to listen to, because the tasks
of formulation and interpretation were performed long ago
by those pioneers who did our thinking for us.

* From *As I Was Saying;* copyright, 1923, by The Macmillan
Company. Reprinted by permission of the author and the publishers.

So dominated are we by a reasonable world that it is not only easy to talk sense, but hard to talk nonsense. Try to talk pure nonsense and willy-nilly (a great-great-great-grandfather of a phrase is Willy-Nilly) you find yourself conveying a meaning! The very effort to avoid the conventional symbols of thought is forcing upon you a most unusual form of mental activity.

Whether axioms and maxims and other crystallized forms of common sense be a symptom or a disease, inevitably they increase as the race grows older and lazier, and everything gets to be said. It is high time that we should attack them by a powerful antidote. With this aim in mind I propose the establishment of Chairs of Nonsense in our colleges and universities—those innermost sanctuaries of the Accepted Truth and the Undisputed Thing. And I stipulate that there should be courses offered to teachers as well as to students.

The ideal university, we are told, is Mark Hopkins at one end of a log and a boy at the other—wisdom on one side of the desk, inquiry and challenge on the other. If wisdom becomes arbitrary, challenge becomes impertinent and useless. If challenge ceases, wisdom deteriorates into dull formula. But a little Nonsense on that log, and what a difference!

"We know what Lewis Carroll was in daily life," writes Gilbert Chesterton: "he was a singularly serious and conventional don, universally respected, but very much of a pedant and something of a Philistine. Thus his strange double life in earth and in dreamland emphasizes the idea that lies at the back of nonsense—the idea of *escape,* of escape into a world where things are not fixed horribly in an eternal appropriateness, where apples grow on pear-trees, and any odd man you meet may have three legs. Lewis Carroll, living one life in which he would have thundered morally against anyone who walked on the wrong plot of grass, and another life in which he would cheerfully call the sun green and the moon blue, was, by his very divided nature, his one foot on both worlds, a perfect type of the position of modern nonsense. His Wonderland is a country popu-

lated by insane mathematicians. We feel the whole is an escape
into a world of masquerade; we feel that if we could pierce their
disguises, we might discover that Humpty Dumpty and the
March Hare were Professors and Doctors of Divinity enjoying a
mental holiday."

Escape!—the word is crowded with joyous suggestion—
escape and revolt. Listen to Algernon Charles Swinburne escaping from the slavery of dull poetic sense:

"From the depth of the dreamy decline of the dawn through a
  notable nimbus of nebulous moonshine,
Pallid and pink as the palm of the flag-flower that flickers with
  fear of the flies as they float,
Are they looks of our lovers that lustrously lean from a marvel of
  mystic miraculous moon shine,
These that we feel in the blood of our blushes that thicken and
  threaten with sobs from the throat?"

And hear Bishop Corbet escaping from theology in the
seventeenth century:

"Like to the fiery tombstone of a cabbage,
  Or like a crab-louse with its bag and baggage,
  Or like the four-square circle of a ring,
  Or like to hey ding, ding-a, ding-a, ding;
  E'en such is he who spake, and yet, no doubt,
  Spake to small purpose, when his tongue was out."

"He must be a fool indeed who cannot at times play the
fool; and he who does not enjoy nonsense must be lacking
in sense," wrote Rolfe, the great Shakespearean scholar.
"None but a man of extraordinary talent," said DeQuincey,
"can write first-rate nonsense." It is easy to prove that great
men of all times have found in nonsense a refreshment of
mind or a challenging test of mental vitality. Wisdom,
grown wiser than its own formulas, turns from introspection
in healthful outbursts of self-contempt. Nonsense is in fact
perpetually challenging Sense. "It's better not to know so

much than to know so many things that ain't so," says Josh Billings defiantly. "Truth is stranger than fiction," says Old Saw. "It is, to most people," says Mark Twain.

> "I never nursed a dear gazelle,"
>   softly quotes Tom Hood,
> "To glad me with its dappled hide,
>   But when it came to know me well,
>   It fell upon the buttered side."

"Think!" cries Nonsense. "Your common sense is clogging the machinery of ratiocination; your axioms soft-pedal the vibrating strings of the mind." Thoughts are not stimulated by any final statement of concrete fact; they are set at rest. But a statement which apparently means nothing at all will at once set them going.

In attempting to justify my chair of Nonsense I am not content to quote DeQuincey or Samuel Johnson or Lord Tennyson in praise of it, or to cite the fact that Ruskin placed Edward Lear at the head of his list of one hundred best books. But we must scrutinize the subject-matter itself and find in nonsense intrinsic values sufficient to entitle it to a place beside the Dead Languages, Higher Mathematics, Household Economics, Paleontology, and others of that sacred company.

First of all, Nonsense bears some peculiar and mysterious relationship to Truth. Perhaps it is fourth dimensional truth. Perhaps it is the truth of to-morrow; undoubtedly, if Professor Einstein's theories hold good, many of the truths of to-day are nonsense. Perhaps it is truth upside down, and classes must stand on their heads to study it. Greater sacrifices have been made in the pursuit of wisdom.

But my theory is that Nonsense embraces All-Truth, even as infinitude embraces the universe. All of the sermons worth preaching could find their texts in Mother Goose, or in Lear, or in those other Bibles, the Alice books. Mr. Don Marquis, in a recent essay extolling the virtues of nursery rhymes, says that he himself forever thinks of royalty in terms of the King who was in his counting house and the Queen who ate bread and honey. And I daresay that the Old Lady Who Lived in a Shoe has wielded upon rising generations an indirect influence compared to which Froebel is negligible. Students might well devote much time to the study of Madam Goose to discover what it is that makes her sayings applicable to all sorts and conditions, generation after generation. Is it merely her simplicity of utterance—a lost art with so many of us—that gives her a cryptic and subtle sound? Edward Lear testified that he had a most difficult time, after he wrote his Nonsense Books, trying to prove that they were not political pamphlets, or at least satires upon current life and manners. Hundreds of readers were certain that they knew personally the "Dong with the Luminous Nose."

It occurs to me that nonsense does not mean anything in particular because it means everything. If this is the case, what other field offers so great opportunities for endless research? "What is it that I mean?" wrote Charles Battell Loomis:

> "What is it that I mean,
> Oh, potent soul of mine?
> Oh, ecstasy divine
> In luscious meadows green!
>
> "When from the void of things
> (What is it that I mean?)
> I sense the joys unseen
> And memory backward flings;
>
> "When I encounter doubt
> And flee th' unquiet scene—
> (What is it that I mean?)
> Friend, hast thou found me out?
>
> "A charnel house at e'en,
> A dusky, reddened sky,
> A tomb where none is nigh—
> (What IS it that I mean?")

This questioning spirit is the basis of all true education. But it must be questioning in perfect honesty of heart; and where is there less evasion and equivocation than in nonsense?

"Not understood? Take me hence! Take me yonder!
    Take me away to the land of my rest—
There where the Ganges and other gees wander,
    And uncles and antelopes act for the best,
And all things are mixed and run into each other
    In a violet twilight of virtues and sins,
With the church-spires below you and no one to show you
    Where the curate leaves off and the pew-rent begins!"

So writes Barry Pain, and W. S. Gilbert echoes, in a burst of perfect frankness:

"His gentle spirit rolls
In the melody of souls,
Which is pretty but I don't know what it means."

Neither do I know what it means, but surely that does not prove it valueless; for I recall that in my own college days, as I painfully struggled through the pages of the "Anabasis," I was assured that I should value the experience in after life not for the information which Xenophon had written down, but for the mental training which I had gained in trying to find out what he meant. Why then, in all of these impressive curricula—set forth in many pages of college catalogues—is there no course deliberately entitled, "Nonsense, Its Literature, Its Uses, and Its Philosophy?" True, now and again some such course exists fortuitously, but its conductor is probably a prophet unawares.

May I be permitted finally to base my appeal for my Chair of Nonsense upon the established arguments of the upholders of higher education as it is? If the Curriculum Committee will but know that nonsense is the chaos out of which all truth was created they will at once grant that an intensive study of its elements may be a means finally of discovering

the very secret of life; at any rate let them think of the
mental training acquired by the student in trying to find out.

That a straight line, for instance, is the shortest distance
between two points is a statement containing one truth, and
one only. What a regrettable paucity of content! Think of
those beautiful lines of the Icelandic poet as set down by
George Ade:

> "To hold is not to have—
> Under the seared firmament
> Where Chaos sweeps, and vast Futurity
> Sneers at these puny Aspirations—
> There is the full Reprisal."

In this statement there may be a thousand truths, for all I
know. The fact that I cannot point out any of them at the
present moment of writing is not in the least significant.
But I am somehow reminded of my own early metrical inter-
pretations of the ancient poets. Doubtless any one skilled in
the examination of undergraduate literal translations could
gain something from it at a single glance.

Certain apologists for our higher education measure everything in terms of service. All studies are of value in so far as
they teach man to know his fellow man. Then let Nonsense
establish herself triumphantly. I may utter sense to a passing
stranger and we pass on as strangers—but let me recite nonsense to him, and at once our relationship becomes positive.
A common knowledge of current literature makes conversation
at afternoon teas. An equal acquaintance with Egyptian
scarabs makes for envy, hatred and all malice. But the discovery of a common familiarity with "Sylvia and Bruno" and
"Gentle Alice Brown" will cause two hearts to beat as one.
"Don't tell me," said William Pitt, "of a man's being able to
talk sense. Everyone can talk sense. Can he talk nonsense?"

I have discovered that if Jones's conversation consists of
nothing but a succession of exact truths, I do not necessarily
get to know Jones. I merely get to know the truths. But

if Jones says something which means nothing at all, I feel that I must know him better. If Robinson tells me all his exact symptoms since he was sick, I know the symptoms, and do not need to know the man. If he offers to tell me how he was since before he was sick, I study him with an aroused curiosity.

We devote the best years of our youth to an examination of the wisdom of the dead, in order that we may better know the living. Why should we not, then, more systematically immerse the minds of our young in a wholly confusing penumbra of ideas, and let them work their way out by natural processes of mental creation into All-Knowledge?

A MAN IN THE HOUSE *

By Winifred Kirkland

THERE persists much of the harem in every well-regulated home. In every house arranged to make a real man happy, that man remains always a visitor, welcomed, honored, but perpetually a guest. He steps in from the great outside for rest and refreshment, but he never belongs. For him the click and hum of the harem machinery stops, giving way to love and laughter, but there is always feminine relief when the master departs and the household hum goes on again. The anomaly lies in the fact that in theory all the machinery exists but for the master's comfort; but in practice, it is much easier to arrange for his comfort when he is not there. A house without a man is savorless, yet a man in a house is incarnate interruption. No matter how closely he incarcerates himself, or how silently, a woman always feels him there. He may hide beyond five doors and two flights of stairs, but his presence somehow leaks through, and unconsciously dominates every domestic detail. He does not mean to; the woman does not mean him to; it is merely the nature of him. Keep a man at home during the working hours of the day, and there is a blight on that house, not obvious, but subtle, touching the mood and the manner of the maidservant and manservant, cat, dog, and mistress, and affecting even the behavior of inanimate objects, so that there is a constraint

* From *The Joys of Being a Woman;* copyright, 1918, by Houghton Mifflin Company. Reprinted by permission of the author and permission of, and special arrangements with, Houghton Mifflin Company, the authorized publishers.

149

about the sewing-machine, a palsy on the vacuum-cleaner, and a *gaucherie* in the stove-lids. Over the whole household spreads a feeling of the unnatural, and a resulting sense of ineffectuality. Let the man go out, and with the closing of the front door, the wheels grow brisk again, and smooth. To enjoy a home worth enjoying, a man should be in it as briefly as possible.

By nature man belongs to the hunt in the open, and woman to the fire indoors, and just here lies one of the best reasons for being a woman rather than a man, because a woman can get along without a man's out-of-doors much better than a man can get along without a woman's indoors, which proves woman of the two the better bachelor, as being more self-contained and self-contented. Every real man when abroad on the hunt is always dreaming of a hearth and a hob and a wife, whereas no real woman, if she has the hearth and the hob, is longing for man's hunting spear or quarry. If she is indeed a real woman she is very likely longing to give a man the comfort of the fire, provided he will not stay too long at a stretch, but get out long enough to give her time to brush up his hearth and rinse his teapot satisfactorily to herself.

A man's home-coming is not an end in itself, its objective is the woman; but a woman's home-making exists both for the man and for itself. A woman needs to be alone with her house because she talks to it, and in a tongue really more natural than her talk with her husband, which is always better for having a little the company flavor, as in the seraglio. The most devoted wives are often those frankest in their abhorrence of a man in the house. It is because they do not like to keep their hearts working at high pressure too long at a time; they prefer the healthy relief of a glorious day of sorting or shopping between the master's breakfast and his dinner.

It is a rare *ménage* that is not incommoded by having its males lunch at home. It is much better when a woman may watch their dear coat-tails round the corner for the day, with an equal exaltation in their freedom for the fray and her

own. A woman whose males have their places of business
neither on the great waters nor in the great streets, but in
their own house, is of all women the most perpetually pitied
by other women, and the most pathetically patient. She
never looks quite like other women, this doctor's, minister's,
professor's, writer's wife. Her eyes have a harassed patience,
and her lips a protesting sweetness, for she does not belong to
her house, and so she does not belong to herself. When a
man's business-making and a woman's home-making live
under the same roof, they never go along in parallel independence: always the man's overlaps, invades. Kitchen and
nursery are hushed before the needs of office and study, and
the professional telephone call postpones the orders to the
butcher. The home suffers, but the husband suffers more, for
he is no longer a guest in his own house, with all a guest's pre-
rogatives; he now belongs there, and must take the consequences.

Fortunately the professional men-about-the-house are in
small minority, and so are their housekeepers, but all women
have sometimes to experience the upheaval incident on a
man's vacation at home; whether father's, or husband's, or
college brother's, or son's, the effect is always the same: the
house stands on its head, and for two days it kicks up its
heels and enjoys it, but after two weeks, two months, that is,
on the removal of the exciting stimulus, it sinks to coma for
the rest of the season. The different professions differ in
their treatment of a holiday, except that all men at home
on a vacation act like fish on land or cats in water, and
expect their womenfolk either to help them pant, or help
them swim. They seem to go out a great deal,—at least they
are always clamoring to have their garments prepared for sor-
ties, social or piscatorial,—and yet they always seem to be
under heel. Some men on a home holiday tinker all day
long, others bring with them a great many books which they
never read, and the result in both cases is that housekeeping
becomes a prolonged picking up. All men at home on a vaca-

tion eat a great deal more than other men, or than at other times; but with the sole exception of the anomalous academic, who is always concerned for his gastronomy, they will eat anything and enjoy it,—and say so. A man at home for his holidays is always vociferously appreciative. His happiness is almost enough to repay a woman for the noise he makes, and the mess; yet statistics would show that during any man's home vacation the women of the house lose just about as many pounds as the man gains. But what are women for, or homes?

After all, you can have a house without a man in it if you are quite sure you want to, but you cannot have a home without one. You cannot make a home out of women alone, or men alone; you have to mix them. Still every woman must admit, and every man with as much sense as a woman, that it's very hard to make a home for any man if he is always in it. Every honest front door must confess that it is glad to see its master go forth in the morning; but this is only because it is so much gladder to see him come back at night.

A CLEAR VIEW OF THE GOVERNMENT AND POLITICS OF ENGLAND *

BY STEPHEN LEACOCK

A LOYAL British subject like myself in dealing with the government of England should necessarily begin with a discussion of the monarchy. I have never had the pleasure of meeting the King,—except once on the G.T.R. platform in Orillia, Ontario, when he was the Duke of York and I was one of the welcoming delegates of the town council. No doubt he would recall it in a minute.

But in England the King is surrounded by formality and circumstance. On many mornings I waited round the gates of Buckingham Palace but I found it quite impossible to meet the King in the quiet sociable way in which one met him in Orillia. The English, it seems, love to make the kingship a subject of great pomp and official etiquette. In Canada it is quite different. Perhaps we understand kings and princes better than the English do. At any rate we treat them in a far more human heart-to-heart fashion than is the English custom, and they respond to it at once. I remember when King George—he was, as I say, Duke of York then—came up to Orillia, Ontario, how we all met him in a delegation on the platform. Bob Curran—Bob was Mayor of the town that year—went up to him and shook hands with him and invited him to come right on up to the Orillia House where he had a room reserved for him. Charlie Janes and Mel Tud-

---

* From *My Discovery of England;* copyright, 1922, by Dodd, Mead and Company. Reprinted by permission of the author and the publishers.

hope and the other boys who were on the town Council gathered round the royal prince and shook hands and told him that he simply must stay over. George Rapley, the bank manager, said that if he wanted a cheque cashed or anything of that sort to come right into the Royal Bank and he would do it for him. The prince had two aides-de-camp with him and a secretary, but Bob Curran said to bring them uptown too and it would be all right. We had planned to have an oyster supper for the Prince at Jim Smith's hotel and then take him either to the Y.M.C.A. Pool Room or else over to the tea social in the basement of the Presbyterian Church.

Unluckily the prince couldn't stay. It turned out that he had to get right back into his train and go on to Peterborough, Ontario, where they were to have a brass band to meet him, which naturally he didn't want to miss.

But the point is that it was a real welcome. And you could see that the prince appreciated it. There was a warmth and a meaning to it that the prince understood at once. It was a pity that he couldn't have stayed over and had time to see the carriage factory and the new sewerage plant. We all told the prince that he must come back and he said that if he could he most certainly would. When the prince's train pulled out of the station and we all went back uptown together (it was before prohibition came to Ontario) you could feel that the institution of royalty was quite solid in Orillia for a generation.

But you don't get that sort of thing in England. There's a formality and coldness in all their dealings with royalty that would never go down with us. They like to have the King come and open Parliament dressed in royal robes, and with a clattering troop of soldiers riding in front of him. As for taking him over to the Y.M.C.A. to play pin pool, they never think of it. They have seen so much of the mere *outside* of his kingship that they don't understand the *heart* of it as we do in Canada.

But let us turn to the House of Commons: for no description of England would be complete without at least some mention of this interesting body. Indeed for the ordinary visitor to London the greatest interest of all attaches to the spacious and magnificent Parliament Buildings. The House of Commons is commodiously situated beside the River Thames. The principal features of the House are the large lunch room on the western side and the tea-room on the terrace on the eastern. A series of smaller luncheon rooms extend (apparently) all round about the premises: while a commodious bar offers a ready access to the members at all hours of the day. While any members are in the bar a light is kept burning in the tall Clock Tower at one corner of the building, but when the bar is closed the light is turned off by whichever of the Scotch members leaves last. There is a handsome legislative chamber attached to the premises from which—so the antiquarians tell us—the House of Commons took its name. But it is not usual now for the members to sit in the legislative chamber as the legislation is now all done outside, either at the home of Mr. Lloyd George, or at the National Liberal Club, or at one or other of the newspaper offices. The House, however, is called together at very frequent intervals to give it an opportunity of hearing the latest legislation and allowing the members to indulge in cheers, sighs, groans, votes and other expressions of vitality. After having cheered as much as is good for it, it goes back again to the lunch rooms and goes on eating till needed again.

It is, however, an entire exaggeration to say that the House of Commons no longer has a real share in the government of England. This is not so. Anybody connected with the government values the House of Commons in a high degree. One of the leading newspaper proprietors of London himself told me that he has always felt that if he had the House of Commons on his side he had a very valuable ally. Many of the labour leaders are inclined to regard the House of Commons as of great utility, while the leading women's organizations, now that women are admitted as members, may be said to regard the House as one of themselves.

Looking around to find just where the natural service of the House of Commons comes in, I am inclined to think that it must be in the practice of "asking questions" in the House. Whenever anything goes wrong a member rises and asks a question. He gets up, for example, with a little paper in his hand, and asks the government if ministers are aware that the Khedive of Egypt was seen yesterday wearing a Turkish Tarbosh. Ministers say very humbly that they hadn't known it, and a thrill runs through the whole country. The members can apparently ask any questions they like. In the repeated visits which I made to the gallery of the House of Commons I was unable to find any particular sense or meaning in the questions asked, though no doubt they had an intimate bearing on English politics not clear to an outsider like myself. I heard one member ask the government whether they were aware that herrings were being imported from Hamburg to Harwich. The government said no. Another member rose and asked the government whether they considered Shakespere or Molière the greater dramatic artist. The government answered that ministers were taking this under their earnest consideration and that a report would be submitted to Parliament. Another member asked the government if they knew who won the Queen's Plate this season at Toronto. They did,—in fact this member got in wrong, as this is the very thing that the government do know. Towards the close of the evening a member rose and asked the government if they knew what time it was. The Speaker, however, ruled this question out of order on the ground that it had been answered before.

The Parliament Buildings are so vast that it is not possible to state with certainty what they do, or do not, contain. But it is generally said that somewhere in the building is the House of Lords. When they meet they are said to come together very quietly shortly before the dinner hour, take a glass of dry sherry and a biscuit (they are all abstemious men), reject whatever bills may be before them at the moment, take another dry sherry and then adjourn for two years.

The public are no longer allowed unrestricted access to the Houses of Parliament; its approaches are now strictly guarded by policemen. In order to obtain admission it is necessary either to (A) communicate in writing with the Speaker of the House, enclosing certificates of naturalization and proof of identity, or (B) give the policeman five shillings. Method B is the one usually adopted. On great nights, however, when the House of Commons is sitting and is about to do something important, such as ratifying a Home Rule Bill or cheering, or welcoming a new lady member, it is not possible to enter by merely bribing the policeman with five shillings; it takes a pound. The English people complain bitterly of the rich Americans who have in this way corrupted the London public. Before they were corrupted they would do anything for sixpence.

This peculiar vein of corruption by the Americans runs like a thread, I may say, through all the texture of English life. Among those who have been principally exposed to it are the servants,—especially butlers and chauffeurs, hotel porters, bell boys, railway porters and guards, all taxi-drivers, pew-openers, curates, bishops, and a large part of the peerage.

The terrible ravages that have been made by the Americans on English morality are witnessed on every hand. Whole classes of society are hopelessly damaged. I have it in the evidence of the English themselves and there seems to be no doubt of the fact. Till the Americans came to England the people were an honest, law-abiding race, respecting their superiors and despising those below them. They had never been corrupted by money and their employers extended to them in this regard their tenderest solicitude. Then the Americans came. Servants ceased to be what they were; butlers were hopelessly damaged; hotel porters became a wreck; taxi-drivers turned out thieves; curates could no longer be trusted to handle money; peers sold their daughters at a million dollars a piece or three for two. In fact the whole kingdom began to deteriorate till it got where it is now. At present after a rich American has stayed in any English country house, its owners find that they can do nothing with the butler; a wildness has come over the man. There is a restlessness in his demeanour and a strange wistful look in his eye as if seeking for something. In many cases, so I understand, after an American has stayed in a country house the butler goes insane. He is found in his pantry counting over the sixpence given to him by a Duke, and laughing to himself. He has to be taken in charge by the police. With him generally go the chauffeur, whose mind has broken down from driving a rich American twenty miles; and the gardener, who is found tearing up raspberry bushes by the roots to see if there is any money under them; and the local curate whose brain has collapsed or expanded, I forget which, when a rich American gave him fifty dollars for his soup kitchen.

There are, it is true, a few classes that have escaped this contagion, shepherds living in the hills, drovers, sailors, fishermen and such like. I remember the first time I went into the English country-side being struck with the clean, honest look in the people's faces. I realised exactly where they got it: they had never seen any Americans. I remember speaking to an aged peasant down in Somerset. "Have you ever seen any Americans?" "Nah," he said, "uz eeard a mowt o' 'em, zir, but uz zeen nowt o' 'em." It was clear that the noble fellow was quite undamaged by American contact.

Now the odd thing about this corruption is that exactly the same idea is held on the other side of the water. It is a known fact that if a young English Lord comes to an American town he puts it to the bad in one week. Socially the whole place goes to pieces. Girls whose parents are in the hardware business and who used to call their father "pop" begin to talk of precedence and whether a Duchess Dowager goes in to dinner ahead of or behind a countess scavenger. After the young Lord has attended two dances and one tea-social in the Methodist Church Sunday School Building (Adults 25 cents, children 10 cents—all welcome.) there is nothing for the young men of the town to do except to drive him out or go further west.

One can hardly wonder then that this general corruption has extended even to the policemen who guard the Houses of Parliament. On the other hand this vein of corruption has not extended to English politics. Unlike ours, English politics,—one hears it on every hand,—are pure. Ours unfortunately are known to be not so. The difference seems to be that our politicians will do anything for money and the English politicians won't; they just take the money and won't do a thing for it.

Somehow there always seems to be a peculiar interest about English political questions that we don't find elsewhere. At home in Canada our politics turn on such things as how much money the Canadian National Railways lose as compared with how much they could lose if they really tried; on whether the Grain Growers of Manitoba should be allowed to import ploughs without paying a duty or to pay a duty without importing ploughs. Our members at Ottawa discuss such things as highway subsidies, dry farming, the Bank Act, and the tariff on hardware. These things leave me absolutely cold. To be quite candid there is something terribly plebeian about them. In short, our politics are what we call in French "peuple."

But when one turns to England, what a striking difference! The English, with the whole huge British Empire to fish in and the European system to draw upon, can always dig up some kind of political topic of discussion that has a real charm about it. One month you find English politics turning on the Oasis of Merv and the next on the hinterland of Albania; or a member rises in the Commons with a little bit of paper in his hand and desires to ask the foreign secretary if he is aware that the Ahkoond of Swat is dead. The foreign secretary states that the government have no information other than that the Ahkoond *was* dead a month ago. There is a distinct sensation in the House at the realisation that the Ahkoond has been dead a month without the House having known that he was alive. The sensation is conveyed to the Press and the afternoon papers appear with large headings, THE AHKOOND OF SWAT IS DEAD. The public who have never heard of the Ahkoond bare their heads in a moment in a pause to pray for the Ahkoond's soul. Then the cables take up the refrain and word is flashed all over the world, *The Ahkoond of Swat is Dead.*

There was a Canadian journalist and poet once who was so impressed with the news that the Ahkoond was dead, so bowed down with regret that he had never known the Ahkoond while alive, that he forthwith wrote a poem in memory of *The Ahkoond of Swat.* I have always thought that the reason of the wide admiration that Lannigan's verses received was not merely because of the brilliant wit that is in them but because in a wider sense they typify so beautifully the scope of English politics. The death of the Ahkoond of Swat, and whether Great Britain should support as his successor Mustalpha El Djin or Kamu Flaj,—there is something worth talking of over an afternoon at tea table. But suppose that the whole of the Manitoba Grain Growers were to die. What could one say about it? They'd be dead, that's all.

So it is that people all over the world turn to English politics with interest. What more delightful than to open an atlas, find out where the new kingdom of Hejaz is, and then violently support the British claim to a protectorate over it. Over in America we don't understand this sort of thing. There is naturally little chance to do so and we don't know how to use it when it comes. I remember that when a chance did come in connection with the great Venezuela dispute over the ownership of the jungles and mud-flats of British Guiana, the American papers at once inserted headings, WHERE IS THE ESSIQUIBO RIVER? That spoiled the whole thing. If you admit that you don't know where a place is, then the bottom is knocked out of all discussion. But if you pretend that you do, then you are all right. Mr. Lloyd George is said to have caused great amusement at the Versailles Conference by admitting that he hadn't known where Teschen was. So at least it was reported in the papers; and for all I know it might even have been true. But the fun that he raised was not really half what could have been raised. I have it on good authority that two of the American delegates hadn't known where Austria Proper was and thought that Unredeemed Italy was on the East side of New York, while the Chinese Delegate thought that the Cameroons were part of Scotland. But it is these little geographic niceties that lend a charm to European politics that ours lack forever.

I don't mean to say the English politics always turn on romantic places or on small questions. They don't. They often include questions of the largest order. But when the English introduce a really large question as the basis of their politics they like to select one that is insoluble. This guarantees that it will last. Take for example the rights of the Crown as against the people. That lasted for one hundred years,—all the seventeenth century. In Oklahoma or in Alberta they would have called a convention on the question, settled it in two weeks and spoiled it for further use. In the same way the Protestant Reformation was used for a hundred years and the Reform Bill for a generation.

At the present time the genius of the English for politics has selected as their insoluble political question the topic of the German indemnity. The essence of the problem as I understand it may be stated as follows:

It was definitely settled by the Conference at Versailles that Germany is to pay the Allies 3,912,486,782,421 marks. I think that is the correct figure, though of course I am speaking only from memory. At any rate, the correct figure is within a hundred billion marks of the above.

The sum to be paid was not reached without a great deal

of discussion. Monsieur Briand, the French Minister, is reported to have thrown out the figure 4,281,390,687,471. But Mr. Lloyd George would not pick it up. Nor do I blame him unless he had a basket to pick it up with.

Lloyd George's point of view was that the Germans could very properly pay a limited amount such as 3,912,486,782,421 marks, but it was not feasible to put on them a burden of 4,281,390,687,471 marks.

By the way, if any one at this point doubts the accuracy of the figures just given, all he has to do is to take the amount of the indemnity as stated in gold marks and then multiply it by the present value of the mark and he will find to his chagrin that the figures are correct. If he is still not satisfied I refer him to a book of Logarithms. If he is not satisfied with that I refer him to any work on conic sections and if not convinced even then I refer him so far that he will never come back.

The indemnity being thus fixed, the next question is as to the method of collecting it. In the first place there is no intention of allowing the Germans to pay in actual cash. If they do this they will merely inflate the English beyond what is bearable. England has been inflated now for eight years and has had enough of it.

In the second place, it is understood that it will not allow the Germans to offer 4,281,390,687,471 marks' worth of coal. It is more than the country needs.

What is more, if the English want coal they propose to buy it in an ordinary decent way from a Christian coal-dealer in their own country. They do not purpose to ruin their own coal industry for the sake of building up the prosperity of the German nation.

What I say of coal is applied with equal force to any offers of food, grain, oil, petroleum, gas, or any other natural product. Payment in any of these will be sternly refused. Even now it is all the British farmers can do to live and for some it is more. Many of them are having to sell off their motors and pianos and to send their sons to college to work. At the same time, the German producer by depressing the mark further and further is able to work fourteen hours a day. This argument may not be quite correct but I take it as I find it in the London Press. Whether I state it correctly or not, it is quite plain that the problem is insoluble. That is all that is needed in first class politics.

A really good question like the German reparation question will go on for a century. Undoubtedly in the year 2000 A.D., a British Chancellor of the Exchequer will still be explaining that the government is fully resolved that Germany shall pay to the last farthing (*cheers*) : but that ministers have no intention of allowing the German payment to take a form that will undermine British industry (*wild applause*) : that the German indemnity shall be paid so that without weakening the power of the Germans to buy from us it shall increase our power of selling to them.

Such questions last forever.

On the other hand sometimes by sheer carelessness a question gets settled and passes out of politics. This, so we are given to understand, has happened to the Irish question. It is settled. A group of Irish delegates and British ministers got together round a table and settled it. The settlement has since been celebrated at a demonstration of brotherhood by the Irish Americans of New York with only six casualties. Henceforth the Irish question passes into history. There may be some odd fighting along the Ulster border, or a little civil war with perhaps a little revolution every now and then, but as a question the thing is finished.

I must say that I for one am very sorry to think that the Irish question is gone. We shall miss it greatly. Debating societies which have flourished on it ever since 1886 will be wrecked for want of it. Dinner parties will now lose half the sparkle of their conversation. It will be no longer possible to make use of such good old remarks as, "After all the

Irish are a gifted people," or "You must remember that fifty per cent of the great English generals were Irish."

The settlement turned out to be a very simple affair. Ireland was merely given dominion status. What that is, no one knows, but it means that the Irish have now got it and that they sink from the high place that they had in the white light of publicity to the level of the Canadians or the New Zealanders.

Whether it is quite a proper thing to settle trouble by conferring dominion status on it, is open to question. It is a practice that is bound to spread. It is rumoured that it is now contemplated to confer dominion status upon the Borough of Poplar and on the Cambridge undergraduates. It is even understood that at the recent disarmament conference England offered to confer dominion status on the United States. President Harding would assuredly have accepted it at once but for the protest of Mr. Briand, who claimed that any such offer must be accompanied by a permission to increase the French fire-brigade by fifty per cent.

It is lamentable, too, that at the very same moment when the Irish question was extinguished, the Naval Question which had lasted for nearly fifty years was absolutely obliterated by disarmament. Henceforth the alarm of invasion is a thing of the past and the navy practically needless. Beyond keeping a fleet in the North Sea and one on the Mediterranean, and maintaining a patrol all round the rim of the Pacific Ocean, Britain will cease to be a naval power. A mere annual expenditure of fifty million pounds sterling will suffice for such thin pretence of naval preparedness as a disarmed nation will have to maintain.

This thing too, came as a surprise, or at least a surprise to the general public who are unaware of the workings of diplomacy. Those who know about such things were fully aware of what would happen if a whole lot of British sailors and diplomatists and journalists were exposed to the hospitalities of Washington. The British and Americans are both alike.   You can't drive them or lead them or coerce them, but if you give them a cigar they'll do anything.

The inner history of the conference is only just beginning to be known.   But it is whispered that immediately on his arrival Mr. Balfour was given a cigar by President Harding.   Mr. Balfour at once offered to scrap five ships, and invited the entire American cabinet into the British Embassy, where Sir A. Geddes was rash enough to offer them champagne.

The American delegates immediately offered to scrap ten ships.   Mr. Balfour, who simply cannot be outdone in international courtesy, saw the ten and raised it to twenty.   President Harding saw the twenty, raised it to thirty, and sent out for more poker chips.

At the close of the play Lord Beatty, who is urbanity itself, offered to scrap Portsmouth Dockyard, and asked if anybody present would like Canada.   President Harding replied with his customary tact that if England wanted the Philippines, he would think it what he would term a residuum of normalcy to give them away.   There is no telling what might have happened had not Mr. Briand interposed to say that any transfer of the Philippines must be regarded as a signal for a twenty per cent increase in the Boy Scouts of France. As a tactful conclusion to the matter President Harding raised Mr. Balfour to the peerage.

As things are, disarmament coming along with the Irish settlement, leaves English politics in a bad way.   The general outlook is too peaceful altogether.   One looks round almost in vain for any of those "strained relations" which used to be the very basis of English foreign policy.   In only one direction do I see light for English politics, and that is over towards Czecho-Slovakia.   It appears that Czecho-Slovakia owes the British Exchequer fifty million sterling.   I cannot quote the exact figure, but it is either fifty million or fifty billion.   In either case Czecho-Slovakia is unable to pay.   The announcement has just been made by M. Sgitzch, the new treasurer, that the country is bankrupt or at least that he sees his way to make it so in a week.

It has been at once reported in City circles that there are "strained relations" between Great Britain and Czecho-Slovakia. Now what I advise is, that if the relations are strained, keep them so. England has lost nearly all the strained relations she ever had; let her cherish the few that she still has. I know that there are other opinions. The suggestion has been at once made for a "round table conference," at which the whole thing can be freely discussed without formal protocols and something like a "gentleman's agreement" reached. I say, don't do it. England is being ruined by these round table conferences. They are sitting round in Cairo and Calcutta and Capetown, filling all the best hotels and eating out the substance of the taxpayer.

I am told that Lloyd George has offered to go to Czecho-Slovakia. He should be stopped. It is said that Professor Keynes has proved that the best way to deal with the debt of Czecho-Slovakia is to send them whatever cash we have left, thereby turning the exchange upside down on them, and forcing them to buy all their Christmas presents in Manchester.

It is wiser not to do anything of the sort. England should send them a good old-fashioned ultimatum, mobilise all the naval officers at the Embankment hotels, raise the income tax another sixpence, and defy them.

If that were done it might prove a successful first step in bringing English politics back to the high plane of conversational interest from which they are threatening to fall.

THE NEWNESS OF THE OLD *

By E. V. Lucas

In an American paper I find this anecdote:

"An old lady was being shown the spot on which a hero fell. 'I don't wonder,' she replied. 'It's so slippery I nearly fell there myself.'"

Now that story, which is very old in England, and is familiar here to most adult persons, is usually told of Nelson and the *Victory*. Indeed it is such a commonplace with facetious visitors to that vessel that the wiser of the guides are at pains to get in with it first. But in America it may be fresh and beginning a new lease of life; it will probably go on forever in all English-speaking countries, on each occasion of its recrudescence finding a few people to whom it is new.

It is a problem why we tend to be so resentful when an editor or a comedian offers us a jest that has done service before. It is, I suppose, in part at any rate, because we have paid our money, either for the paper or the seat, and we experience the sense of having been defrauded. We have been done, we feel, because the bargain, as we understood it, was that we were purchasing novelty. So that when suddenly an old, old jape, which perhaps we have ourselves related—and that of course is an aggravation of the grievance—confronts us, we are indignant. But what, one wonders, would a comic paper or a revue that had nothing old in it be like? We can never know.

The odd thing is that we not only resent the age of the joke, even though it is in our own repertory, but we resent the laughter of those to whom it is new—perhaps three-quarters of the audience. How dare they also not have heard it before? is our unspoken question. Not long ago, seated in a theatre next a candid and normally benignant and tolerant friend, I found myself laughing at what struck me as a distinctly humorous remark made by one of London's non-sensical funny men. Engaged in a competition with another as to which had the longer memory, he clinched the discussion by saying that he personally could remember London Bridge when it was a cornfield. To me that was as new as it was idiotic, and I behaved accordingly; but my friend was furious with me. "Good Heavens!" he exclaimed with the click of the tongue that usually accompanies such criticism, "fancy digging that up again! It's as old as the hills." And his face grew dark and stern.

What we have to remember, and what might have softened my friend's granite anger had he remembered it, is that a new audience is always coming along to whom nothing is a chestnut. It is not the most reassuring of thoughts to those who are a little fastidious about ancientry in humour; but it is nature and therefore a fact. Just as every moment (so I used to be told by a solemn nurse) a child is born (she added also that every moment some one dies, and she used to hold up her finger and hush! for me to realise that happy thought), so nearly every moment (allowing for a certain amount of infant mortality) an older child attains an age when it can understand and relish a funny story. To those children every story is original. With this new public, clamourous and appreciative, why do humourists try so hard to be novel? (But perhaps they don't.)

I suppose that there are theories as to what is the oldest story, but I am not acquainted with them. That people are, however, quite prepared for every story to be old is proved by the readiness with which, when Mark Twain's "Jumping

Frog" was translated into Greek for a School Reader, a number of persons remarked upon the circumstance that the humourist had gone to ancient literature for his jest. For by a curious twist we are all anxious that stories should not be new. Much as we like a new story, we like better to be able to say that to use it was familiar.

Many stories come rhythmically round again. Such, for example, during the Great War, as those with a martial background. I remember during the Boer War hearing of a young man who was endeavoring to enlist, and was rejected because his teeth were defective. "But I want to fight the Boers," he said, "not eat them." Between 1914 and 1918 this excellent retort turned up again, only this time the young man said that he did not want to eat the Germans. I have no doubt that in the Crimean War a similar applicant declared that he did not want to eat the Russians, and a hundred years ago another was vowing that he did not want to eat the French. Probably one could trace it through every war that ever was. Probably a young Hittite with indifferent teeth proclaimed that his desire was to fight the Amalekites and not to eat them. The story was equally good each time; and there has always been a vast new audience for it. And so long as war continues and teeth exist in the human head, which I am told will not be for ever, so long will this anecdote enjoy popularity. After that it will enter upon a new phase of existence based upon defects in the applicant's râtelier, and so on until universal peace descends upon the world, or, the sun turning cold, life ceases.

A DEFENCE OF SUPERSTITION *

By Robert Lynd

It was announced shortly before the production of *The Golden Moth* that the name of the play was to be changed because the company believe that the presence of the word "golden" in a title is unlucky. A little later the management of the theatre decided to defy superstition and the play was produced with the original title after all. The stage is perhaps the most superstitious institution in England, after the racecourse. The latter is so superstitious that to wish a man luck when on his way to a racemeeting is considered unlucky. Instead of saying "Good luck!" you should say something insulting, such as, "May you break your leg!" Actors and actresses have not only all the ordinary superstitions about picking up of pins, breaking looking-glasses, and the unluckiness of certain numbers. They have also a number of professional superstitions. It is unlucky, they say, for instance, to quote *Macbeth*. Actors dare not say to each other at parting: "When shall we three meet again?" No good actress would advise a nervous fellow-artist to "screw her courage to the sticking-place." It is unlucky during rehearsals to quote the catchword of a forthcoming play in casual conversation. It is unlucky to carry a make-up box, like an amateur actress. Then there are certain theatres that are regarded as unlucky, and the superstitious actor is depressed at the prospect of having to appear at one of them.

The luck may turn, we are told, if the name of the theatre is changed; this was probably the cause of the change of the name of one London theatre which has since been successful.

Most of us are accustomed to regard superstitious people as unenlightened, and there is no one who feels more eminently wise than the man who rises first from a table at which thirteen guests have sat down. So far as I have discovered, however, the dividing line between those who are superstitious and those who are not is not at all the same as the line that divides enlightenment from unenlightenment. Some of the world's wisest men have been superstitious. Some of the world's greatest dunderheads have been free from superstition. Plutarch was a wise man, not only for his own age, but for any age, yet he believed in superstitions that a modern bus-conductor would laugh at. Many of those who laugh at superstitions do so from narrowness of mind. They are incredulous of everything that their eyes have not seen. They cannot imagine anything outside the day's work and the football results. Their unbelief in black cats is simply a form of dull materialism. I do not, I may say, contend that the superstitious man is wiser than the unsuperstitious. All I contend is that freedom from superstition is not necessarily a form of wisdom, but that it frequently results from thoughtlessness. Perfect wisdom, I believe, gives perfect freedom from superstition, but it probably involves belief in a good many things that will seem superstitious to a thoughtless man.

Consider, for a moment, how the first superstition came into the world. Man found himself cast into a chaos of drifting phenomena without the slightest notion of what they meant or whether they meant anything. He could not distinguish between things and their shadows. He was as ignorant as a child as to how children were born. He did not know what was happening to his friends when they died. He was frightened of many things, because some things hurt him, and he did not know which did and which did not. All that he knew was that queer things were constantly happening, but they happened, not according to any rule that he could see, but in a confused and terrifying jumble. One day, in the forest, however, he casually picked up a pin—or, let us say, a sharp pine-needle—and immediately afterwards he came on the most delightful bunch of bananas he had ever tasted This did not at the moment strike him as being remarkable. But the next day he noticed the same sort of pine-needle lying on the ground and picked it up. Immediately afterwards he discovered another bunch of bananas even more delightful than the first. His brain swam with the sense of discovery. He beat his forehead with his hands—hairy, prehensile hands—for the birth of something absolutely new in his mind was making his head ache. He muttered: "I pick up pine-needles and find sweet bananas! I pick up pine-needles and find sweet bananas!" It was some time before even this conveyed a clear message to a brain unaccustomed to act. But as he repeated the words in a sort of trance, the truth suddenly flashed upon him. When he uncovered his face he was looking ten years older, but he was wearing a smile that was almost human. He did not exactly say to himself, "I have found a pattern in the universe," but he had made the first move towards the happiest of all Eurekas. He was never quite simian again. He was like a child who, after long contemplation of the stars in the night sky, that seem to lie about haphazard like fallen apples, suddenly picks out the certain pattern of a constellation. He, too, has seen a pattern: the stars are no longer an abracadabra to him, but reveal meaning to him in a speech that he continually learns to understand better. In the same way, primitive man in his superstitions was slowly learning to put two and two together. What matter if they often came to five? It is better to put two and two together wrong than to believe that they cannot be put together at all.

This, it may be said, may account for the reign of superstition, but it does not therefore justify the superstitions of civilized men and women. We have surer means nowadays of discovering the pattern in life. We cannot be content with apparent cause and effect, but we employ intelligent tests for the discovery of the real cause. The child in arms may believe that the watch flies open because it blows hard on its back, but a grown-up man would be an imbecile to imagine that this is the real reason why the watch flies open. This is true enough. When the real pattern of cause and effect is known, there is no room for fantastic explanations. We have not the right to believe that the crowing of cocks causes the sun to rise, or that railway trains are propelled, not by steam, but by the waving of a green flag or a green light. One might as well doubt the pattern of the Seven Stars. Such patterns are established once for all. On the other hand, the greater part of the universe is undiscovered and uncharted, as the greater part of the sky is. Our lives are still a voyage amid chance and confusion, and there are many things of which we know as little as the first monkey. While this continues, men will go on being superstitious—casting their fancies into the unknown in search of signs. For superstition is mainly a belief in signs. The superstitious man does not believe that bringing blackthorn in flower into a house actually causes a death in the house; what he believes is that it announces a death. It is the same with telling fortunes with the cards. The cards are not supposed to control events but only to prophesy them. I know that the superstitious do not always adopt this comparatively philosophical attitude. Some of them will put the blame of their misfortunes on a friend, for instance, who has sent them a gift of white flowers without a mixture of other colours. But this is unreasonable. The only reasonable defence of modern superstition I have ever heard was that certain signs show the direction of events as a weather-cock shows the direction in which the wind is blowing.

Even so, in practice, it is at times almost impossible to distinguish between the prophet of bad news and the causer of bad events. In the old days the prophets were stoned because they were hated as a woman hates a broken mirror. I have heard superstitious people arguing gravely as to whether President Wilson's downfall was caused by his association with the number thirteen, or whether his association with the number thirteen was a prophecy of his downfall. It will be remembered that on his arrival in France he was entertained at a dinner at which thirteen persons sat down, because he had announced that he regarded thirteen as a lucky number. It will also be remembered that, though he originally published his Fourteen points, they were afterwards reduced to Thirteen, owing to the objections of the Allies to the "Freedom of the Seas." The superstitious find it difficult to think that this was only an omen. They half believe at the back of their minds that another guest and another point might have made the world safe for democracy.

The ordinary man's reply to superstitions of the kind is seldom based on reason. He is content to say "Rot!" and will no more argue about it than if you told him that a runner duck in your back-yard had been heard quoting *Paradise Lost*. As a matter of fact, neither the attack on superstition nor the defence of it has very much to do with reason. We believe or disbelieve according to our temperaments. Two men, equal in brain and courage, will behave quite differently when it comes to walking under a ladder or lighting a cigarette from a match from which two cigarettes have been already lit. Parnell was eminent for moral courage, but he believed that green was an unlucky colour, and was horror-stricken—and not on æsthetic grounds—when he was presented with a green smoking-cap by a too patriotic lady. During the war the men who carried mascots were not noticeably inferior to the men who did not. By a curious irony, it was in the country which instituted the worship of reason that mascots were most popular. An interesting essay could be written on the theme that an increase of rationalism leads automatically to an increase of superstition. I doubt whether the religious Victorians, who sneered at ghosts and picked up pins only on grounds of economy, were quite so superstitious as their irreligious successors. After all, the human mind cannot be content to accept the unknown as unknowable. Life is a mystery, but most of us feel that, like a jigsaw puzzle, it may yield a solution if only we keep trying to put the apparently incoherent pieces together. Superstition will never give us the whole pattern, but is a pardonable attempt to unite two or three of the pieces in a sub-pattern. All science and art is but the piecing together of a sub-pattern out of chaos. Be not censorious if an inhabitant of chaos finds a meaning you do not in two magpies or a dog's howl or a slice of bread-and-butter that falls with its face in the dust.

JOSEPH CONRAD *

By John Macy

To the newest generation of adult readers the dawn of a literary light is a rare experience. It is as if the courses of our literature were Arctic in their slowness, as if the day came at long intervals, and then without warmth or brilliance. Our fathers knew the joy of welcoming the latest novel of Dickens or a new volume of essays by Carlyle. The only † great day whose beginning young men have witnessed is the day of Kipling; his light mounted rapidly to a high noon, and if the afternoon shadows have begun to deepen prematurely, that sun is still beautiful and strong. Other lights have kindled in the last fifteen years, and have gone out before they had fairly dislodged the darkness, or have continued to burn dimly.

Eyes accustomed only to darkness and uncertain lights are in condition to be deluded by the phantoms of false dawn; it is therefore unwise to greet with too much enthusiasm the arrival of Mr. Joseph Conrad. Even if the dawn is real, it is certainly overcast with heavy clouds, and it has not proved bright enough to startle the world. Nevertheless, his light is of unique beauty in contemporary literature, and the story of its kindling makes interesting biography.

Joseph Conrad Korzeniowski was born fifty years ago in Poland. His father, a critic and poet, and his mother, who was exiled to Siberia, were engaged in revolutionary journalism. At nineteen Conrad left home, to escape an unsettled life, and also, it is fair to assume, to satisfy his love of ad-

† I ask the reader to remember that this was written in 1906.

venture. He found work on English vessels, and this fact gave to contemporary English letters a man who might otherwise have written in French. To-day he appears in handbooks of biography as Master in the British Merchant Service, and Author. At nineteen he had not mastered English; at thirty-eight he had published no book. Since then he has published about a volume a year. In preparation for his books he sailed as able seaman, mate, and master, for twenty years, on steam and sailing craft, and meanwhile he was reading deep in French and English literature,—all, we are told, with no intent to become a writer. Indeed it was a period of ill health resulting in an enforced idleness from the familiar sea that gave him opportunity to put some of his adventures into words. Perhaps he is a lesser illustration of a theory of Thoreau's that a word well said "must have taken the place of a deed by some urgent necessity, even by some misfortune, so that the truest writer will be some captive knight, after all." However that may be, the intellectual and physical adventures of Conrad's life were abundant, and they reappear, discernible though transfigured, in the substance and the qualities of his work.

His ten books are for the most part concerned with the waters of the earth, and the men that sail on the face of the waters, and with lands, far from English readers, to be reached only by long journeyings in ships.* His first book,

* *Almayer's Folly.* The Macmillan Co. 1895.
An Outcast of the Islands. Tauchnitz. 1896.
The Nigger of the Narcissus (*Children of the Sea*). Dodd, Mead & Co. 1897.
Tales of Unrest. Charles Scribner's Sons. 1898.
Lord Jim. McClure, Phillips & Co. 1899.
The Inheritors (with F. M. Hueffer). McClure, Phillips & Co. 1901.
Typhoon. G. P. Putnam's Sons. 1902.
Falk. McClure, Phillips & Co. 1903.
Youth. McClure, Philips & Co. 1903.
Romance (with F. M. Hueffer). McClure, Phillips & Co. 1904.
Nostromo. Harper & Brothers. 1904.

"Almayer's Folly," tells the story of a disappointed Dutch trader in Borneo, whose half-caste daughter runs away with a Malay chief. His second book, "An Outcast of the Islands," deals further with the career of Almayer and with that of another exiled Dutchman. "Nostromo" has for its scene an imaginary South American state, and its heroes are an Englishman and an Italian. "The Nigger of the Narcissus" (published in America as "The Children of the Sea") and "Typhoon" are each the chronicle of a voyage. "Lord Jim" is the story of a young mate who disgraces himself by one unseaman-like act, and becomes a wanderer in the eastern islands, and finally a kind of king in a village of savages. "Tales of Unrest" contains five stories, two of which are about Malays, and another about white traders in an African station. The hero of "Falk"—the title story of a volume of three pieces—is a Scandinavian sailor who has been a cannibal, and who wins the daughter of a German ship captain in an Eastern port. "Youth," the first story in a volume of three, is the memory of a young mate's voyage in an unseaworthy ship, which burns and leaves the crew to seek an Eastern seaport in the boats. The second story, "The Heart of Darkness," is an account of a journey into the Belgian Congo State and a curious study of the effect of solitude and the jungle and savagery on a white trader. The third piece in the volume is the story of a ship-captain who steers his ship with the help of a Malay servant and lets no one guess until the end that he is blind. Of two books written in collaboration with Mr. Ford M. Hueffer, the only one worth considering, "Romance," comes the nearest to being the kind of fiction that the advertisements announce as "full of heart interest, love, and the glamour of a charming hero and heroine." It begins with a smuggler's escapade in England, and ends in an elopement in the West Indies; the best parts, probably Mr. Conrad's share in the work, are those about the sea and all that on it is, fogs, ships, and bearded pirates. In these books are men and women of all civilized nations, the acquaintance of a globe-trotter, and there are, besides, enough Malays, Chinamen, and Negroes to make the choruses of several comic operas. But in Conrad they are serious people, every Malay with a soul and a tragedy; even the Nigger of the Narcissus is equipped with psychological machinery.

Conrad's subject-matter, the secretion of experience, is rich enough and of sufficiently strange and romantic quality to endow a writer of popular fiction; and his style,—that is, the use of words for their melody, power, and charm,—is fit for a king of literature. Stevenson, who found so little sheer good writing among his contemporaries, would have welcomed Conrad and have lamented that he could not or would not tell his stories in more brief, steady, and continuous fashion.

For there is the rub. Conrad is not instinctively a story-teller. Many a writer of less genius surpasses him in method. He has no gift of what Lamb calls a bare narrative.

There are writers with magnificent power of language who do not attain that combination of literary and human qualities which is readableness, and there are others who interest many people in many generations, and yet do not write well. To most readers Dickens is as delightful when he writes slovenly sentences as when he writes at his best. Scott, the demigod, pours out his great romances in an inexpressive fluid. On the other hand, Walter Pater writes infallibly well. These illustrations are intended to suggest a difference which is a fact in literature, and are not to be carried to any conclusive comparison. The difference exists and it is not a strange fact. It is strange, however, that Conrad, who spins yarns about the sea, master of a kind of subject-matter that would make his books as popular as "Robinson Crusoe" and "Treasure Island," should be one of those who can write but cannot make an inevitably attractive and winning book for the multitude.

Either he knows his fault and cannot help it, or he wills it and does not consider it a fault. There is evidence on this question. Several of his stories are put in the mouth of Marlow, an eloquent, reflective, world-worn man. In one place Conrad says, "We knew that we were fated, before the ebb began to run, to hear about one of Marlow's *inconclusive* experiences." The story Marlow tells is no more inconclusive and rambling than most of the other stories, so that one is forced to conclude that Marlow's character as narrator is Conrad's concession to his own self-observed habit of mind. In another place Conrad says: "The yarns of seamen have a direct simplicity, the whole meaning of which lies within the shell of a cracked nut. But Marlow was not typical (if his propensity to spin yarns be excepted), and to him the meaning of an episode was not inside a kernel, but outside, enveloping the tale which brought it out as a glow brings out a haze, in the likeness of one of these misty halos that sometimes are made visible by the spectral illumination of moonshine." Evidently Conrad prefers or pretends to prefer the haze to the kernel.

In an essay on Henry James he openly scorns the methods usual to fiction of "solution by rewards and punishments, by crowned love, by fortune, by a broken leg or sudden death," and says: "Why the reading public, which as a body has never laid upon the story-teller the command to be an artist, should demand from him this sham of divine omnipotence is utterly incomprehensible." Thus Mr. Conrad flings down the gauntlet to those demands of readers which greater men than he and Mr. James have been happy to satisfy without sacrifice of wisdom and reality.

A further announcement of his literary creed he made in a kind of artistic confession published a few years ago. "His (the prose writer's) answer to those who in the fulness of a wisdom which looks for immediate profit, demand specifically to be edified, consoled, amused, who demand to be promptly improved or encouraged, or frightened, or shocked, or charmed, must run thus: 'My task which I am trying to achieve is by the power of the written word to make you hear, to make you feel—it is before all to make you see. . . . If I succeed, you shall find there, according to your deserts, encouragement, consolation, fear, charm—all you demand; perhaps also that glimpse of truth * for which you have forgotten to ask."

A writer with ideals so high and strongly felt commits himself for trial by exacting standards. It is necessary to remind Mr. Conrad that if a reader is to feel, he must first understand; if he is to hear, he must hear distinctly; and if he is to see, his eye must be drawn by interest in the object, and it can look only in one direction at once. "Nostromo" is told forward and backward in the first half of the book, and the preliminary history of the silver mine is out of all proportion to the story of Nostromo, the alleged hero of the book. "Lord Jim" is confused.† The first few chapters are narrated in the third person by the author. Then for three hundred pages Marlow, a more or less intimate spectator of Jim's career, tells the story as an after-dinner yarn. It would have taken three evenings for Marlow to get through the talk, and that talk in print involves quotation within quotation beyond the legitimate uses of punctuation marks. In other stories the point of view fails. In "The Nigger of the Narcissus" are conferences between two people in private which no third person could overhear, yet the narrative seems to be told in the first person by one of the crew. In "Typhoon," where a steamer with deck almost vertical is plunging through a storm, we are on the bridge beside the simple dogged captain while he shouts orders down to the engine-room through the tube. Without warning we are down in the engine-room, hearing the captain's voice from above, and as suddenly we are back on the bridge again. A man crawls across the deck in a tempest so black that he cannot see whose legs he is groping at. We are immediately informed that he is a man of fifty, with coarse hair, of immense strength, with great

* These Slavs (see above on Tolstoy) are all for Truth, but they are not Chadbandians. They are artists. And so was the Anglo-Saxon who made Chadband.

† No, it is not. It is clear as daylight.

lumpy hands, a hoarse voice, easy-going and good-natured,
—as if the man were visible at all, except as a blot in the
darkness!

Conrad has a mania for description. When anything is mentioned in the course of narrative, though it be a thousand miles
from the present scene, it must be described. Each description
creates a new scene, and when descriptions of different and
separated places appear on the same page, the illusion of
events happening before the eye is destroyed. If a writer is
to transport us instantaneously from one quarter of the globe
to another he should at least apprise us that we are on the
magic rug, and even then the space-o'erleaping imagination
resents being bundled off on hurried and inconsequential
journeys. Often when Conrad's descriptions are logically in
course, they are too long; the current of narrative vanishes
under a mountain (a mountain of gold, perhaps, but difficult
to the feet of him who would follow the stream); and when
the subterranean river emerges again, it is frequently ob-
structed by inopportune, though subtle, exposition.

Conrad's propensity for exposition is allied, no doubt, with
his admiration for Mr. Henry James, of whom he has
written an extremely "literary" appreciation. Too much interest in masters like Flaubert and Mr. James is not gentle-
manly in a sailor, and it cannot help a sailor turned writer,
who pilots a ship through a magnificent struggle with a typhoon, leads us into the bewitching terror of the African
jungle, and guides us to Malay lands where the days are full
of savage love, intrigue, suicide, murder, piracy, and all forms
of picturesque and terrific death. Mr. Conrad finds that there
are "adventures in which only choice souls are involved, and
Mr. James records them with a fearless and insistent fidelity
to the *péripéties* of the contest and the feelings of the com-
batants." That is true and fine, no doubt, but the price which
Mr. Conrad pays for his ability to discover it is the fact that
hundreds of thousands of readers of good masculine romance
are not reading "Lord Jim," or finding new "Youth" in a

young mate's wondrous vision of the East, or welcoming a new hero in Captain Whalley. A man who can conceive the mournful tale of Karain and the fight between the half crazy white men at an African trading post has a kind of adventure better, as adventure, than the experiences of Mr. James's choice souls. Stevenson knew all about Mr. James and his "péripéties," but he could stow that knowledge on one side of his head, and from the other side spin "Treasure Island" and "The Wrecker." "The Sacred Fount" never could have befuddled the chronicle of the amiable John Silver, but in Mr. Conrad's "An Outcast of the Islands," where it seems to be a question which white man will kill the other, after a dramatic meeting in the presence of a Malay heroine, each man stands still before our eyes and radiates states of mind.

The lover who finds fault with his sweetheart because he is so proud of her is perfectly human and also perfectly logical. So my reason for dwelling on Mr. Conrad's shortcomings is because his books are thoroughly worth consideration. His advent is really important. More than any other new writer he is master of the ancient eloquence of English style; no one since Stevenson has surpassed in fiction the cadence and distinction of his prose. Never has an English sailor written so beautifully, never has artist had such full and authoritative knowledge of the sea, not even Pierre Loti. Stevenson and Kipling are but observant landsmen after all. Marryat and Clark Russell never write well, though they tell absorbing tales. There was promise in Jack London, but he was not a seaman at heart. Herman Melville's eccentric genius, greater than any of these, never led him to construct a work of art, for all his amazing power of thought and language. Conrad stands alone with his two gifts of sea experience and cultivation of style. He has lived on the sea, loved it, fought it, believed in it, been baffled by it, body and mind. To know its ways, to be master of the science of its winds and waves and the ships that brave it, to have seen men and events and the lands and waters of the earth with the eye of a sailor, the heart of a poet, the mind of a psychologist—artist and ship-captain in one—here is a combination through which Fate has conspired to produce a new writer about the most wonderful of all things, the sea and the mysterious lands beyond it.

If we grant that he is not master of the larger units of style, that is, of construction, we can assert that in the lesser units, sentence for sentence, he is a master of the English tongue. There is a story that he learned English first from the Bible, and his vigorous primal usages of words, his racial idioms and ancient rich metaphors warrant the idea that he came to us along the old highway of English speech and thought, the King James version. His sentences, however, are not biblical as Stevenson's and Kipling's often are, but show a modern sophistication and intellectual deliberateness. He frequently reminds us that he is a Slav who learned French along with his native tongue, that he has read Flaubert and Maupassant and Henry James. Approaching our language as an adult foreigner, he goes deep to the derivative meanings of words, their powerful first intentions, which familiarity has disguised from most of us native-born to English. He has achieved that ring and fluency which he has declared should be the artist's aim. Conrad's prose lifts to passages of great poetic beauty, in which the color of the sea, its emotional aspects, its desolation and its blitheness, are mingled with its meaning for the men who sail it, its "austere servitude," its friendliness and its treachery.

"The ship, a fragment detached from the earth, went on lonely and swift like a small planet. Round her the abysses of sky and sea met in an unattainable frontier. A great circular solitude moved with her, ever changing and ever the same, always monotonous and always imposing. Now and then another wandering white speck, burdened with life, appeared far off,—disappeared, intent on its own destiny. . . . The august loneliness of her path lent dignity to the sordid inspiration of her pilgrimage. She drove foaming to the southward, as if guided by the courage of a high endeavor. The smiling greatness of the sea dwarfed the extent of time."

No fairer temptation can be offered to a reader who does not know Conrad than to quote a passage from the end of "Youth," and no more honest praise can be offered to Conrad than to say that it is a selected, but by no means unique, specimen of his genius.

A crew that have left a burning ship in boats find an Eastern port at night. The weary men tie to the jetty and go to sleep. This is the young mate's narrative years after, the narrative of the reflective and eloquent Marlow: "I was lying in a flood of light, and the sky had never looked so far, so high, before. I opened my eyes and lay without moving. And then I saw the men of the East—they were looking at me. The whole length of the jetty was full of people. I saw brown, bronze, yellow faces, the black eyes, the glitter, the color of an Eastern crowd. And all these beings stared without a murmur, without a sigh, without a movement. They stared down at the boats, at the sleeping men who at night had come to them from the sea. Nothing moved. The fronds of palms stood still against the sky. Not a branch stirred along the shore, and the brown roofs of hidden houses peeped through the green foliage, through the big leaves that hung shining and still like leaves forged of heavy metal. This was the East of the navigators, so old, so mysterious, resplendent and somber, living and unchanged, full of danger and promise. . . . I have known its fascinations since: I have seen the mysterious shores, the still water, the lands of brown nations, where a stealthy Nemesis lies in wait, pursues, overtakes so many of the conquering race, who are proud of their wisdom, of their knowledge, of their strength. But for me all the East is contained in that vision of my youth. It is all in that moment when I opened my young eyes on it. I came upon it from a tussle with the sea—and I was young—and I saw it looking at me. And this is all that is left of it! Only a moment of strength, of romance, of glamour, of youth!"

THE OLD SOAK'S HISTORY—MORE EVILS
OF PROHIBITION *

By Don Marquis

WELL, another kick I got on the abolition of the barroom is the fact that you got to stay around home so much and that naturally leads to having a row with your wife.

When there was barrooms my wife used to jaw me every time I come home anyways lit up and I just let her jaw me and there wasn't any row for I figured better let her get away with it who knows maybe she thinks she is right about it.

But now I stick around home a good deal of the time and it leads to words.

Well, she says to me, why don't you go and get a job of work of some kind.

Well, I tell her, mind your own business. I always been a good pervider ain't I. You have got five or six children working for you ain't you and a man that pervides his wife with five or six children to work for her is not going to listen to no back talk.

Well, she says, you ought to be ashamed to loaf around home all the time.

Well, I says, I'm thinking up a big business deal but that's the way with women they never understand they got to keep their mouth shut and give a man peace and quiet to do his thinking in so he can make them a good living all they think about is new-fangled ways to spend the money after he has slaved himself half to death making it .

Well, she says, I ain't seen you slaving lately.

Well, I tells her, I done all my hard slaving when I was young and I got a little money coming in right along from them two houses I own, and I ain't going to work myself into the grave for no extravagant woman, and me with a heart pappitation you can hear half a mile on a clear day.

Well, she says, what rent money them two houses brings in don't any more than pay for the booze you drink.

Well, I says, you Prohibitionists done that to me. You went and made it plumb impossible to get good liquor for any reasonable price. That there rent money used to pay for three times the booze I drink.

Well, she says, you oughta get a job.

If I was to tie myself down to a job, I tells her, what chance would I have to trade and dicker around and make little turnovers, let alone thinking up this big business deal I am working on.

You are a liar, She said, and if I knowed where your whiskey was hid I'd bust every bottle and what kind of a business deal are you thinking up.

It is an invention I says to her and you mind your own business just because I have stood for you intrupting me for forty years is no sign I am going to stand for it forty years more.

You can quit any time she says and good riddance the children will keep me and there will be one less to cook for besides being ashamed of you before all my own friends and the nice people the children know.

Well, I said, here I set turning over the leaves of the Bible and you attack me that way and me trying to think up a business deal to buy you an automobile and the pappitation in my heart that bad it shakes the chair I am setting in and if a man with one foot in the grave can't get any peace and quiet to read his Bible in his own home against the time he is going to cash in then I will say that Prohibition has brought this country to a pretty pass.

Well, she says, what is that pappitation from but all the liquor you drunk.

It is from my constitution, I says, as the doctor will tell you if it hadn't been for a little mite of stimulant now and then I would have cashed in long ago and you would now have the life insurance money.

Well, she says, what kind of an invention is this you claim you are thinking up all the time.

Yes, I says, I would see myself telling you, wouldn't I and you blabbing it the next time a lot of them church women meets at our house and some old church deacon getting hold of it and getting rich off it and me wandering the streets in destitution with the rain running down offen my beard and the end of my nose because you and the children cast me into the street.

Well, she says, where is that thousand dollars that my uncle Lemuel willed to me and I give it to you for one of them inventions nearly thirty years ago and never seen hide nor hair on it since then.

Well, I says, that thousand dollars is gone and it went the same way as that money I loaned to your cousin Dan when he failed in business and would have starved to death him and his family if I hadn't come across with the cash that is where that thousand dollars is.

Well, that's the way it goes, until I get tired of trying to make her see any sense and sneak out to where my stuff is hid and fill me a pint bottle for my hip pocket and go and find a friend somewheres.

And in just that way Prohibition is breaking up millions and millions of homes every day.

THE GENTLE ART OF REPARTEE *

By Brander Matthews

I

Doctor Holmes once declared that the bound volumes of comic papers were "cemeteries of hilarity, interspersed with cenotaphs of wit and humor." Probably he would have admitted that only the cypress and the yew could supply appropriate shelving for the second-rate comic plays of the immediate past, brisk enough in the performance not so very long ago, and yet sadly old-fashioned now that our taste in jokes has changed. Still, a wise word or a witty may be gleaned even from these forlorn pieces, which we may dismiss with what the colored gentleman aptly called "despisery." In a forgotten English comedy of the second half of the nineteenth century, a man, describing the only kind of woman he would be willing to marry, asserted that she must be a clever woman, a very clever woman—"a woman clever enough to begin a conversation with a repartee!" This is evidence that bachelors are ever unreasonable in the demands they make upon spinsters, since there never was a woman clever enough to open a conversation with a retort. Any dictionary will remind us that a mere smart saying, a glittering epigram, a brilliant witticism, is not entitled to be received as a repartee unless it is a rejoinder. The exact definition of repartee is "a clever, ready, and witty retort."

In one of the Leatherstocking tales, Cooper narrates that Natty Bumppo was engaged in single combat with an adroit Indian foe, and that the redskin finally cast his tomahawk at the white hunter. Leatherstocking swiftly stepped aside, and with inconceivable dexterity caught the glittering weapon as it flew through the air, and with unerring aim hurled it back, to sink into the brain of his supple enemy. That was a true repartee—the rejoinder of the backwoods, the retort in kind, which closes a conversation and renders all further discussion unnecessary. It is therefore quite different from Leatherstocking's marvelous feats of marksmanship, when he drew a bead on a distant foe and dropped him in his tracks before the enemy knew what had hit him.

If we accept this distinction, as I think we must, we are forced to rule out a host of unexpected witticisms, spontaneously generated, and yet devoid of this element of rejoinder. They may be as rapid and as recreative as the true repartee, but they lack this necessary element of self-defense, of legitimate reprisal. Congreve once told Colley Cibber that there were many witty speeches in one of Cibber's comedies, and also many speeches that looked witty and yet were not really what they seemed at first sight. So there are delightfully sudden flashes of wit which look like repartees, and yet are not when they are examined more closely. They are none the less delightful, but they are to be classified under another head. Here is an example of the instantaneous quip which is not a true repartee, felicitous as it is. Some years ago a friend of Mr. Oliver Herford's was going to Europe on the "Celtic," and the evening before his departure Mr. Herford called him up on the telephone to say good-by. He asked what ship his friend was going on, and some imp of the perverse prompted the friend to answer that he was sailing on the "Keltic." Mr. Herford promptly responded, "Don't say that, or you will have a hard C all the way across!"

We come a little closer to the genuine rejoinder, and again without attaining it, in a sharp turn attributed to Voltaire.

That arch-wit was once speaking in praise of a certain contemporary man of letters, and a bystander remarked that it was very good of M. de Voltaire to say pleasant things of this man, since he was always saying unpleasant things of Voltaire; whereupon Voltaire smiled sweetly and suggested, "Perhaps we are both of us mistaken." This may be accepted as a retort to an absent adversary. It has the obvious element of self-defense, which is ever the essential quality of the true repartee, and it recalls the wise saying that it is the man who returns the first blow that begins the quarrel.

Voltaire's rejoinder is characteristically neat. It has the dexterity of the Oriental executioner, who seemed only to be flourishing his sword until he presented his snuff-box, whereupon the victim promptly sneezed his amputated head from his unsuspecting shoulders. It is in marked contrast to the surly brutality of Doctor Johnson's verbal boxing. After all, the proper weapon for the accomplished master of fence is the delicate duelling-sword and not the bludgeon or the boomerang, even if these more vulgar instruments may also be wielded with deadly effect. At bottom, what gives to the true repartee its utmost effect is the fact that the engineer has been hoist by his own petard; he is summarily disposed of while the rest of us are dazzled by the unforeseen sparks of the explosion.

Speaker Reed was once discussing the merits of President Harrison with a fellow-congressman, who, remembering that Reed's well-known dislike of the President was heightened by the fact that in the appointment of a collector of the port of Portland Reed's candidate had been turned down in favor of the Maine senator's, said:

"Of course, Mr. Reed, I know that Mr. Harrison can't say 'No' gracefully."

At which Reed flashed out: "Oh, it's worse than that. He can't say 'Yes' gracefully."

The mention of Reed leads naturally to the mention of Bismarck, also a master of debate in his own lordly fashion.

In the days when the Seven Weeks' War with Austria was already looming in the distance, a French minister at one of the German courts protested against Prussia's conduct and warned Bismarck that, if it continued, it would lead Prussia straight to Jena. Bismarck looked the Frenchman in the eye and asked the simple question, "Why not to Waterloo?"

In like manner the mention of Waterloo leads naturally to the mention of Napoleon and Talleyrand, who were necessary to each other, but who crossed swords often, none the less. When Talleyrand was created Prince of Bénévent, he presented his wife to the emperor. Napoleon knew that the new princess resembled the heroine of the modern problem-play in that she was

> A lady with a record
> Whose career was rather checkered,

so he expressed his hope that her conduct in the future would be in accord with her exalted rank. And Talleyrand bowed, and responded that Mme. de Talleyrand would undoubtedly pattern her conduct on that of the empress. He knew, and he knew that Napoleon knew that he knew, how much scandal had attached to the conduct of Josephine even after she had married Napoleon.

In one of the bitter scenes of altercation which were not infrequent between Napoleon and his indispensable minister, the emperor declared that Talleyrand probably expected to be chief of the regency if Napoleon died. "But remember this," threatened the irate sovereign, "if I fall dangerously ill, you will be dead before me." And Talleyrand bowed ceremoniously and answered, "Sire, I did not need this warning to address to heaven my most ardent wishes for the conservation of Your Majesty's health."

On another occasion Talleyrand heard a certain general talking contemptuously of a class of persons whom he designated as *pékins*. Talleyrand asked who were the creatures so curtly dismissed as unworthy of regard. The general gladly explained that, "We soldiers call everybody a *pékin* who is not military." And Talleyrand accepted the explanation with his usual suavity. "I see," he said, "it is just like what we do when we call anybody military who is not civil."

Many of the best of Talleyrand's good things are to be classed as true repartee; but on occasion he was tempted by his readiness of wit to puncture pretenders even when he himself had not been attacked. When a silly young fellow, seated between Mme. de Staël and Mme. Récamier, had the folly to insult both ladies by the remark that he was now between wit and beauty, Talleyrand could not resist the temptation. "Yes," he remarked, "and without possessing either." At first glance this may look like an unprovoked assault; and yet it may really be defended as a repartee, since it was due to the desire to avenge a thoughtless slur on two ladies to whom he was greatly attracted. Indeed, Mme. de Staël, when she was most intimate with Talleyrand, was not a little jealous of Mme. Récamier. Once she inquired of Talleyrand which of them he would fish out of the water if she and Mme. Récamier happened to fall in at the same time. And again Talleyrand was equal to the occasion. With his most flattering smile he replied, "Ah, Madame, you swim so well."

II

There is a charming subtlety about this which seems characteristically French. Yet we can now and again attain to an easy felicity that a Frenchman might envy. When the late Maurice Barrymore was once holding forth with his exuberant humor, an intoxicated bystander rudely interrupted by crying out, "You're a liar!" Barrymore was known to be a handy man with his fists, and the spectators expected a swift blow from the shoulder. It came only from the lips. Barrymore saw the man's condition, and with a light laugh responded, "Surely not—if *you* say so!"

This may be accepted as the repartee in all its nakedness. In fact, the repartee is almost always an ingenious variation of the everlasting retort, "You're another!" It is contained in its simplest form in the ancient and honorable dialogue which begins, "You're no gentleman!" and which ends, "You're no judge!" There is a variant of this which describes the fisticuffs of two rude fellows of the baser sort, one of whom is heard to declare, "I'll learn you to behave like a gentleman!" whereat the other insists, "I defy you to do it." And we may discover an analogy between these two masculine repartees and a feminine repartee credited to a British suffragette. A puny male offensively thrust himself forward and interrupted the lady's eloquent address with the irrelevant query, "Wouldn't you jolly well like to be a man?" And the champion of the fair sex instantly proved its superiority by the counter-question, "Wouldn't you?"

By the side of this intersexual retort may be placed several international repartees, all credited to that anonymous but fascinating entity, the American Girl. Once when a Beefeater at the Tower of London was displaying its treasures to a party of transatlantic pilgrims, he drew special attention to a certain gun, "captured at the battle of Bunker Hill, ladies and gentlemen!" And then the American Girl rose to the occasion. "I see," she said meekly, "you have the cannon, and we have the hill." This is perhaps a little sharper and less obvious than another of her retorts, called forth by the remark of an English lady to the effect that she could see "no reason why you Americans seem to think so much of your own country." Then the American Girl replied languidly, "I suppose it must be because we have seen some of the other countries." Closely akin to this is her swift response to another British dame who had read in the London papers horrible details about evil doings in the United States and who was thereby moved to suggest that if things did not improve, it might be necessary to send over an army to chastise us. Whereupon the American Girl affected surprise and asked, "What—again?"

When Oscar Wilde came to the United States to lecture on esthetics in his highly esthetic velvet costume,—and incidentally to prepare the public mind for the proper appreciation of Gilbert and Sullivan's 'Patience,' in which the esthetic movement was held up to ridicule,—he used to complain that America was very uninteresting since it had "no antiquities and no curiosities." But he ventured on this disparagement once too often, for in the course of his travels he uttered it to the American Girl, and she replied with the demure depravity of candid innocence that this was not quite a fair reproach, since "we shall have the antiquities in time, and we are already importing the curiosities."

Lamb once declared that it was some compensation for growing old that in his youth he had seen the 'School for Scandal' acted by the incomparable cast that illuminated the original performance; and perhaps the present writer may discover a like compensation in the fact that he can recall the elder Sothern's rich and mellow rendering of the 'Crushed Tragedian.' Hazlitt—writing, it is true, before the full flowering of the modern novel—asserted that "to read a good comedy is to keep the best company in the world, where the best things are said and the most amusing happen." Yet even better than the reading of a good comedy, entertaining as that may be, is the recalling of its performance, with the echo of its best things in our ears and with the memory of its amusing happenings rising unbidden before our eyes. The 'Crushed Tragedian' was not a very good comedy, taken as a whole; but Sothern's performance of the broken-down old actor was a delight that no one who ever enjoyed it would willingly forget. Rising on the top wave of joyous recollection is the superb attitude of triumph assumed by Sothern as the old actor transfixes one of the other characters with what he believes to be a master stroke of repartee. The other character is an old banker, who, when he learns that Sothern is an actor, makes the lordly remark that "it is twenty years since I have been in a theater." This gives the crushed tragedian his chance, and with immense scorn he hurls back the withering words, "It is about the same time since *I* have been in a *bank!*"

This is transcendental in its sublimity. It is very much more felicitous than the more obvious rejoinder in one of Augier's comedies, in the course of which two friends discover that they have made a mistake. "What fools we have been!" one of them admits; and the other, a little nettled, replies, "Put that in the singular." "Certainly," the first retorts, "what a fool *you* have been!" Obvious as this is, and inexpensive as it must be considered, it falls completely within the definition of the repartee. Not a few other examples might be picked from the pages of the younger Dumas and Beaumarchais, as well as from those of Sheridan and Congreve. Perhaps it is because actors are in the habit of taking part in the amusing happenings of good comedies, and of uttering the good things prepared for them by the authors, that they are encouraged to achieve good things of their own. During the run of the 'Blue Bird' in New York last winter, a friend of the late Jacob Wendell (who played the part of the faithful Dog in Maeterlinck's fairy allegory) met him at The Players. This friend praised Wendell's performance of the canine character, with the sole reservation of the barking. That, the volunteer critic insisted, was not so true to life as it should be; he declared finally, "I could just naturally bark better than that myself." And Wendell gravely expostulated, "Ah, but, you see, I had to learn *my* bark."

III

This may be taken as an example of the retort courteous, altho it is not as gentle as one of Thackeray's. When the novelist made his single attempt to be elected to Parliament, he happened one day to meet the rival candidate, who parted from him with the familiar Anglo-Saxon phrase, "May the best man win!" To this Thackeray instantly responded, "I hope *not!*" Thackeray's collaborator in the pages of *Punch,* Douglas Jerrold, was incapable of a suave rejoinder of this sort. Jerrold was in fact a little like Doctor Johnson, in his disregard for the feelings of others and in his willingness to give pain for the pleasure of his own wit. When Bentley the publisher told Jerrold that he had at first intended to call his new magazine the *Wit's Miscellany* but had finally decided to style it *Bentley's Miscellany,* Jerrold smiled bitterly and said, "Well, you needn't have gone to the other extreme." This is not a true repartee, since it was wholly gratuitous, being entirely without provocation.

The sole justification for the bold retort is that it is a weapon of self-defense. Tennyson, so we were told, used to delight in narrating a rejoinder of a certain more or less disreputable man about town, named Trumpington, who was a crony of George IV. Once when the king came down to a seaside resort, he met his friend with the remark, "I hear you are the biggest blackguard in the place." And Trumpington bowed and responded, "I hope Your Majesty has not come down here to take away my character." By the side of this may be put a remark of Ben Butler's during the Crédit Mobilier debate of 1873, perhaps not strictly a repartee by the definition insisted upon in these pages, and yet so near to the margin of the definition that it deserves mention here. Butler had objected to an elaborate and unduly distended speech of an opponent, who expostulated with the plea that he had expected to divide time with the honorable gentleman opposite. To this Butler retorted: "Divide time? It looks to me more like dividing eternity."

There is an epigram often attributed to Sheridan, but really composed by Lewis, the author of the 'Monk,' which preserves in rime a repartee that may have been due originally to Sheridan himself:

> Lord Erskine, at woman presuming to rail,
> Called a wife, "a tin canister tied to one's tail."
> And fair Lady Anne, while the subject he carries on,
> Seems hurt by his lordship's degrading comparison.
> But wherefore degrading?   Considered aright,
> A canister's useful and polished and bright;
> And should dirt its original purity hide—
> That's the fault of the puppy to whom it is tied.

On one occasion, at least, Sheridan and Lewis sparred, and the author of the 'School for Scandal' countered neatly on the author of the 'Castle Specter.' This last piece was a tawdry melodrama which had proved very attractive at Drury Lane, although it had not brought to Lewis what he believed to be a proportionate share of its profits. By chance the manager and the author had a dispute about some question of the hour, and Lewis offered to back his opinion with a bet. "I'll make a big bet," he cried; "I'll bet you what you have made by my play." "No," retorted Sheridan, "I'll make only a little bet. I'll bet you what your play is really worth."

It is an interesting fact that Sheridan, prodigal as he was of wit, in life as in literature, was sparing of repartee, or at least that his repartee was rarely or never offensive. His humor was good humor also, and that can rarely be said of a wit. Moore, in his memorial poem, declared that Sheridan's wit

> Ne'er carried a heart-stain away on its blade.

Sheridan was liked by those he laughed at. He was that rare character, a wit, ready at repartee, and yet not feared. He was popular, notwithstanding Chesterfield's wise remark that to be known as a wit "is a very unpopular denomination, as it carries terror along with it; and people in general are as much afraid of a live wit, in company, as a woman is of a gun, which she thinks may go off of itself and do her a mischief." If wit is a gun, repartee is sometimes a gun that kicks and sorely bruises the shoulder of him who fires it. A weapon of self-defense it may be, but, like other weapons, it sometimes proves a dangerous possession. Perhaps a time may come when men will not be allowed to carry wit concealed about their persons without a special permit from the municipal authorities, to be granted only to those who can bring testimonials to the gentleness of their character.

THE AMERICAN MAGAZINE *

By H. L. Mencken

It is astonishing, considering the enormous influence of
the popular magazine upon American literature, such as it is,
that there is but one book in type upon magazine history in
the republic. That lone volume is "The Magazine in America," by Professor Dr. Algernon Tassin, a learned birchman
of the great university of Columbia, and it is so badly written
that the interest of its matter is almost concealed—almost, but
fortunately not quite. The professor, in fact, puts English
to paper with all the traditional dullness of his flatulent order,
and, as usual, he is most horribly dull when he is trying most
kittenishly to be lively. I spare you examples of his writing;
if you know the lady essayists of the United States, and their
academic imitators in pantaloons, you know the sort of arch
and whimsical jocosity he ladles out. But, as I have hinted,
there is something worth attending to in his story, for all the
defects of its presentation, and so his book is not to be sniffed
at. He has, at all events, brought together a great mass of
scattered and concealed facts, and arranged them conveniently
for whoever deals with them next. The job was plainly
a long and laborious one, and rasping to the higher cerebral
centers. The historian had to make his mole-like way
through the endless files of old and stupid magazines;
he had to read the insipid biographies and autobiographies of

* From *Prejudices: First Series;* copyright, 1919, by Alfred A.
Knopf, Inc. Reprinted by permission of the author and the publishers.

dead and forgotten editors, many of them college professors, preachers out of work, pre-historic uplifters and bad poets; he had to sort out the facts from the fancies of such incurable liars as Griswold; he had to hack and blast a path across a virgin wilderness. The thing was worth doing, and, as I say, it has been done with commendable pertinacity.

Considering the noisiness of the American magazines of to-day, it is rather instructive to glance back at the timorous and bloodless quality of their progenitors. All of the early ones, when they were not simply monthly newspapers or almanacs, were depressingly "literary" in tone, and dealt chiefly in stupid poetry, silly essays and artificial fiction. The one great fear of their editors seems to have been that of offending some one; all of the pioneer prospectuses were full of assurances that nothing would be printed which even "the most fastidious" could object to. Literature, in those days,—say from 1830 to 1860—was almost completely cut off from contemporary life. It mirrored, not the struggle for existence, so fierce and dramatic in the new nation, but the pallid reflections of poetasters, self-advertising clergymen, sissified "gentlemen of taste," and other such donkeys. Poe waded into these *literati* and shook them up a bit, but even after the Civil War the majority of them continued to spin pretty cobwebs. Edmund Clarence Stedman and Donald G. Mitchell were excellent specimens of the clan; its last survivor was the lachrymose William Winter. The "literature" manufactured by these tear-squeezers, though often enough produced in beer cellars, was frankly aimed at the Young Person. Its main purpose was to avoid giving offense; it breathed a heavy and oleaginous piety, a snug niceness, a sickening sweetness. It is as dead to-day as Baalam's ass.

The *Atlantic Monthly* was set up by men in revolt against this reign of mush, as *Putnam's* had been a few years before, but the business of reform proved to be difficult and hazardous, and it was a long while before a healthier breed of authors could be developed, and a public for them found. "There is not much in the *Atlantic,"* wrote Charles Eliot Norton to Lowell in 1874, "that is likely to be read twice save by its writers, and this is what the great public likes. . . . You should hear Godkin express himself in private on this topic." *Harper's Magazine,* in those days, was made up almost wholly of cribbings from England; the *North American Review* had sunk into stodginess and imbecility; *Putnam's* was dead, or dying; the *Atlantic* had yet to discover Mark Twain; it was the era of *Godey's Lady's Book.* The new note, so long awaited, was struck at last by *Scribner's,* now the *Century* (and not to be confused with the *Scribner's* of to-day). It not only threw all the old traditions overboard; it established new traditions almost at once. For the first time a great magazine began to take notice of the daily life of the American people. It started off with a truly remarkable series of articles on the Civil War; it plunged into contemporary politics; it eagerly sought out and encouraged new writers; it began printing decent pictures instead of the old chromos; it forced itself, by the sheer originality and enterprise of its editing, upon the public attention. American literature owes more to the *Century* than to any other magazine, and perhaps American thinking owes almost as much. It was the first "literary" periodical to arrest and interest the really first-class men of the country. It beat the *Atlantic* because it wasn't burdened with the *Atlantic's* decaying cargo of Boston Brahmins. It beat all the others because it was infinitely and obviously better. Almost everything that is good in the American magazine of to-day, almost everything that sets it above the English magazine or the Continental magazine, stems from the *Century.*

At the moment, of course, it holds no such clear field; perhaps it has served its function and is ready for a placid old age. The thing that displaced it was the yellow magazine of the *McClure's* type—a variety of magazine which surpassed it in the race for circulation by exaggerating and vulgarizing all its merits. Dr. Tassin seems to think, with William

Archer, that S. S. McClure was the inventor of this type, but the truth is that its real father was the unknown originator of the Sunday supplement. What McClure—a shrewd literary bagman—did was to apply the sensational methods of the cheap newspaper to a new and cheap magazine. Yellow journalism was rising and he went in on the tide. The satanic Hearst was getting on his legs at the same time, and I daresay that the muck-raking magazines, even in their palmy days, followed him a good deal more than they led him. McClure and the imitators of McClure borrowed his adept thumping of the tom-tom; Munsey and the imitators of Munsey borrowed his mush. *McClure's* and *Everybody's,* even when they had the whole nation by the ears, did little save repeat in solemn, awful tones what Hearst had said before. As for *Munsey's,* at the height of its circulation, it was little more than a Sunday "magazine section" on smooth paper, and with somewhat clearer half-tones than Hearst could print. Nearly all the genuinely original ideas of these Yankee Harmsworths of yesterday turned out badly. John Brisben Walker, with the *Cosmopolitan,* tried to make his magazine a sort of national university, and it went to pot. Ridgway, of *Everybody's,* planned a weekly to be published in a dozen cities simultaneously, and lost a fortune trying to establish it. McClure, facing a situation to be described presently, couldn't manage it, and his magazine got away from him. As for Munsey, there are many wrecks behind him; he is forever experimenting boldly and failing gloriously. Even his claim to have invented the all-fiction magazine is open to caveat; there were probably plenty of such things, in substance if not in name, before the *Argosy.* Hearst, the teacher of them all, now openly holds the place that belongs to him. He has galvanized the corpse of the old *Cosmopolitan* into a great success, he has distanced all rivals with *Hearst's,* he has beaten the English on their own ground with *Nash's,* and he has rehabilitated various lesser magazines. More, he has forced the other magazine publishers to imitate him. A glance at *McClure's* to-day offers all the proof that is needed of his influence upon his inferiors.

Dr. Tassin, apparently in fear of making his book too nearly good, halts his chronicle at its most interesting point, for he says nothing of what has gone on since 1900—and very much, indeed, has gone on since 1900. For one thing, the *Saturday Evening Post* has made its unparalleled success, created its new type of American literature for department store buyers and shoe drummers, and bred its school of brisk, business-like, high-speed authors. For another thing, the *Ladies' Home Journal,* once supreme in its field, has seen the rise of a swarm of imitators, some of them very prosperous. For a third thing, the all-fiction magazine of Munsey, Robert Bonner and Street & Smith has degenerated into so dubious a hussy that Munsey, a very moral man, must blush every time he thinks of it. For a fourth thing, the moving-picture craze has created an entirely new type of magazine, and it has elbowed many other types from the stands. And for a fifth thing, to make an end, the muck-raking magazine has blown up and is no more.

Why this last? Have all the possible candidates for the rake been raked? Is there no longer any taste for scandal in the popular breast? I have heard endless discussion of these questions and many ingenious answers, but all of them fail to answer. In this emergency I offer one of my own. It is this: that the muck-raking magazine came to grief, not because the public tired of muck-raking, but because the muck-raking that it began with succeeded. That is to say, the villains so long belabored by the Steffenses, the Tarbells and the Phillipses were either driven from the national scene or forced (at least temporarily) into rectitude. Worse, their places in public life were largely taken by nominees whose chemical purity was guaranteed by these same magazines, and so the latter found their occupation gone and their following with it. The great masses of the plain people, eager to swallow denunciation in horse-doctor doses, gagged at the first spoonful of praise. They chortled and read on when Aldrich, Boss Cox, Gas Addicks, John D. Rockefeller and the other bugaboos of the time were belabored every month, but they promptly sickened and went elsewhere when Judge Ben B. Lindsey, Francis J. Heney, Governor Folk and the rest of the bogus saints began to be hymned.

The same phenomenon is constantly witnessed upon the lower level of daily journalism. Let a vociferous "reform" newspaper overthrow the old gang and elect its own candidates, and at once it is in a perilous condition. Its stock in trade is gone. It can no longer give a good show—within the popular meaning of a good show. For what the public wants eternally —at least the American public—is rough work. It delights in vituperation. It revels in scandal. It is always on the side of the man or journal making the charges, no matter how slight the probability that the accused is guilty. The late Roosevelt, perhaps one of the greatest rabble-rousers the world has ever seen, was privy to this fact, and made it the corner-stone of his singularly cynical and effective politics. He was forever calling names, making accusations, unearthing and denouncing demons. Dr. Wilson, a performer of scarcely less talent, has sought to pursue the same plan, with varying fidelity and success. He was a popular hero so long as he confined himself to reviling men and things—the Hell Hounds of Plutocracy, the Socialists, the Kaiser, the Irish, the Senate minority. But the moment he found himself on the side of the defense, he began to wobble, just as Roosevelt before him had begun to wobble when he found himself burdened with the intricate constructive program of the Progressives. Roosevelt shook himself free by deserting the Progressives, but Wilson found it impossible to get rid of his League of Nations, and so, for a while at least, he presented a quite typical picture of a muck-raker ham-strung by blows from the wrong end of the rake.

That the old appetite for bloody shows is not dead but only sleepeth is well exhibited by the recent revival of the

weekly of opinion. Ten years ago the weekly seemed to be absolutely extinct; even the *Nation* survived only as a half-forgotten appendage of the *Evening Post*. Then, of a sudden, the alliance was broken, the *Evening Post* succumbed to Wall Street, the *Nation* started on an independent course—and straightway made a great success. And why? Simply because it began breaking heads—not the old heads of the *McClure's* era, of course, but nevertheless heads salient enough to make excellent targets. For years it had been moribund; no one read it save a dwindling company of old men; its influence gradually approached *nil*. But by the elementary device of switching from mild expostulation to violent and effective denunciation it made a new public almost over-night, and is now very widely read, extensively quoted and increasingly heeded. . . . I often wonder that so few publishers of periodicals seem aware of the psychological principle here exposed. It is known to every newspaper publisher of the slightest professional intelligence; all successful newspapers are ceaselessly querulous and bellicose. They never defend any one or anything if they can help it; if the job is forced upon them, they tackle it by denouncing some one or something else. The plan never fails. Turn to the moving-picture trade magazines: the most prosperous of them is given over, in the main, to bitter attacks upon new films. Come back to daily journalism. The New York *Tribune*, a decaying paper, well nigh rehabilitated itself by attacking Hearst, the cleverest muck-raker of them all. For a moment, apparently dismayed, he attempted a defense of himself—and came near falling into actual disaster. Then, recovering his old form, he began a whole series of counter attacks and cover attacks, and in six months he was safe and sound again. . . .

INTELLECTUAL SNOBBERY *

By A. A. Milne

A GOOD many years ago I had a painful experience. I was discovered by my house-master reading in bed at the unauthorized hour of midnight. Smith *minor* in the next bed (we shared a candle) was also reading. We were both discovered. But the most annoying part of the business, as it seemed to me then, was that Smith *minor* was discovered reading Alton Locke, and that I was discovered reading *Marooned Among Cannibals.* If only our house-master had come in the night before! Then he would have found *me* reading *Alton Locke.* Just for a moment it occurred to me to tell him this, but after a little reflection I decided that it would be unwise. He might have misunderstood the bearings of the revelation.

There is hardly one of us who is proof against this sort of intellectual snobbery. A detective story may have been a very good friend to us, but we don't want to drag it into the conversation; we prefer a casual reference to *The Egoist,* with which we have perhaps only a bowing acquaintance; a reference which leaves the impression that we are inseperable companions, or at any rate inseparable until such day when we gather from our betters that there are heights even beyond *The Egoist.* Dead or alive, we would sooner be found with a copy of Marcus Aurelius than with a copy of Marie Corelli. I used to know a man who carried always with him a Russian novel in the original; not because he read Russian, but because a day might come when, as a result of some accident, the

* From *Not That It Matters;* copyright, 1920, by E. P. Dutton & Company. Reprinted by permission of the author and the publishers.

"pockets of the deceased" would be exposed in the public Press. As he said, you never know; but the only accident which happened to him was to be stranded for twelve hours in August at a wayside station in the Highlands. After this he maintained that the Russians were overrated.

I should like to pretend that I myself have grown out of these snobbish ways by this time, but I am doubtful if it would be true. It happened to me not so long ago to be travelling in company of which I was very much ashamed; and to be ashamed of one's company is to be a snob. At this period I was trying to amuse myself (and, if it might be so, other people) by writing a burlesque story in the manner of an imaginary collaboration by Sir Hall Caine and Mrs. Florence Barclay. In order to do this I had to study the works of these famous authors, and for many week-ends in succession I might have been seen travelling to, or returning from, the country with a couple of their books under my arm. To keep one book beneath the arm is comparatively easy; to keep two is much more difficult. Many was the time, while waiting for my train to come in, that one of those books slipped from me. Indeed there is hardly a junction in the railway system of the southern counties at which I have not dropped on some Saturday or other a Caine or a Barclay; to have it restored to me a moment later by a courteous fellow-passenger—courteous, but with a smile of gentle pity in his eye as he glimpsed the author's name. "Thanks very much," I would stammer, blushing guiltily, and perhaps I would babble about a sick friend to whom I was taking them, or that I was running out of paper-weights. But he never believed me. He knew that he would have said something like that himself.

Nothing is easier than to assume that other people share one's weaknesses. No doubt Jack the Ripper excused himself on the ground that it was human nature; possibly, indeed, he wrote an essay like this, in which he speculated mildly as to the reasons which made stabbing so attractive to us all. So I realize that I may be doing you an injustice in suggesting

that you who read may also have your little snobberies. But
I confess that I should like to cross-examine you. If in conversation with you, on the subject (let us say) of heredity,
a subject to which you had devoted a good deal of study, I
took it for granted that you had read Ommany's *Approximations,* would you make it quite clear to me that you had not
read it? Or would you let me carry on the discussion on the
assumption that you knew it well; would you, even, in answer
to a direct question, say shamefacedly that though you had
not—er—actually read it, you—er—knew about it, of course,
and had—er—read extracts from it? Somehow I think I
could lead you on to this; perhaps even make you say that
you had actually ordered it from your library, before I had
told you the horrid truth that Ommany's *Approximations* was
an invention of my own.

It is absurd that we (I say "we," for I include you now)
should behave like this, for there is no book over which we
need be ashamed, either to have read it or not to have read
it. Let us, therefore, be frank. In order to remove the unfortunate impression of myself which I have given you, I will
confess that I have only read three of Scott's novels, and
begun, but never finished, two of Henry James'. I will also
confess—and here I am by way of restoring that unfortunate
impression—that I do quite well in Scottish and Jacobean
circles on those five books. For, if a question arises as to
which is Scott's masterpiece, it is easy for me to suggest one
of my three, with the air of one who has chosen it, not over
two others, but over twenty. Perhaps one of my three is
the acknowledged masterpiece; I do not know. If it is, then,
of course, all is well. But if it is not, then I must appear
rather a clever fellow for having rejected the obvious. With
regard to Henry James, my position is not quite so secure;
but at least I have good reason for feeling that the two novels
which I was unable to finish cannot be his best, and with a
little tact I can appear to be defending this position hotly
against some imaginary authority who has declared in favour

of them. One might have read the collected works of both authors, yet make less of an impression.

Indeed, sometimes I feel that I *have* read their collected works, and Ommany's *Approximations,* and many other books with which you would be only too glad to assume familiarity. For in giving others the impression that I am on terms with these masterpieces, I have but handed on an impression which has gradually formed itself in my own mind. So I take no advantage of them; and if it appears afterwards that we have been deceived together, I shall be at least as surprised and indignant about it as they.

212   ESSAYS BY PRESENT-DAY WRITERS

THE AUTOGENESIS OF A POET *

By Christopher Morley

THE mind trudges patiently behind the senses. Day by day a thousand oddities and charms outline themselves tenderly upon consciousness, but it may be long before understanding comes with brush and colour to fill in the tracery. One learns nothing until he rediscovers it for himself. Every now and then, in reading, I have come across something which has given me the wild surmise of pioneering mingled with the faint magic of familiarity—for instance, some of the famous dicta of Wordsworth and Coleridge and Shelley about poetry. I realized, then, that a teacher had told me these things in my freshman year at college—fifteen years ago. I jotted them down at that time, but they were mere catchwords. It had taken me fifteen years of vigorous living to overhaul those catchwords and fill them with a meaning of my own. The two teachers who first gave me some suspicion of what lies in the kingdom of poetry—who gave "so sweet a prospect into the way as will entice any man to enter into it"—are both dead. May I mention their names?—Francis B. Gummere and Albert Elmer Hancock, both of Haverford College. I cannot thank them as, now, I would like to. For I am (I think) approaching a stage where I can somewhat understand and relish the things of which they spoke. And I wonder afresh at the patience and charity of those who go on lecturing, unabated in zest, to boys of whom one in ten may perhaps, fifteen years later, begin to grasp their message.

* From *Plum Pudding;* copyright, 1921, by Doubleday, Page & Company. Reprinted by permission of the author and the publishers.

In so far as any formal or systematic discipline of thought was concerned, I think I may say my education was a complete failure. For this I had only my own smattering and desultory habit of mind to blame and also a vivid troublesome sense of the beauty of it all. The charm of the prismatic fringe round the edges made juggling with the lens too tempting, and a clear persistent focus was never attained. Considered (oddly enough) by my mates as the pattern of a diligent scholar, I was in reality as idle as the idlest of them, which is saying much; though I confess that my dilettantism was not wholly disreputable. My mind excellently exhibited the Heraclitean doctrine: a constant flux of information passed through it, but nothing remained. Indeed, my senses were so continually crammed with new enchanting impressions, and every field of knowledge seemed so alluring, it was not strange I made little progress in any.

Perhaps it was unfortunate that both in America and in England I found myself in a college atmosphere of extraordinary pictorial charm. The Arcadian loveliness of the Haverford campus and the comfortable simplicity of its routine; and then the hypnotizing beauty and curiosity and subtle flavour of Oxford life (with its long, footloose, rambling vacations)—these were aptly devised for the exercise of the imagination, which is often a gracious phrase for loafing. But these surroundings were too richly entertaining, and I was too green and soft and humorous (in the Shakespearean sense) to permit any rational continuous plan of study. Like the young man to whom Coleridge addressed a poem of rebuke, I was abandoned, a greater part of the time, to "an Indolent and Causeless Melancholy"; or to its partner, an excessive and not always tasteful mirth. I spent hours upon hours, with little profit, in libraries, flitting aimlessly from book to book. With something between terror and hunger I contemplated the opposite sex. In short, I was discreditable and harmless and unlovely as the young Yahoo can be. It fills me with amazement to think that my preceptors must have seen, in that ill-conditioned creature, some shadow of human semblance, or how could they have been so uniformly kind?

Our education—such of it as is of durable importance—comes haphazard. It is tinged by the enthusiasm of our teachers, gleaned by suggestions from our friends, prompted by glimpses and footnotes and margins. There was a time, I think, when I hung in tender equilibrium among various possibilities. I was enamoured of mathematics and physics: I went far enough in the latter to be appointed undergraduate assistant in the college laboratory. I had learned, by my junior year, exploring the charms of integral calculus, that there is no imaginable mental felicity more serenely pure than suspended happy absorption in a mathematical problem. Of course I attained no higher than the dregs of the subject; on that grovelling level I would still (in Billy Sunday's violent trope) have had to climb a tree to look a snake in the eye; but I could see that for the mathematician, if for any one, Time stands still withal; he is winnowed of vanity and sin. French, German, and Latin, and a hasty tincture of Xenophon and Homer (a mere lipwash of Helicon) gave me a zeal for philology and the tongues. I was a member in decent standing of the college classical club, and visions of life as a professor of languages seemed to me far from unhappy. A compulsory course in philosophy convinced me that there was still much to learn; and I had a delicious hallucination in which I saw myself compiling a volume of commentaries on the various systems of this queen of sciences. "The Grammar of Agnostics," I think it was to be called: it would be written in a neat and comely hand on thousands of pages of pure white foolscap: I saw myself adding to it night by night, working *ohne Hast, ohne Rast*. And there were other careers, too, as statesman, philanthropist, diplomat, that I considered not beneath my horoscope. I spare myself the careful delineation of these projects, though they would be amusing enough.

But beneath these preoccupations another influence was working its inward way. My paramount interest had always been literary, though regarded as a gentle diversion, not degraded to a bread-and-butter concern. Ever since I had fallen under the superlative spell of R. L. S., in whom the cunning enchantment of the written word first became manifest, I had understood that books did not grow painlessly for our amusement, but were the issue of dexterous and intentional skill. I had thus made a stride from Conan Doyle, Cutcliffe Hyne, Anthony Hope, and other great loves of my earliest teens; those authors' delicious mysteries and picaresques I took for granted, not troubling over their method; but in Stevenson, even to a schoolboy the conscious artifice and nicety of phrase were puzzlingly apparent. A taste for literature, however, is a very different thing from a determination to undertake the art in person as a means of livelihood. It takes brisk stimulus and powerful internal fevers to reduce a healthy youth to such a contemplation. All this is a long story, and I telescope it rigorously, thus setting the whole matter, perhaps, in a false proportion. But the central and operative factor is now at hand.

There was a certain classmate of mine (from Chicago) whose main devotion was to scientific and engineering studies. But since his plan embraced only two years at college before "going to work," he was (in the fashion traditionally ascribed to Chicago) speeding up the cultural knick-knacks of his education. So, in our freshman year, he was attending a course on "English Poets of the Nineteenth Century," which was, in the regular schedule of things, reserved for sophomores (supposedly riper for matters of feeling). Now I was living in a remote dormitory on the outskirts of the wide campus (that other Eden, demi-paradise, that happy breed of men, that little world!) some distance from the lecture halls and busy heart of college doings. It was the custom of those quartered in this colonial and sequestered outpost to make the room of some central classmate a base for the day, where books might be left between lectures, and so on. With the Chicagoan, whom we will call "J——," I had struck up a mild friendship; mostly charitable on his part, I think, as he was from the beginning one of the most popular and influential men in the class, whereas I was one of the rabble. So it was, at any rate; and often in the evening, returning from library or dining hall on the way to my distant Bœotia, I would drop in at his room, in a lofty corner of old Barclay Hall, to pick up note-books or anything else I might have left there.

What a pleasant place is a college dormitory at night! The rooms with their green-hooded lights and boyish similarity of decoration, the amiable buzz and stir of a game of cards under festoons of tobacco smoke, the wiry tinkle of a mandolin distantly heard, sudden clatter subsiding again into a general humming quiet, the happy sense of solitude in multitude, these are the partial ingredients of that feeling no alumnus ever forgets. In his pensive citadel, my friend J—— would be sitting, with his pipe (one of those new "class pipes" with inlaid silver numerals, which appear among every college generation toward Christmas time of freshman year). In his lap would be the large green volume ("British Poets of the Nineteenth Century," edited by Professor Curtis Hidden Page) which was the textbook of that sophomore course. He was reading Keats. And his eyes were those of one who has seen a new planet swim into his ken.

I don't know how many evenings we spent there together. Probably only a few. I don't recall just how we communed, or imparted to one another our juvenile speculations. But I plainly remember how he would sit beside his desk-lamp and chuckle over the Ode to a Nightingale. He was a quizzical and quickly humorous creature, and Keats' beauties seemed to fill him not with melancholy or anguish, but with a delighted prostration of laughter. The "wormy-circumstance" of the Pot of Basil, the Indian Maid nursing her luxurious sorrow, the congealing Beadsman and the pal-

sied beldame Angela—these and a thousand quaintnesses of
phrase moved him to a gush of glorious mirth. It was not
that he did not appreciate the poet, but the unearthly strange-
ness of it all, the delicate contradiction of laws and behaviours
known to freshmen, tickled his keen wits and emotions until
they brimmed into puzzled laughter. "Away! Away!" he
would cry—

> For I will fly to thee,
> Not charioted by Bacchus and his pards,
> But on the viewless wings of Poesy,
> Though the dull brain perplexes and retards—

and he would shout with merriment. Beaded bubbles winking
at the brim; Throbbing throats' long, long melodious moan;
Curious conscience burrowing like a mole; Emprison her
soft hand and let her rave; Men, slugs and human serpentry;
Bade her steep her hair in weird syrops; Poor weak palsy-
stricken churchyard thing; Shut her pure sorrow-drops with
glad exclaim—such lines were to him a constant and ex-
hilarating excitement. In the very simplicity and unsophisti-
cation of his approach to the poet was a virgin naïveté of
discernment that an Edinburgh Reviewer would rarely attain.
Here, he dimly felt, was the great key

> To golden palaces, strange minstrelsy,
> . . . aye, to all the mazy world
> Of silvery enchantment.

And in line after line of Endymion, as we pored over them
together, he found the clear happiness of a magic that dis-
solved everything into lightness and freedom. It is agreeable
to remember this man, preparing to be a building contractor,
who loved Keats because he made him laugh. I wonder if
the critics have not too insistently persuaded us to read our
poet in a black-edged mood? After all, his nickname was
"Junkets."

So it was that I first, in any transcending sense, fell under the empire of a poet. Here was an endless fountain of immortal drink: here was a history potent to send a young mind from its bodily tenement. The pleasure was too personal to be completely shared; for the most part J—— and I read not together, but each by each, he sitting in his morris chair by the desk, I sprawled upon his couch, reading, very likely, different poems, but communicating, now and then, a sudden discovery. Probably I exaggerate the subtlety of our enjoyment, for it is hard to review the unself-scrutinizing moods of freshmanhood. It would be hard, too, to say which enthusiast had the greater enjoyment: he, because these glimpses through magic casements made him merry; I, because they made me sad. Outside, the snow sparkled in the pure winter night; the long lance windows of the college library shone yellow-panelled through the darkness, and there would be the occasional interruption of light-hearted classmates. How perfectly it all chimed into the mood of St. Agnes' Eve! The opening door would bring a gust of lively sound from down the corridor, a swelling jingle of music, shouts from some humorous "rough-house" (probably those sophomores on the floor below)—

> The boisterous, midnight, festive clarion
> The kettle-drum, and far-heard clarionet
> Affray his ears, though but in dying tone—
> The hall-door shuts again, and all the noise is gone.

It did not take very long for J—— to work through the fifty pages of Keats reprinted in Professor Hidden Page's anthology; and then he, a lone and laughing faun among that pack of stern sophomores—so flewed, so sanded, out of the Spartan kind, crook-knee'd and dewlapped like Thessalian bulls—sped away into thickets of Landor, Tennyson, the Brownings. There I, an unprivileged and unsuspecting hanger-on, lost their trail, returning to my own affairs. For some reason—I don't know just why—I never "took" that course in Nineteenth Century Poets, in the classroom at any rate. But just as Mr. Chesterton, in his glorious little book, "The Victorian Age in Literature," asserts that the most important event in English history was the event that never happened at all (you yourself may look up his explanation) so perhaps the college course that meant most to me was the one I never attended. What it meant to those sophomores of the class of 1909 is another gentle speculation. Three years later, when I was a senior, and those sophomores had left college, another youth and myself were idly prowling about a dormitory corridor where some of those same sophomores had previously lodged. An unsuspected cupboard appeared to us, and rummaging in it we found a pile of books left there, forgotten, by a member of that class. It was a Saturday afternoon, and my companion and I had been wondering how we could raise enough cash to go to town for dinner and a little harmless revel. To shove those books into a suitcase and hasten to Philadelphia by trolley was the obvious caper; and Leary's famous old bookstore ransomed the volumes for enough money to provide an excellent dinner at Lauber's, where, in those days, the thirty-cent bottle of sour claret was considered the true, the blushful Hippocrene. But among the volumes was a copy of Professor Page's anthology which had been used by one of J——'s companions in that poetry course. This seemed to me too precious to part with, so I retained it; still have it; and have occasionally studied the former owner's marginal memoranda. At the head of The Eve of St. Agnes he wrote: "Middle Ages. N. Italy. Guelph, Guibilline." At the beginning of Endymion he recorded: "Keats tries to be spiritualized by love for celestials." Against Sleep and Poetry: "Desultory. Genius in the larval state." The Ode on a Grecian Urn, he noted: "Crystallized philosophy of idealism. Embalmed anticipation." The Ode on Melancholy: "Non-Gothic. Not of intellect or disease. Emotions."

Darkling I listen to these faint echoes from a vanished lecture room, and ponder. Did J—— keep his copy of the book, I wonder, and did he annotate it with lively commentary of his own? He left college at the end of our second year, and I have not seen or heard from him these thirteen years. The last I knew—six years ago—he was a contractor in an Ohio city; and (is this not significant?) in a letter written then to another classmate, recalling some waggishnes of our own sophomore days, he used the phrase "Like Ruth among the alien corn."

In so far as one may see turning points in a tangle of yarn, or count dewdrops on a morning cobweb, I may say that a few evenings with my friend J—— were the decisive vibration that moved one more minor poet toward the privilege and penalty of Parnassus. One cannot nicely decipher such fragile causes and effects. It was a year later before the matter became serious enough to enforce abandoning library copies of Keats and buying an edition of my own. And this, too, may have been not unconnected with the gracious influence of the other sex as exhibited in a neighbouring athenæum; and was accompanied by a gruesome spate of florid lyrics: some (happily) secret, and some exposed with needless hardihood in a college magazine. The world, which has looked leniently upon many poetical minorities, regards such frenzies with tolerant charity and forgetfulness. But the wretch concerned may be pardoned for looking back in a mood of lingering enlargement. As Sir Philip Sidney put it, "Self-love is better than any gilding to make that seem gorgeous wherein ourselves be parties."

There is a vast deal of nonsense written and uttered about poetry. In an age when verses are more noisily and fluently circulated than ever before, it might seem absurd to plead in the Muse's defence. Yet poetry and the things poets love are pitifully weak to-day. In essence, poetry is the love of life—not mere brutish tenacity of sensation, but a passion for all the honesties that make life free and generous and clean. For two thousand years poets have mocked and taunted the cruelties and follies of men, but to what purpose? Wordsworth said: "In spite of difference of soil and climate, of language and manners, of laws and customs, in spite of things silently gone out of mind, and things violently destroyed, the Poet binds together by passion and knowledge the vast empire of human society, as it is spread over the whole earth, and over all time." Sometimes it seems as though "things violently destroyed," and the people who destroy them, are too strong for the poets. Where, now, do we see any cohesive binding together of humanity? Are we nearer these things than when Wordsworth and Coleridge walked and talked on the Quantock Hills or on that immortal road "between Porlock and Linton"? Hardy writes "The Dynasts," Joseph Conrad writes his great preface to "The Nigger of the *Narcissus,*" but do the destroyers hear them? Have you read again, since the War, Gulliver's "Voyage to the Houyhnhnms," or Herman Melville's "Moby Dick"? These men wrote, whether in verse or prose, in the true spirit of poets; and Swift's satire, which the textbook writers all tell you is so gross and savage as to suggest the author's approaching madness, seems tender and suave by comparison with what we know to-day.

Poetry is the log of man's fugitive castaway soul upon a doomed and derelict planet. The minds of all men plod the same rough roads of sense; and in spite of much knavery, all win at times "an ampler ether, a diviner air." The great poets, our masters, speak out of that clean freshness of perception. We hear their voices—

I there before thee, in the country that well thou knowest,
Already arrived am inhaling the odorous air.

So it is not in vain, perhaps, to try clumsily to tell how this delicious uneasiness first captured the spirit of one who, if not a poet, is at least a lover of poetry. Thus he first looked beyond the sunset; stood, if not on Parnassus, tiptoe upon a little hill. And overhead a great wind was blowing.

THE TOO-PERFECT THEATRE *

By George Jean Nathan

THE professors who are indefatigable in their effort further to improve the contemporary theatre seem to overlook one important thing. And this is that the theatre has already been improved to a degree where—unless someone soon takes measures to check the danger—it will be irretrievably ruined. One may improve certain things so far, and no farther; and the theatre is one of these. If one sought to improve George Ade's excellent "Fables in Slang" by converting them into the more substantial and exquisite English of Walter Pater one would, clearly, subvert them. Or if one sought to improve Chopin's buoyant scherzo in E, op. 54, by deepening its emotional content, or the compositions of Domenico Scarlatti by muscularizing their beautifully slight structure one would, just as clearly, devastate them. It is the same with the theatre. If one seeks to improve it by taking from it all the infractions and crudities that compose its very soul, one damages it out of all recognition.

All consideration of the box-office aside, it remains that not only the first, but the highest, aim of the theatre is as a showhouse. It is a showhouse whether it offers Shakespeare à la Gordon Craig or Avery Hopwood à la A. H. Woods. It is a showhouse whether it offers "L'Aiglon" or "Twin Beds." To attempt to make the theatre something more than a show-

house is to attempt to make the Flonzaley Quartette the Boston Symphony Orchestra. A showhouse is essentially a showhouse; a quartette is essentially a quartette; each is good
enough in its own way. Yet what do the professors seek to accomplish; what have they already accomplished? They have
already so distorted the theatre by improving it that it is to-
day less a theatre, less a house of unadulterated diversion, than
an austere annex to the art gallery, the college lecture hall and
the library. Its fine old youthful barbarism, its beloved old
gracelessness, all the old flaws that made it dear to the heart—
these all are gone from it. And in their stead have come a
polish, a hard and fast beauty and a proximity to life that
have taken from it so much of its erstwhile remote romance,
its erstwhile mystery, and its erstwhile wonderful old smell.

When one went to the theatre twenty-five and thirty years
ago one knew that one was in a theatre: and when one goes to
a theatre, that is obviously what one wants to know and to
feel. For the theatre is an escape from reality. But today,
once the curtain of a dramatic theatre is up, one is subcon-
sciously uncertain whether one is in a theatre or whether
one is in close contact with life. Or, in a musical comedy
theatre, whether one is in the studio of some extraordinarily
successful scene painter or in the display room of some Fifth
Avenue modiste. Seeing the crude drama of other days, one
was sure that one was sitting in a showhouse. Seeing the
remarkably suave drama of this day, one's subconscious self
is tricked and deceived. Is this the theatre, it asks; is this a
play, or is this life—life that I came here to avoid? When
one used to see "The Romany Rye" or "The Marble Heart" or
"The Corsican Brothers," one knew every minute that one
was in a theatre. When now one sees "Jane Clegg" or
"Hindle Wakes" or "The Easiest Way," one doesn't feel that
one is peeking into a theatre at romance and unreality so
much as one feels that one is peeking out of a theatre at life
and reality.

Twenty-five years ago every effort was made to make a

person feel that he was in a theatre. Today every effort is made to make him forget that he is in a theatre. When I used to go to the old Lyceum Theatre and see a character on the stage lift a window-shade and then see the room flooded by a Daniel Frohman bunchlight with a magenta and green sunshine, I knew that I was in a theatre. Now when I go to the new Lyceum Theatre and see a character lift a window-shade and then see the room flooded by a Belasco fabrication with a sunlight as realistic as the real thing, I am fooled for the moment into believing that I am out of a theatre and in an actual scene. And I don't relish it. Nor, I dare say, does any one else who forgets the single instance and considers the situation in its broadest sweep.

Nothing seems to me so absurd as the cry for the theatre to mirror life. Life is precisely what the theatre should not mirror. It should mirror fancy, illusion, hypnotic romance, impossible adventure—everything but life. It should be a world of make-believe, as it was born. It should give us not trees and moons that look real, not William Falders and Laura Murdocks that are real, but trees of shaky canvas and wiggling moons and false-whiskered Hawkshaws and theatrical Lady Gay Spankers. That is, in essence: it is the spirit of the theatre, not its content, that I refer to. A circus belongs in a tent: it is not the same when it is dolled up in a Madison Square Garden. The theatre and its exhibits, once glorying in their own small circus air, are rapidly becoming Madison Square Gardened. Electrical equipment developed to a point where its dawns and twilights compete with nature's, scenic inventions that convert paint and canvas into landscapes completely deceptive, dramatists and actors who duplicate life so closely that the illusion is too complete, auditoriums so shrewdly designed that not a trace of the old-time theatre feel remains in them—all these things have contributed to a rapidly become too-perfect institution. An institution, in a word, akin to a woman who has painted, penciled, powdered, coiffed and massaged herself to the point of artificial perfection where she is less a human woman than a walking wax model.

It is doubtless this knowledge, felt if unphrased, that lies at the bottom of the artistic revolts against the theatre of to-day, the revolts of such men as Craig and Fuchs on the scenic side, such men as Bakst and Pankok on the costume side, such men as Appia and Ottomar Starke on the lighting side, and such men as Georg Kaiser and Jean Cocteau on the dramatic and technical side. And, further, to turn to the musical side, such men as Erik Satie and Georges Auric. Of these, Craig, of course, is the most articulate: he most clearly knows what he is driving at. Where the majority of the others feel that something is wrong, their cures have not yet been perfected: Cocteau, for example, is a mere Greenwich Villager who happens to have been born in Paris; and Bakst, though he has done some beautiful and excellent work, intrinsically a Russian Roycrofter. But Craig's eye, if not always his pen, is sure and clear. His theory is sharp, vital, unerring, even if his attempts to phrase that theory for the reading public are not always so felicitous. Give us back the theatre! he cries—and soundly. It is when he employs the word beauty without a qualifying footnote that he appears sometimes to confound himself. For what Craig would bring back to the theatre is not the hard, set beauty of truth but the gorgeous, liquid beauty of theatrical artificiality. He sees the theatre as a great showhouse, not—like the great majority of advanced theatre bolsheviks—as a sort of combined Louvre, Bibliothèque Nationale and Paquin's. He sees that what it needs at the present time is a rich dose of old-fashioned castor oil to purge it of its mechanically perfect fol-de-rols, its amazing pretenses and realisms, its confusing encroachments upon life and reality. He sees that what it needs—if it is to live and if its future is to regain all the glory of its past—is its self of yesterday seen through an imagination of today. Filter the old theatre through a sieve of beauty—that is the Craig credo.

The paint and canvas room in Polonius' house in an Edmund Kean production of "Hamlet" surely looked no more to a theatre audience of the last century like an actual room in an actual house than the portièred room in Polonius' house in a Craig-Stanislavski production of "Hamlet" looks to a theatre audience of the present century like an actual room in an actual house. Both are purely "theatre"; both are grounded in a secure theory of the theatre; Craig's room is beautiful "theatre" where the Kean room was ugly "theatre." This is Craig's theory in simple illustration. An audience must ever be reminded that it is in a theatre: that was the sound theory of Augustin Daly. An audience must ever be beautifully reminded that it is in a theatre: that is the sounder theory of Craig. An audience must ever be made to forget that it is in a theatre: that is the theory of the Messrs. Hornimans and Belascos, a theory akin to one which would hold that a thirsty man who rushes eagerly into a brewery with his mouth open and his tongue hanging out should be cleverly persuaded that he is in a Baptist Sunday School.

I believe in realism to a certain extent—I am by no means an impressionist patriot—but did I believe in it to the complete exclusion of everything else I should yet not be able to convince myself that it wasn't a bad thing for the theatre. That way lies a theatre that is kin to the poetry of Robert Service, with its idiotic and alien literality, and to the music of Raymond Hubbell, with its water-whistle imitation of birds and resined-string imitation of bull-frogs. The realistic theatre is as much of an anomaly as an impressionistic laundry. One doesn't put on a dinner jacket, fasten a boutonnière to one's lapel, hail a crooked-metred taxicab and hasten to hand a man behind a grilled window $2.50 in order to get into a place to see something that looks very much like what one has already often seen gratis outside in one's street clothes. And, as I have several times written, the theatre mood is the dinner jacket mood, whether one has on a dinner jacket or not. And, as I have also written, this theatre mood may be catered to aptly and equally by a Reinhardt or an A. H. Woods, by an Antoine or a J. J. Shubert. But whether by Max or Al, by André or Jake, whether in terms of realism, impressionism or any other ism, whether sound or unsound, good or bad—and this is the point—it must be catered to by the theatre in terms of the artificial theatre rather than by the theatre in terms of the realistic theatre. Belasco has doubtless been uniformly successful in making a lot of money out of his extravagant stage realism not, as so many believe, because of that extravagant stage realism but because his theatre and auditorium are themselves twice as extravagantly unrealistic and theatrical as any of the romantic stages of his contemporaries. Belasco's theatre in West Forty-fourth Street, with its lighting à la Murray's restaurant, its ankle-deep carpet, its unexpectedly encountered mirrors and general, mysterious phrenologist's parlour atmosphere, counteracts whatever untheatrical realism he discloses upon its stage, and so insures no violation of the audience's theatre mood. When one is in the Belasco Theatre, one knows that one is in a theatre, sometimes even after the curtain has gone up. When one is in the gaunt, bare Garrick Theatre at some such persuasive production as "Jane Clegg," one's active mind periodically doesn't distinguish whether one is in a theatre seeing a play or in a provincial English house seeing a family's bickerings.

Does all this seem to be a contradiction of certain of my critical attitudes in the past? No matter. The fact that my personal critical tastes at times run to things that are inimical to what are perhaps the highest interests of the theatre has utterly nothing to do with the integrity of the present argument. The circumstance that I personally enjoy a good loud burlesque show more than "Plody Prosvyeschcheniya" doesn't necessarily mean that Al Reeves has worked a greater benefit to the theatre than Tolstoi. Nor does the circumstance that the naturalistic and realistic "Weavers" happens to be a better and theatrically more enjoyable play than the symbolic and impressionistic "Death of Tintagiles." Some of the very things that are least to our tastes are the best for us: regular hours, a light diet, a hard pillow, Hunyadi Janos. And some of the very things that are most to our tastes are the worst for the theatre: the drama of Hauptmann, the naturalistic acting of the Barnowski direction, the lighting of Belasco, the architecture of the Little Theatre.

The stage is properly not the playground of the Zolas and the Dreisers, but of the Hewletts and the Cabells. It is the church of human joys and human forgetfulness. It is the eternal boy of the arts. It is never, and never must be, the professor. Let us have back its old canvas mountains that bend in the middle when the villain leans against them, its old proscenium arch of pea-green canvas foliage for summer and winter scenes alike, its old tin crowns and wooden swords and papier machè locomotives. *They* are the soul of the theatre!

"20" *

By A. Edward Newton

WE were in London—a maiden uncle and a presumably maiden aunt and I—and I was showing my relatives the town, which I knew well, with a fine air of proprietorship. It happened years ago. There were omnibuses in those days—not huge, self-propelled motorbusses, driven at a breakneck pace through the crowded streets, but gayly painted, lazy, rotund coaches, like huge beetles, driven by men who bore a strong family resemblance to the elder Weller.

With my party I had been climbing from the top of a bus going east to the top of another going west, when the suggestion was made that the next sight should be a bit of the roast beef of Old England. We were for a moment off the beaten track of the busses, and the only vehicle in sight was a disreputable-looking four-wheel cab, usually denominated a "growler," no doubt from the character of the driver. Rather against my judgment we entered it and I gave the order, "Simpson's, in the Strand." The driver roused himself and his beast, and we started; but we had gone only a short distance when, in some inexplicable way, the man, who was subsequently discovered to be drunk, locked the wheels of the cab in attempting to make a sharp turn, and completely upset the ramshackle vehicle. Within, there was a great confusion. Just how it happened I never knew, but in some way my foot got outside the broken window; the horse moved; I heard

* From *A Magnificent Farce;* copyright, 1921, by The Atlantic Monthly Press. Reprinted by permission of the author and the publishers.

something snap, felt a sharp pain, and knew that my leg was broken.

A crowd gathered, but the omnipresent policeman was on the spot in a moment, and order was quickly brought out of confusion. My companions were unhurt, but it was instantly realized that I was in real trouble. More policemen arrived, numbers were taken, explanations demanded and attempted; but accidents happen in the crowded streets of London at the rate of one a minute or so, and the rules are well understood. A shrill blast on a whistle brought several hansoms dashing to the scene. I had become the property of the Corporation of the City of London in general, and of St. Bartholomew's Hospital in particular. The custom is, when one is hurt in the streets of London, that he is taken at once to the nearest hospital. His not to reason why: "It's an 'ard, fast rule."

Fortunately, the hospital was near at hand, and in a very few moments, I found myself lying on a bench in the casualty ward, writhing in agony, and surrounded by a crowd of young men curious to know how it happened. The general opinion, as voiced by a young cockney, who seemed to be in authority, was that I had had a "naasty one," and that Mr. Peterson would probably "take it hoff at the knee." It was my intention to expostulate with Mr. Peterson when he arrived and I hoped he would come quickly; but when he appeared, he seemed so intelligent and sympathetic, that I indulged myself in the hope that I and "it" would be safe in his hands. The entrance of a seriously injured man into a London hospital confers no distinction upon him—he is regarded, not as an individual, but simply as another casualty, making six, or sixteen, taken to the operating room that morning. My arrival, therefore, was taken quite as a matter of course. A few questions were asked by a recorder, and as soon as I had told him who I was, where I lived, my age and best friend, I was picked up, placed on a stretcher, and carried away, I knew not whither.

Within the hospital there was neither surprise, confusion,

nor delay. They might have been expecting me. Almost before I knew it, I was being rapidly but skillfully undressed. I say undressed, but in point of fact my trousers and one shoe were being removed with the aid of several pairs of shears in skillful hands. I was curious to see for myself the extent of the injury that seemed so interesting to those about me, but this was not permitted. Someone ventured the opinion, for which I thanked him, that as I was young and clean, I had more than an even chance to save my leg; another remarked that there was no place in the world like "Bart's," for fractures, and that with luck my wound might begin to heal "by first intention."

Meanwhile I divined rather than saw that preparations for a serious operation were under way. Nurses with ominous-looking instruments wrapped up in towels made their appearance, and I heard the word "chloroform" used several times; then a rubber pad was put over my face, I felt someone fumbling at my wrist and I was told to take a deep breath. In a moment I was overcome by a sickening sensation occasioned by something sweetish; I felt lifted higher, higher, higher—until suddenly something seemed to snap in my head, and I awoke, in exquisite pain and very sick at the stomach.

Several hours had elapsed; I found myself quite undressed and in a bed in a large room in which were many other beds similar to mine, most of them occupied. Leaning over me was a white-capped nurse, and at the foot of the bed was a very kindly-looking woman, a lady of mature years, wearing an elaborate cap, whom I heard addressed as "Sister." I had lost my identity and had become merely "20", Pitcairn Ward, St. Bartholomew's Hospital, London—one of the oldest and, as I was to discover, one of the best hospitals in the world.

I was in great agony and very lonely. Things had happened with such rapidity that I could scarcely realize how I came to be where I was. I inquired for my relatives, and was told that they would "be here presently." I asked for Dr.

Peterson, and was told that he, too, would be here "presently." From the pain I felt I made no doubt that he had after all taken "it" off at the knee, as prophesied.

"Presently" I heard outside the door a great scuffling of feet, as of the approach of a considerable crowd; then the door opened and there entered a group of students, led by an elderly and distinguished looking man who, visiting a row of cots in turn, finally came to mine and, without speaking to me, took my chart from a nurse and studied it attentively. A moment later Mr. Peterson came up and explained what he had done, to all of which the distinguished man, addressed as Mr. Willett, listened attentively, expressing his satisfaction and saying "exactly" several times.

Finally, Mr. Willett addressed the crowd gathered in a semi-circle about my bed. "The patient is suffering from a compound comminuted fracture of the tibia and fibula; he was fished out of an overturned four-wheeler just by the Charterhouse Gate. Mr. Peterson has just performed an operation. He has—" Here followed a rapid and technical account of what had been done to me,—and it seemed ample,— what complications might ensue, and what was hoped for, ending with congratulations to Mr. Peterson on having done a very good job. "Six hundred yards of plaster bandage, eh? good, very good."

I was in great pain and too ill to listen with much attention to what more he said. At last, as an afterthought, Mr. Willett again took the chart from the nurse and, glancing at it indifferently for a moment, said, "Ah, an American, eh?" Then, turning to me he added, "They've brought you to the right shop for fractures, my lad; there's no place in the world where you would be better off than just where you are, and Mr. Peterson had made as clean a job as the best surgeon in" —glancing at the chart again—"Philadelphia could have done."

"But, doctor," I piped (I did not then know that surgeons in England are always addressed as Mister), "it's not to be forgotten that Dr. Peterson has been working on excellent American material."

Mr. Willett almost dropped the chart in amazement and Sister told me to "Sh-h, don't talk back." Such a thing was unheard of, for a poor devil lying on a cot in a great charity hospital of London to bandy words with one of the greatest surgeons in England. Mr. Willett was too surprised to say anything; he simply turned on his heel and walked away, followed by his students and the Sister, leaving the nurse to tell me that I must never, never, never talk back to Mr. Willett again. "He's never to be spoke to 'nless he asks a question."

At half-past five supper was served. I didn't get any, didn't want any. By eight o'clock we were being prepared for the night. How I dreaded it! We were a lot of poor, forlorn men and boys, twenty-four of us, all more or less broken somewhere, all suffering; some groaning and complaining, some silently bearing their agony. In the cot next to mine there was a great burly fellow, who called me Matey and said I was in luck. I didn't care much to pursue the subject, but asked him how he made that out.

"You've had one leg broke twice Hi 'ear: that haain't nuthin'. Hi've 'ad both legs hoff at the knee, and Hi've a missus and six kiddies."

I was inclined to agree with him; but a Susan-Nipper-like person said, "No talking," and I was glad she did.

The pain was dreadful. I wanted a great many little attentions, and got them, from a nurse whose name after all these years I here record with respect and affection—Nurse Hare. Midnight came; I was suffering terribly. Finally I asked Nurse if I could not have a hypodermic. She said she thought I could, and presently came and jabbed a little needle into my arm, at the same time telling me to be very quiet in order that the drug might take effect. At last, I fell into a troubled sleep, only to start out of it again. Still, I got a little sleep from time to time, and finally morning came. A few days later, when Nurse Hare and I were exchanging confidences, she told me the hypodermic was of cold water only. "I couldn't 'ave given you a 'ypodermic without orders," she said.

Morning comes slowly in London; sometimes in December it can hardly be said to come at all; but breakfast comes. By six o'clock the gas was lit, and hot water and basins and towels were passed about to those who could use them. Confusion took the place of comparative quiet. I had not tasted food for almost twenty-four hours. I was hungry. The pain in my leg was a deep throbbing pain, but it could be borne. I began to look about me. Someone said, "Good-morning, Twenty," and I replied, "Good-morning, Seventeen. What kind of a night did you have?"—"Rotten, 'ad the 'ump." It occurred to me that I had always wanted to talk to a pure and undefiled cockney and that I now had an excellent opportunity to learn. Breakfast, which came to me on a tray, was delicious: porridge and milk, tea, bread, butter, and jam. I wanted a second round, but something was said about temperature, and I was forced to be content.

Late in the day, as it seemed, but actually about nine o'clock, my uncle came to see me. Poor fellow, he too had passed a sleepless night and showed it. What could he do for me? There was just one man I wanted to see above all others —my friend Hutt, or as he pronounced it, 'Utt, the bookseller in Clements Inn Passage. Would my uncle go and bring him to me? He would; he did not say so, but he would have fetched me a toothpick from the furtherest inch of Asia if I had asked for it. He had never seen Mr. Hutt, he did not know his way around, and was as nervous as a hen. I told him as well as I could where Hutt's shop was and he started off; as he went, I noticed he was carrying my umbrella, which had a rather curious horn handle studded with round-headed silver tacks—quite an unusual-looking handle. I am telling the exact truth when I say that my uncle promptly lost his way and an hour later, my friend Hutt, hurrying along the crowded Strand, saw a man wandering about, apparently

looking for someone or something, *and carrying my umbrella.*
He went up and, calling my uncle by name (he had heard me
speak of him), asked if he could direct him anywhere. My
uncle was amazed, as well he might be, and conducted my
friend, or rather was conducted by him, to my bedside.

When Mr. Willett came in on his rounds later in the day,
my uncle entered upon a rather acrimonious discussion with
him on the subject of my being a charity patient in a public
ward. Mr. Willett explained very patiently that I should have
every attention, but as for private rooms, there was none.
Whatever I needed, the hospital would supply, but under the
rules nothing could be brought in to me, nothing of any kind
or character, and no tips or fees were permitted. Finally my
uncle, dear old man, broke down and cried; and then Mr. Willett, like the gentleman he was, said, "I tell you what I'll do.
There are no private rooms, but so sure I am that your nephew
would not in a week's time go into one if there were, that I
promise that, when he can be moved without danger, I will
personally put him in a nursing home and take care of him
myself if he wishes it; but I know from experience that your
nephew will find so much of interest going on about him that
he will wish to remain here. We have had gentlemen here before—why, sir, nobility even."

With this we were forced to be content, and it turned out
exactly as Mr. Willett prophesied.

My greatest discomfort arose from my being compelled to
remain always in one position. With my leg in a plaster-cast,
in which were two windows through which my wounds were
observed and dressed, and securely fastened in a cradle, I was
compelled to remain on my back and could move only my
upper body without assistance. At first I found this desper-
ately irksome, but I gradually became accustomed to it. I
was greatly helped by a simple device which I thought at the
time a great blessing; I have never seen it elsewhere, and
wonder why. In the wall about eight feet above the head of
each bed was set a stout iron bracket, a bracket strong enough

to bear the weight of a heavy man. From the end of the bracket, about thirty inches from the wall, hung a rope, perhaps five feet long; a handle-bar with a hole in it, through which the rope passed, enabled one to adjust the handle at any height desired above the bed. A knot at the end of the rope prevented the handle slipping off and fixed the lower limit of its travel, but it could be adjusted by another knot at any higher point desired. The primary object of this device, which was called a pulley, was to enable the patient to lift himself up in bed without subjecting his lower body to strain of any kind. But it had many other purposes. From it one could hang one's newspaper, or watch, or handkerchief, and it served also as a harmless plaything. Have you seen a kitten play with a ball of wool? In a like manner have I seen great men relieve the monotony with their pulley, spinning it, swinging it, sliding the handle up and down, for hours at a time.

Without suggesting that I was in any way a conspicuous person in the ward, I am bound to say that my fellow patients treated me as a "toff"—in other words, a swell. This was due solely to the fact that I had a watch. Such a possession in a public ward of a London hospital is like keeping a carriage or a gig; to use Carlyle's word, it is a mark of respectability. Frequently during the night I would hear some poor helpless sufferer say, "Hi siay, 20, wot time his hit?" It occurred to me that it would be a nice thing to have one of my friends go to Sir John Bennett's, the famous clockmaker, and buy a small clock with a very soft strike, which would mark the hours without disturbing anyone. I spoke to Nurse Hare about it, and she to someone in authority. The answer came: no gifts could be accepted while I was in the hospital. After my discharge any gifts I might see fit to make should be sent to the hospital, to be used as the authorities thought best, and not to any ward in particular. Another " 'ard, faast rule," and a good one.

Before a week had passed, Christmas was upon us. The

afternoon before, I sent out for a copy of "The Christmas Carol," which I had read so often before, and have read so often since, on Christmas Eve. Through this little book Dickens has, more than any other man, given Christmas its character of cheer and good-will; but it reads better in London than elsewhere.

"How's the weather outside?" I asked, looking up from my book, of a "dresser" who had just come in.

"There's snow on the ground and a regular 'London particular' [fog], and it's beginning to sleet."

I thanked my lucky stars that I was in bed, as warm as toast, and wondered what I would get for a "Christmas box," —that is to say, a Christmas present,—for we were all looking forward to something. There was to be a tree in the adjoining ward, but, as I could not be moved, I was to have my presents brought to me. I can still see the gifts I received from kindly disposed ladies! Useful gifts! A little game of cards played with Scripture texts; a handkerchief primarily intended for mental stimulation, with the alphabet and numbers up to ten printed thereon; a pair of socks, hand-knitted, of a yarn of the consistency of coarse twine; a pair of pulse-warmers, and a book,—a copy of "The British Workman,"—and last, but not least, a pair of stout hobnailed shoes. Ladies, too, came and offered to read to me, assuming that I could not read to myself, and in other ways showed their kindness of heart. God bless them every one.

No one ever worked harder at a foreign language than I did at learning cockney. I drawled my *o's* and *i's,* and broadened my *a's,* and dropped my *h's* and picked them up again and put them in the wrong place; and I had the best instructors in London. A few in the ward could read, but more could not; and almost without exception they spoke that peculiar dialect which is the curious inheritance of the Londoner. Those of us whose memories go back twenty-five years or so remember it as the medium of that great music-hall artist, Albert Chevalier. His songs were then all the rage, as were, too, Gus Ellen's. As we became better acquainted, we sang them together, and I then acquired an accomplishment which has even yet not entirely deserted me. (I should have said that it was the custom for the surgical wards of St. Batholomew's Hospital to take in accident cases continuously until all the beds were full; as a result most of the patients entered about the same time, and we came to know one another, by number, very intimately in the two or four or six weeks' residence.)

Mr. Willett was quite right: I would not have been moved into a private room for something handsome. There were so many men worse off than myself, that I forgot myself in thinking of others. "Twenty-one" had lost both feet; I certainly was fortunate compared with him. "Seventeen," while cleaning a plate-glass window from a ladder, had slipped and plunged through the window, damaging himself horribly in half a dozen ways; I certainly was lucky compared with him. "Eight" had undergone three serious operations, and another one was contemplated. In short, as soon as I became reasonably comfortable I began to feel quite at home. I had my books and papers and magazines, and spent hours in playing checkers for a penny a game with a poor chap who had lost an arm. He almost always beat me, but a shilling was not much to pay for an afternoon's diversion.

No one could spend two months or so in St. Bartholomew's Hospital,—"Bart's," as it is affectionately called,—without seeking to know something of its history. Its origin is shrouded in antiquity. In the church St. Batholomew the Great, wedged into a corner of Smithfield just outside of the gate, is the tomb of its founder, Rahere, a minstrel, or court jester, of Henry I. While on a pilgrimage to Rome, he was stricken with a serious illness, during which he made a vow, if he lived to get back to London, he would build a hospital in thanksgiving. Thus it was that, in the year 1102, a priory and hospital were founded. Thanks to the protests of the citizens of London, it not only escaped the attentions of Henry

VIII, when he entered upon his period of destruction, but it was even said to have been reëstablished by him. Thenceforth it came to be regarded as the first of royal hospitals. In receipt of a princely income, it has from time out of mind been the scene of great events in surgical and medical science. Harvey, physician of Charles I, the discoverer of the circulation of the blood, was chief physician of the hospital for more than thirty years. A roll of the distinguished names would be tedious; but Mr. Willett was quite right when he said that I had come to the right shop for fractures. "We make a specialty of fractures" might have been adopted as a slogan, had slogans been in vogue when the famous surgeon, Percival Pott, was thrown from his horse and sustained a compound fracture, and with difficulty prevented a brother surgeon from giving him first aid with a knife and a saw. How he directed the treatment of his own case and saved his leg is one of the many legends of the place.

But to return to Pitcairn Ward. It was a large room, with a high ceiling, and with two rows of beds, twelve to a row, on either side of a wide aisle. It was heated by a soft-coal-burning device, something like a range, but with a large open grate, the smoke from which curled lazily up the chimney. One morning it was discovered that the fire was out; and as this seemed to indicate neglect, and certainly meant work for the ward-maid, each patient as he woke and made this discovery sang out cheerily, "Fire's out." To these remarks the maid usually replied by asking the speaker to mind his own business; or perhaps she contented herself by making faces or sticking her tongue out at him.

Presently a curious sound was heard from the chimney, as of a fluttering of birds, followed by a curious cry, "Peep, peep, peep," which was instantly recognized by those familiar with it as being the professional cry of the chimney-sweep. Someone cried, "Sweeps!" The effect was instantaneous. As when one discovers a ship in mid-ocean and announces the fact, all rush to the rail, so all who could crowded in wheel-chairs around the fireplace, only to be told to "Be hoff" by the ward-maid.

Presently the sounds grew louder, until, at last, a tall, slender lad, black with soot from head to foot, armed with brushes and brooms, slid down into the grate, leaped out, gave a little scream, bowed, and disappeared, almost before we could clap our eyes upon him. My intention had been to ask the little urchin to get into a bed next to mine, at that moment vacant, and give an imitation of Charles Lamb's chimney-sweep "asleep like a young Howard in the state bed of Arundel Castle." I probably saved myself a lot of trouble by being so surprised at his quick entrance and get-away that I said not a single word. "A chimney-sweeper quickly makes his way through a crowd by being dirty."

Anything kinder, anything more considerate than the authorities of the hospital, from Mr. Willett down to the ward-maid, could hardly be imagined. There was, however, one ordeal against which I set my face like flint—namely, shaving. Shaving was I think an extra; its cost, a penny. Every day a man and a boy entered the ward, the boy carrying a small tub filled with thick soap-suds, the man with a razor incredibly sharp. One cried, "Shaves?" and perhaps from two or half a dozen beds came the word, "Yus." No time was lost in preliminaries. A common towel was tied around one's neck, and a brush like a large round paint-brush was dipped into the thick lather. With a quick movement, the result of much practice, the boy made a pass or two from ear to ear; with a twist and a return movement, the cheeks, lips, mouth, and chin were covered with soap. The man wielded a razor in much the same manner, and the victim spent the next hour or two patting his face with his hands, then withdrawing them and looking at them, as if he expected to see them covered with blood. The operation was complete. I use the word "operation" advisedly; although chloroform was not administered, I always insisted that it should have been. The first surgeons were barbers; at least the two trades were closely allied, and in England they seem to be allied still. Thanks to the kindness of one of the "dressers," when I became well enough to be shaved, I had a real barber from a near-by shop. It cost me half a crown, and was a prolonged agony rather than a brief one; that was the chief difference; in essentials the operation was the same. Is it surprising that in England gentlemen invariably shave themselves?

Some men make excellent patients, I am told, when they are very ill, and allow their bad traits to come to the surface when they become convalescent. It was so in my case. I grew tired of the life and began inquiring how much longer my leg was to be kept in plaster. Fortunately I had no idea of the ordeal of removing a plaster-cast which reached from one's toes to one's hip. At last the day came, and I shall never forget it. I had first been permitted to limp around the ward on crutches for a few days, and soon learned to manage them very nicely; and when a time was set for my leg to come out of plaster, I was very thankful. It was the work of hours: every tiny hair on my leg was firmly set in plaster of Paris, and the removal of the cast occasioned such continuous pain that several times I thought I should faint. At last, however, the task was accomplished and I looked down at the leg which had been the subject of so much discussion, which had been dressed so often. It was a poor thing, but mine own; no one else would have had it; a poor, shrunken, shortened, emaciated member, but whole, thank God! I did not then know that a year after the accident happened I should be walking as well as ever; and let me say that I have never had a twinge of pain in it since. Mr. Willett and Mr. Peterson and "Sister" and Nurse Hare, I doff my hat to you.

Measurements were taken for a leather stocking, which was a work of art; and finally a date was set for my dismissal. A room had been secured for me in a not-distant lodging; for I still had to go to the hospital once or twice a week to have the rapidly healing wounds dressed. I made my departure from the hospital early one afternoon, in what was called a private ambulance; but I am certain that the vehicle was usually used as a hearse. The stretcher on which I was laid was on casters and was pushed into the rear door of a long low contrivance with glass sides. As we prepared to drive away from the hospital gate, an effigy, that of Henry, the Eighth of that name, looked down upon me from his niche over Smithfield Gate. A crowd gathered, and from my horizontal position the unusual sight of so many people moving about in perpendicular made me dizzy. I closed my eyes and heard someone inquire, "Is he dead?" I was very unhappy, and still more so when, half an hour later, I found myself in a very tiny bedroom, as it seemed to me, and in *a bed with no pulley.* I could have cried; indeed, I think I did. I wanted to go back to the hospital; I felt that I was being neglected and should die of suffocation.

A maid came in and asked me if I wanted anything. "Want anything!" I certainly did, and I gave her a list of things I wanted, in the most approved cockney. As she left my room, I heard her say to another maid just outside the door, " 'Ave you 'eard that bloke hin there talk? Faancy 'im trying to paass hisself hoff has comin' from New York!"

THE CHEERFUL BREAKFAST TABLE *

"A good, honest, wholesome, hungry breakfast."
—The Compleat Angler.

By Meredith Nicholson

"One fine morning in the full London season, Major Arthur Pendennis came over from his lodgings, according to his custom, to breakfast at a certain club in Pall Mall, of which he was a chief ornament." This has always seemed to me the noblest possible opening for a tale. The zest of a fine morning in London, the deliberation of a gentleman taking his ease in his club and fortifying himself against the day's events with a satisfying breakfast, are communicated to the reader in a manner that at once inspires confidence and arouses the liveliest expectations. I shall not go the length of saying that all novels should begin with breakfast, but where the disclosures are to be of moment, and we are to be urged upon adventures calculated to tax our emotions or our staying powers, a breakfast table serves admirably as a point of departure. We thus begin the imaginary day where the natural day begins, and we form the acquaintance of the characters at an hour when human nature is most satisfactorily and profitably studied.

It is only a superstition that night alone affords the proper atmosphere for romance, and that the curtain must fall upon the first scene with the dead face of the king's messenger upturned to the moon and the landlord bawling from an upper window to know what it's all about. Morning is the beginning of all things. Its hours breathe life and hope. "Pistols and coffee!" The phrase whets the appetite both for the encounter and the cheering cup. The duel, to be sure, is no longer in favor, and it is not for me to lament its passing; but I mention it as an affair of dewy mornings, indelibly associated with hours when the hand is steady and courage runs high.

It may be said with all assurance that breakfast has fallen into sad neglect, due to the haste and rush of modern life—the commuter's anxiety touching the 8.27, the city man's fear that he may not be able to absorb the day's news before his car is at the door. Breakfast has become a negligible item of the day's schedule. An increasing number of American citizens are unfit to be seen at the breakfast hour; and a man, woman, or child who cannot present a cheery countenance at breakfast is living an unhealthy life upon the brink of disaster. A hasty visit to the table, the gulping of coffee, the vicious snapping of teeth upon food scarcely looked at, and a wild rush to keep the first appointment noted on the calendar, is the poorest possible preparation for a day of honest work. The man who follows this practice is a terror to his business associates. Reports that "the boss isn't feeling well this morning" pass about the office, with a disturbance of the morale that does not make for the efficiency of the establishment. The wife who reaches the table dishevelled and fretful, under compulsion of her conscience, with the idea that the lord of the house should not be permitted to fare forth without her benediction, would do better to keep her bed. If the eggs are overdone or the coffee is cold and flavorless, her panicky entrance at the last moment will not save the situation. A growl from behind the screening newspaper is a poor return for her wifely self-denial, but she deserves it. There is guilt upon her soul; if she had not insisted on taking the Smiths to supper after the theatre the night before, he would have got the amount of sleep essential to his well-being and the curtaining paper would not be camouflaging a face to which the good-by kiss at the front door is an affront, not a caress.

"Have the children come down yet?" the lone breakfaster growlingly demands. The maid replies indifferently that the children have severally and separately partaken of their porridge and departed. Her manner of imparting this information signifies rebellion against a system which makes necessary the repeated offering of breakfast to persons who accept only that they may complain of it. No happier is the matutinal meal in humbler establishments where the wife prepares and serves the food, and buttons up Susie's clothes or sews a button on Johnny's jacket while the kettle boils. If the husband met a bootlegger in the alley the previous night it is the wife's disagreeable duty to rouse him from his protracted slumbers; and if, when she has produced him at the table, he is displeased with the menu, his resentment, unchecked by those restraints presupposed of a higher culture, is manifested in the playful distribution of the tableware in the general direction of wife and offspring. The family cluster fearfully at the door as the head of the house, with surly resignation, departs for the scene of his daily servitude with the smoke of his pipe trailing behind him, animated by no love for the human race but only by a firm resolution not to lift his hand until the last echoes of the whistle have died away.

It is foreign to my purpose to indict a whole profession, much less the medical fraternity, which is so sadly harassed by a generation of Americans who demand in pills and serums what its progenitors found in the plough handle and the axe, and yet I cannot refrain from laying at the doors of the doctors some burden of responsibility for the destruction of the breakfast table. The astute and diplomatic physician, perfectly aware that he is dealing with an outraged stomach and that the internal discomfort is due to overindulgence, is nevertheless anxious to impose the slightest tax upon the patient's self-denial. Breakfast, he reflects, is no great shakes anyhow, and he suggests that it be curtailed, or prescribes creamless coffee or offers some other hint equally banal. This is wholly satisfactory to Jones, who says with a sigh of relief that he never cared much for breakfast, and that he can very easily do without it.

About twenty-five years ago some one started a boom for the breakfastless day as conducive to longevity. I know persons who have clung stubbornly to this absurdity. The despicable habit contributes to domestic unsociability and is, I am convinced by my own experiments, detrimental to health. The chief business of the world is transacted in the morning hours, and I am reluctant to believe that it is most successfully done on empty stomachs. Fasting as a spiritual discipline is, of course, quite another thing; but fasting by a tired business man under medical compulsion can hardly be lifted to the plane of things spiritual. To delete breakfast from the day's programme is sheer cowardice, a confession of invalidism which is well calculated to reduce the powers of resistance. The man who begins the day with a proscription that sets him apart from his neighbors may venture into the open jauntily, persuading himself that his abstinence proves his superior qualities; but in his heart, to say nothing of his stomach, he knows that he has been guilty of a sneaking evasion. If he were a normal, healthy being, he would not be skulking out of the house breakfastless. Early rising, a prompt response to the breakfast-bell, a joyous breaking of the night's fast is a rite not to be despised in civilized homes.

Old age rises early and calls for breakfast and the day's news. Grandfather is entitled to his breakfast at any hour he demands it. He is at an age when every hour stolen from the night is fairly plucked from oblivion, and to offer him breakfast in bed as more convenient to the household, or with a well-meant intention of easing the day for him, is merely to wound his feelings. There is something finely appealing in the thought of a veteran campaigner in the army of life who doesn't wait for the bugle to sound reveille, but kindles his fire and eats his ration before his young comrades are awake.

The failure of breakfast, its growing ill repute and dis-favor are not, however, wholly attributable to the imperfections of our social or economic system. There is no more reason why the homes of the humble should be illumined by a happy breakfast table than that the morning scene in abodes of comfort and luxury should express cheer and a confident faith in human destiny. Snobbishness must not enter into this matter of breakfast reform; rich and poor alike must be persuaded that the morning meal is deserving of all respect, that it is the first act of the day's drama, not to be performed in a slipshod fashion to spoil the rest of the play. It is the first chapter of a story, and every one who has dallied with the art of fiction knows that not merely the first chapter but the first line must stir the reader's imagination.

Morning has been much sung by the poets, some of them no doubt wooing the lyre in bed. A bard to my taste, Benjamin S. Parker, an Indiana pioneer and poet who had lived in a log cabin and was, I am persuaded, an early and light-hearted breakfaster, wrote many verses on which the dew sparkles:

> "I had a dream of other days,—
>   In golden luxury waved the wheat;
> In tangled greenness shook the maize;
>   The squirrels ran with nimble feet,
> And in and out among the trees
>   The hangbird darted like a flame;
> The catbird piped his melodies,
>   Purloining every warbler's fame:
> And then I heard triumphal song,
>   'Tis morning and the days are long."

I hope not to imperil my case for the cheerful breakfast table by asserting too much in support of it, but I shall not hesitate to say that the contemptuous disregard in which breakfast is now held by thousands of Americans is indisputably a cause of the low state to which the family tie has fallen. It is a common complaint of retrospective elderly persons that the family life, as our grandparents knew it, has been destroyed by the haste and worry incident to modern conditions. Breakfast—a leisurely, jolly affair as I would have it, with every member of the household present on the stroke of the gong—is unequalled as a unifying force. The plea that everybody is in a hurry in the morning is no excuse; if there is any hour when haste is unprofitable it is that first morning hour.

It is impossible to estimate at this writing the effect of the daylight-saving movement upon breakfast and civilization. To add an hour to the work-day is resented by sluggards who, hearing seven chime, reflect that it is really only six, and that a little self-indulgence is wholly pardonable. However, it is to be hoped that the change, where accepted in good spirit, may bring many to a realization of the cheer and inspiration to be derived from early rising.

A day should not be "jumped into," but approached tranquilly and with respect and enlivened by every element of joy that can be communicated to it. At noon we are in the midst of conflict; at nightfall we have won or lost battles; but in the morning "all is possible and all unknown." If we have slept like honest folk, and are not afraid of a dash of cold water, we meet the day blithely and with high expectation. If the day dawn brightly, there is good reason for sharing its promise with those who live under the same roof; if it be dark and rain beats upon the pane, even greater is the need of family communion, that every member may be strengthened for valiant wrestling with the day's tasks.

The disorder of the week-day breakfast in most households is intensified on Sunday morning, when we are all prone to a very liberal interpretation of the meaning of a day of rest. There was a time not so long ago when a very large proportion of the American people rose on Sunday morning with no other thought but to go to church. Children went to Sunday-school, not infrequently convoyed by their parents. I hold no brief for the stern inhibitions of the monstrous Puritan Sunday which hung over childhood like a gray, smothering cloud. Every one has flung a brick at Protestantism for its failures of reconstruction and readjustment to modern needs, and I am not without my own shame in this particular. The restoration of breakfast to its rightful place would do much to put a household in a frame of mind for the contemplation of the infinite. Here, at least, we are unembarrassed by the urgency of the tasks of every day; here, for once in the week, at an hour that may very properly be set forward, a well-managed family may meet at table and infuse into the gathering the spirit of cheerful yesterdays and confident tomorrows.

No better opportunity is afforded for a friendly exchange of confidences, for the utterance of words of encouragement and hope and cheer. Tommy, if he has been dealt with firmly in this particular on earlier occasions, will not revive the old and bothersome question of whether he shall or shall not go to Sunday-school. If he is a stranger to that institution by reason of parental incompetence or apostasy, the hour is not a suitable one for mama to make timid suggestions as to the importance of biblical instruction. Nor will eighteen-year-old Madeline renew her demand for a new party dress when this matter was disposed of definitely Saturday night. Nor will the father, unless he be of the stuff of which brutes are made, open a debate with his wife as to whether he shall accompany her to church or go to the club for a luxurious hour with the barber. A well-ordered household will not begin the week by wrangling on a morning that should, of all mornings, be consecrated to serenity and peace.

Great numbers of American households are dominated by that marvel of the age, the Sunday newspaper. For this prodigious expression of journalistic enterprise I have only the warmest admiration, but I should certainly exclude it from the breakfast table as provocative of discord and subversive of discipline. Amusing as the "funny page" may be, its color scheme does not blend well either with soft-boiled eggs or marmalade. Madeline's appetite for news of the social world may wait a little, and as there is no possibility of buying or selling on the Sabbath-day, the gentleman at the head of the table may as well curb his curiosity about the conclusions of the weekly market review. Fragments of Sunday newspapers scattered about a breakfast table are not decorative. They encourage bad manners and selfishness. A newspaper is an impudent intrusion at the table at any time, but on Sunday its presence is a crime. On an occasion, the late William Graham Sumner was a guest in my house. Like the alert, clear-thinking philosopher he was, he rose early and read the morning paper before breakfast. He read it standing, and finding him erect by a window with the journal spread wide for greater ease in scanning it quickly, I begged him to be seated. "No," he answered; "always read a newspaper standing; you won't waste time on it that way."

With equal firmness I should exclude the morning mail from the table. The arrival of the post is in itself an infringement upon domestic privacy, and the reading of letters is deadly to that conversation which alone can make the table tolerable at any meal. Good news can wait; bad news is better delayed until the mind and body are primed to deal with it. If the son has been "canned" at school, or if the daughter has overstepped her allowance, or if some absent member of the family is ill, nothing can be done about it at the breakfast table. On the first day of the month, the dumping of bills on the table, to the accompaniment of expostulations, regrets, and perhaps tears, should be forbidden. Few homes are so controlled by affection and generous impulses as to make possible the distribution of bills at a breakfast table without poisoning the day. A tradesman with the slightest feeling of delicacy will never mail a bill to be delivered on the morning of the first day of the month. Anywhere from the third or fourth to the twentieth, and so timed as to be delivered in the afternoon—such would be my suggestion to the worthy merchant. The head of the house knows, at dinner time, the worst that the day has for him; if fortune has smiled, he is likely to be merciful; if fate has thrown the dice against him, he will be humble. And besides, a discreet wife, receiving an account that has hung over her head ever since she made that sad, rash purchase, has, if the bill arrive in the afternoon post, a chance to conceal the odious thing until such time as the domestic atmosphere is clear and bright. Attempts to sneak the dressmaker's bill under the coffee-pot are fraught with peril; such concealments are unworthy of American womanhood. Let the hour or half-hour at the breakfast table be kept free of the taint of bargain and sale, a quiet vestibule of the day, barred against importunate creditors.

As against the tendency, so destructive of good health and mental and moral efficiency, to slight breakfast, the food manufacturers have set themselves with praiseworthy determination to preserve and dignify the meal. One has but to peruse the advertising pages of the periodicals to learn of the many tempting preparations that are offered to grace the breakfast table. The obtuse, inured to hasty snatches, nibbles, and sips, are assisted to a proper appreciation of these preparations by the most enchanting illustrations. The art of publicity has spent itself lavishly to lure the world to an orderly and contemplative breakfast with an infinite variety of cereals that have been subjected to processes which make them a boon to mankind. When I hear of an addition to the long list, I fly at once to the grocer to obtain one of the crisp packages, and hurry home to deposit it with the cook for early experiment. The adventurous sense is roused not only by the seductive advertisement but by the neatness of the container, the ears of corn or the wheat sheaf so vividly depicted on the wrapper, or the contagious smile of a radiant child brandishing a spoon and demanding more.

Only a slouchy and unimaginative housewife will repeat

monotonously a breakfast schedule. A wise rotation, a con-
tinual surprise in the food offered, does much to brighten the
table. The damnable iteration of ham and eggs has cracked
the pillars of many a happy home. There should be no ground
for cavil; the various items should not only be well-chosen,
but each dish should be fashioned as for a feast of high ceremony. Gluttony is a grievous sin; breakfast, I repeat, should
be a spiritual repast. If fruit is all that the soul craves, well
enough; but let it be of paradisaical perfection. If coffee and
a roll satisfy the stomach's craving, let the one be clear and
not so bitter as to keep the imbiber's heart protesting all day,
and the other hot enough to melt butter and of ethereal lightness. The egg is the most sinned against of all foods. It
would seem that no one could or would wantonly ruin an egg,
a thing so useful, so inoffensive; and yet the proper cooking
of an egg is one of the most difficult of all culinary arts.
Millions of eggs are ruined every year in American kitchens.
Better that the whole annual output should be cast into the
sea than that one egg should offend the eye and the palate
of the expectant breakfaster.

It grieves me to be obliged to confess that in hotels and on
dining-cars, particularly west of Pittsburgh, many of my
fellow citizens are weak before the temptation of hot cakes,
drenched in syrup. I have visited homes where the griddle is
an implement frequently invoked through the winter months,
and I have at times, in my own house, met the buckwheat
cake and the syrup jug and meekly fallen before their combined assault; but the sight of a man eating hot cakes on a
flying train, after a night in a sleeper, fills me with a sense
of desolation. Verily it is not alone the drama that the
tired business man has brought to low estate!

Sausage and buckwheat cakes have never appealed to me as
an inevitable combination like ham and eggs. Beefsteak and
onions at the breakfast hour are only for those who expect
to devote the remainder of the day to crime or wood-chopping.
The scent in itself is not the incense for rosy-fingered morn;

and steak at breakfast, particularly in these times of perpendicular prices, speaks for vulgar display rather than generosity.

The history of breakfast, the many forms that it has known, the customs of various tribes and nations, assist little in any attempt to re-establish the meal in public confidence. Plato may have done his loftiest thinking on an empty stomach; I incline to the belief that Sophocles was at all times a light breakfaster; Horace must regret that he passed into the Elysian Fields without knowing the refreshing qualities of a grapefruit. If my post-mortem terminal were less problematical, I should like to carry him a grapefruit—a specimen not chilled to death in cold storage—and divide it with him, perhaps adding a splash of Falernian for memory's sake. But the habits of the good and great of olden times are not of the slightest importance to us of twentieth-century America. Still, not to ignore wholly the familiar literary associations suggested by my subject, Samuel Rogers and his weakness for entertaining at breakfast shall have honorable mention. Rogers's breakfasts, one of his contemporaries hinted, were a cunnning test of the fitness of the guests to be promoted to the host's dinner table—a process I should have reversed, on the theory that the qualifications for breakfast guests are far more exacting than those for a dinner company. We have testimony that Rogers's breakfasts, informal and with every one at ease, were much more successful than his dinners. Wordsworth, Coleridge, Byron and Moore, Southey and Macaulay, the Duke of Wellington and Lord John Russell were fellows to make a lively breakfast table. At one of these functions Coleridge talked for three hours on poetry, an occasion on which, we may assume, the variety or quality of the food didn't matter greatly.

Breakfast as a social medium has never flourished in America, chiefly because of our lack of leisure. Where recognized at all it is thrown into the middle of the day where it becomes an anomaly, an impudent intrusion. A breakfast that is a luncheon is not a breakfast, but a concession to the Philistines. Once, with considerable difficulty, I persuaded a lady of my acquaintance to undertake to popularize breakfast by asking a company, few and fit, for eight o'clock. The first party was delightful, and the second, moved along to nine, was equally successful. But the hostess was so pleased with her success that she increased the number of guests to a dozen and then to fifteen, and advanced the hour to noon, with the result that the felicity of the earlier hours was lost. One must have a concrete programme to be of service in these reforms, and I shall say quite fearlessly that a round table set for six is the ideal arrangement.

A breakfast must be planned with greatest care. It should never be resorted to as a means of paying social debts, but arranged with the utmost independence. Where a wife is a desirable guest and the husband is not, there is no reason why a plate should be wasted. On the other hand, I should as rigidly exclude the wife who is socially a non-conductor. The talk at a breakfast table must be spirited, and it will not be otherwise if the company is well chosen. It's an absurd idea that candle-light is essential to sociability and that wit will not sparkle in the early morning. Some of the best talk I ever listened to has been at breakfast tables, where the guests conversed freely under the inspiration of a mounting sun. Doctor Holmes clearly believed the breakfast hour appropriate for the disclosure of the sprightliest philosophy.

An American novelist once explained that he did his writing in the afternoon because he couldn't make love in the morning. Not make love in the morning! The thought is barbarous. Morning is of sentiment all compact. Morning to the lover who possesses a soul is washed with Olympian dews. The world is all before him where to choose and his heart is his only guide. Love is not love that fears the morning light. . . . There was a house by the sea, whence a girl used to dart forth every morning for a run over the rocks. We used to watch her from our windows, admiring the lightness of her step, her unconscious grace as she was silhouetted on some high point of the shore against the blue of the sea and sky. It was to think of him, her lover, in the free sanctuary of the new, clean day that she ran that morning race with her own spirits. And he, perhaps knowing that she was thus preparing herself for their first meeting, would fly after her, and they would come running back, hand in hand, and appear with glowing cheeks and shining eyes at the breakfast table, to communicate to the rest of us the joy of youth.

There are houses in which participation in the family breakfast is frankly denied to the guest, who is informed that by pressing a button in his room coffee will appear at any hour that pleases his fancy. Let us consider this a little. The ideal guest is rare; the number of persons one really enjoys having about, free to penetrate the domestic arcana, is small indeed. This I say who am not an inhospitable soul. That a master and mistress should keep the morning free is, however, no sign of unfriendliness; the shoving of breakfast into a room does not argue necessarily for churlishness, and I have never so interpreted it. A hostess has her own affairs to look after, and the despatch of trays upstairs enables her to guard her morning from invasion. Still, in a country house, a guest is entitled to a fair shot at the morning. The day is happier when the household assembles at a fixed hour not to be trifled with by a lazy and inconsiderate guest.

Moreover, we are entitled to know what our fellows look like in the morning hours. I have spoken of lovers, and there is no sterner test of the affections than a breakfast-table inspection. Is a yawn unbecoming? We have a right to know with what manner of yawn we are to spend our lives. Is it painful to listen to the crunching of toast in the mouth of the adored? Is the wit laggard in the morning hours when it should be at its nimblest? These are grave matters not lightly to be brushed aside. At breakfast the blemish in the damask cheek publishes itself shamelessly; an evil temper that is subdued by candle-light will betray itself over the morning coffee. At breakfast we are what we are, and not what we may make ourselves for good or ill before the stars twinkle.

I protest against breakfast in bed as not only unsocial but unbecoming in the children of democracy. I have never succumbed to this temptation without experiencing a feeling of humiliation and cowardice. A proper punishment for such self-indulgence is inflicted by the stray crumbs that lodge between the sheets unless one be highly skilled in the handling of breakfast trays. Crumbs in bed! Procrustes missed a chance here. The presence of emptied dishes in a bedroom is disheartening in itself; the sight of them brings to a sensitive soul a conviction of incompetence and defeat. You cannot evade their significance; they are the wreck of a battle lost before you have buckled on your armor or fired an arrow at the foe. My experiments have been chiefly in hotels, where I have shrunk from appearing in a vast hall built for banqueting and wholly unsuitable for breakfasting; but better suffer this gloomy isolating experience than huddle between covers and balance a tray on stubborn knees that rebel at the indignity.

The club breakfast is an infamous device designed to relieve the mind of what should be the pleasant privilege of selection. I am uninformed as to who invented this iniquity of numbered alternatives, but I unhesitatingly pronounce him an enemy of mankind. Already too many forces are operating to beat down the imagination. I charge this monstrosity upon the propagandists of realism; certainly no romanticist in the full possession of his powers would tolerate a thing so deadly to the play of fancy. I want neither the No. 7 nor the No. 9 prescribed on the card; and the waiter's index finger wabbling down the margin in an attempt to assist me is an affront, an impudence. Breakfast should be an affair between man and his own soul; a business for the initiative, not the referendum.

Breakfast out of doors is the ideal arrangement, or in winter under an ample screen of glass. My own taste is for a perspective of sea or lake; but a lusty young river at the elbow is not to be despised. The camper, of course, has always the best of it; a breakfast of fresh-caught trout with an Indian for company serves to quicken such vestiges of the primitive as remain in us. But we do not, if we are wise, wait for ideal conditions. It is a part of the great game of life to make the best of what we have, particularly in a day that finds the world spinning madly "down the ringing grooves of change."

The breakfast table must be made a safe place for humanity, an inspirational center of democracy. A land whose people drowsily turn over for another nap at eight o'clock, or languidly ring for coffee at eleven, is doomed to destruction. Of such laziness is unpreparedness born—the vanguard of the enemy already howling at the postern; treason rampant in the citadel; wailing in the court. Breakfast, a sensible meal at a seasonable hour; sausage or beefsteak if you are capable of such atrocities; or only a juicy orange if your appetite be dainty; but breakfast, a cheerful breakfast with family or friends, no matter how great the day's pressure. This, partaken of in a mood of kindliness and tolerance toward all the world, is a definite accomplishment. By so much we are victors, and whether the gulfs wash us down or we sight the happy isles we have set sail with flags flying and to the stirring roll of drums.

THE CARY GIRLS *

By Edmund Lester Pearson

THERE was once a bashful old professor of literature at Yale, who ended a course of lectures on American Writers by uttering a deprecatory cough, and an apology. "Gentlemen," he explained, "when I commenced these lectures, I intended if time allowed, to embrace both Phoebe and Alice Cary."

As I write this, I am sitting at a window from which I have many times seen the Cary sisters—their blue veils flying—go by to their work. Not Phoebe and Alice, but Miss Hattie and Miss Ellen Cary, who were much concerned with the art of literature in our town.

The Twentieth Century has altered Lanesport. The town hall where we used to see Ullie Akerstrom, "Lanesport's Favorite Actress," in "Uncle Tom's Cabin" (with the bloodhounds led through the street in procession before the show), is now a Community Hall, housing the Plaza Picture Palace. Mrs. Bagley's millinery establishment is replaced by the Up-To-Date Garage; and Mr. Davenport's little shop, with its low and dingy ceiling, where he would sell you delicious molasses candy, or open at your demand innumerable oysters which he or his son had taken from their beds early that morning— this place now appears with flamboyant decoration and enlarged area as Kondokoupolos Brothers' House of Sweets. But more than anything I resent the transformation of Miss Cary's circulating library into La Fortune's Phonograph Parlor and Souvenir Post-card Emporium.

* From *Books in Black and Red;* copyright, 1923, by the Macmillan Company. Reprinted by permission of the author and the publishers.

About twenty minutes before nine every morning the Cary girls would trot down our street, Miss Hattie to open the reading-room in the public library, and Miss Ellen to her own little circulating library, where she sat all morning and afternoon, renting books at two cents a day. They were white-haired women when I first knew them, but they had never married, and so by the custom of the town, they were and would remain the "Cary *girls,*" even though they lived to fourscore and ten.

Miss Hattie was tall and slender; Miss Ellen, short and stout. Miss Ellen might have posed for Queen Victoria. Indeed, some years later, when the fashion for "Living Pictures" reached Lanesport, I am not sure she was not induced to put on a black gown and a widow's cap, and impersonate that diminutive and dignified monarch. Both sisters parted their hair in the middle, and wore long blue cloaks in summer and "fur-lined circulars" in the winter. Their bonnets were not unlike those now worn by the Salvation Army girls, except that they were complicated by the windings of yards and yards of blue veils.

You may be inclined to dismiss them as a couple of "New England old maids," since spinsters, it is well known, exist only in New England. They appear to you, perhaps, as relics of that Puritanism which so many people are now engaged in deriding. But it is not in this light that I remember them. They had their standards and their limitations, and their points of conservatism, but that they were just as eager for human progress as many of the platitudinous "liberals" and "radicals" who haunt the book-shops of Greenwich Village, there is not in my mind an atom of doubt.

Like those radicals, they were opposed to bloodshed. But instead of the healthy and necessary bloodshed of Germans in Belgium and France—which so disturbed the radicals—the trial of brute force which horrified Miss Hattie and Miss Ellen was the projected fight between John L. Sullivan and Corbett in New Orleans. They thought it disgraceful that such a spectacle should be allowed "in this nineteenth century." They grieved at my interest in it. But when I met them, on my way to school the morning after the fight, their concerted, excited, and altogether human inquiry was: "Who won the fight?"

Miss Ellen Cary's circulating library was all contained in a small room. The walls were lined and the floor-space covered with book-cases and the books were protected and disguised by brown-paper covers. Surely *The Purple Pagan,* the radical book-shop near Washington Square, which I occasionally visit nowadays, is a brighter, more vivid, and apparently more exciting place. But for all its color and uneasy exploitation of various egotisms, it does not inspire my imagination as much as Miss Cary's dismal-looking collection. And this is curious, since all its art is supposed to set the imagination afire; its sculptors scorn to model more of a human figure than an elbow sticking out of a solid block of clay. Your imagination is called upon to supply the rest of the figure.

In Miss Cary's library you stood and wondered what was behind those paper covers. What strange voyage or extraordinary chapters of wonder might be disclosed if you took one of those volumes home? There had been some great moments. A tale of a suicide club, and the story of a rajah's diamond had been found in one called "The New Arabian Nights," by a Scotchman whose life was then drawing to a close in the South Sea Islands. There were some crisp and tingling little stories about India by a newspaper man from Lahore, who had just offended America by his flippant account of his visit to this country. My brother had recently come home with two poems which he had committed to memory—two extraordinary poems which filled me with delight. They were also by this newspaper man from India, and they were called "Gunga Din" and "Mandalay." And for the next ten years I never hesitated to horrify my elders by saying that Kipling and Stevenson were far better than Sir Walter Scott.

Now it is my turn to be horrified and disgusted when I hear that boys in school and college think that only old fogies read Kipling and Stevenson. What is better? I tremulously cry. Not ——? or ——? Don't make me laugh!

Miss Cary lent me a book called "The Three Imposters," by Arthur Machen (who had been reading "The New Arabian Nights," I could see), and it was very much to my taste. The proprietor of *The Blue Pagan* has just discovered Arthur Machen (more than twenty-five years after Miss Ellen Cary) and offers me his books at a fancy price.

It would be wrong to say that the Cary girls have no representatives today. There is Mr. Falcon, the owner of a quiet book-shop in New York. He is the gravest book-dealer in the city. He raises his head from his desk and surveys me with his mild blue eyes. He bows courteously as I come in his shop, and asks how he may serve me. His hair and beard are so fine and silvery that I would liken him to an etching by—but I never can remember who did the etching. The Curator of Prints, to whom I submitted the question, says that Seymour Haden is not the man. The Curator does not know my old book-dealer, and I am shaky about Seymour Haden. So the point may never be settled.

"I would like to look about," I tell the book-dealer.

"Is there some subject in which you are particularly interested?"

There are fifteen subjects, and this news is imparted to the dealer. He shows polite disbelief and fatherly amusement. I am still under sixty, and I can see that the old book-dealer thinks it distressing that so young a reader should play with the truth. I mention one or two of my interests, but it does no good. He regards them as frivolous. Mine is not a case needing learned guidance. Jimmie—who is about thirteen—is called, and instructed to lead me to see some of the books I have indicated. Jimmy and I walk down the shop together, and I feel grateful not to be given a fairy-tale and told to trot away home.

It is not surprising that many book-dealers arrive at this frame of mind. Shyness in the presence of books is not peculiar to one side of the counter.

The older and more experienced dealers may carry too far their manner of paternal tolerance for the limitations of the young. I knew a girl who was attracted by the pretty edition of *"The Compleat Angler,"* edited by Mr. Le Gallienne, and published a dozen years ago by Mr. Lane. Happening to be in a strange city—famed for its book-shops—she decided to buy a copy as a gift. She was neither wrinkled, gray, nor be-spectacled—far from any of these—but she had spent two or three years in the order division of a public library, during its organization, and more books new and old had passed through her hands and under her observation in a week than the clerks in the book-shop to which she applied were apt to handle in a month. A nice old gentleman came to wait on her, and to him she mentioned her wish, saying that it was a new edition, and adding some details about it.

His eyes twinkled behind his gold eye-glasses. Here was a funny story to tell his friends. This pretty young school girl, who had gone about as far into literature as Richard Harding Davis's romances! His voice was so soothing as he replied, that she expected him to pat her hands.

"My dear young lady," he said, prolonging the word "dear," " 'The Compleat Angler' is a very, *very* old book, written a great many years ago——"

"Yes, I know," she interrupted, "but there is a new edition——"

"By Izaak Walton," he continued, and having informed her so far, and wagging his head in a sort of solemn merriment, to show that he was not angry at her preposterous inquiry, he fairly backed her out of the shop, closed the door, and left her to go and acquire age and wisdom.

My searches in the shop of the old dealer was not often successful. As soon as Jimmie and I pass the section near the door, devoted to novels of the present year, we are immersed in the Black Walnut period of American literature. That fascinating decade when Andrew Lang and Austin Dobson were writing ballades, when Frank Stockton was writing and A. B. Frost picturing the comedies of American country life—this pleasant era seems to be despised by my old gentleman. He has no past except that of the Beecher trial and the Danbury News Man. I may buy a biography of Adoniram Judson, if I wish, or "Dred, a Tale of the Great Dismal Swamp." Miss Madeleine Smith, the Edinburgh beauty, read the latter, by the way, about a year after its publication, and nearly at the same time when she was refreshing her lover, M. L'Angelier, with cocoa thoughtfully mixed (so it was asserted) with arsenic. She did not enjoy the novel, but it was all the amusement she had on a rainy Sunday.

It is a matter of fifty-one blocks in distance to *The Purple Pagan,* and the change is from Clarissa Harlowe to Ann Veronica. The place is bright with new bookcovers, and posters full of yellows and greens. It is the "greenery-yallery, Grosvenor Gallery" school of English æstheticism, dished up again forty years later and enlivened by one jigger of Cubism, one of Vorticism, a dash of Communism, the whole mingled with that which Keats long ago saw upon a Grecian urn two thousand years old—the spirit of youth, "forever panting and forever young."

It is all giddy and bright and a little loony. Here comes Alys, the very spirit of America's Bohemia. Born in Nebraska, she has moved to New York "to live her own life." To her fellow-townsmen this suggests awful memories of George Sand and her carryings on, but it really means nothing worse than dining when she feels so inclined on chocolate caramels, cooked on an alcohol flame in the bath-tub. She has a dear friend called Bernice who is even more modern. Back in 1920 I saw Bernice one afternoon turning into Eighth Street; she was dressed in a kind of green burlap. She wore no stockings but had carefully painted pansies on her ankles. Two dogs backed growling into an area as she passed by, and a baby in a perambulator, seeing her, set up a terrific howl. "I hope you don't think we dress with *attractiveness* in mind!" she said to her brother, who had come on to visit her. "Well, what do you dress for?" he replied faintly; "political reasons?"

Poor Bernice! She is so busy in being modern that there is no chance that she will ever discover how ancient she really is. As she is vowed never to read anything a year old she will never see herself as Lady Jane, Angela, Saphir and all the others in W. S. Gilbert's "Patience." Yet there she was forty years ago, green burlap and all—or as Lady Jane said: "a cobwebby grey velvet, with a tender bloom like cold gravy, which made Florentine Fourteenth Century, trimmed with Venetian leather and Spanish altar lace, and surmounted with something Japanese—it matters not what—" And Bernice has much in common with Mrs. Cimabue Brown, a creation of a social satirist named Du Maurier, of whom, however, she has never heard. *She* offended the eye with peacock-feathers; Bernice does it with *batik;* but they look alike as two string-beans.

Alys and Bernice are much "intrigued" (for they still use that base-born verb) by Morris, who came a few years ago, when he was fifteen, from southern Russia. There he had to be revolutionary in order not to be classed with the stupid and the illiterate. Here he keeps on being revolutionary to prove that he is still intellectual, and as nobody asks him what he wishes to revolutionize, the mental effort is almost negligible. Looking about for tyrants, he describes in the President another Nicholas II, and thinks that the Governor of New York is practically as good, for his purposes, as the old Pro-curator of the Holy Synod. All the people he knew in south-ern Russia were very gloomy, and he is convinced that it is so with the Americans. An annoying cheerfulness, which is sometimes forced upon his attention, is easily dismissed. The Intellectuals are not that way, he reflects. For reasons con-nected with his digestion, it is not difficult for Morris to fight off cheerfulness, and so there he is, both intellectual and pessimistic, without the slightest exertion.

And yet they are uneasy. Alys and Morris and Bernice are perpetually uncomfortable, are suffering pangs which are no part of their programme. Partly this is because they need exercise and a change from eccentric food. The biliousness of their art is symbolic. But their troubles are deeper than that; they live in constant dread—dread of being conventional, of being called Puritanical or Mid-Victorian. Life is difficult in a circle where the rules for poetry or painting are laid down anew each Monday afternoon, upset by another authority on Wednesday in favor of a new code of laws, which are, in turn, declared Mid-Victorian on Thursday morning. Like a girl from the country, who dreads to be called a prude, and so hastens to light a cigarette before she has even had time to get settled at her table in a Bohemian restaurant, they have subjected themselves to a tyranny of ideas as cruel as those of the Puritans.

The books which cover the tables in *The Purple Pagan,* fresh, bright, and attractive—show that the writers are fearful that somebody may not remember that "male and female created He them." There has been a lapse into forgetfulness about sex on the part of the human race, it appears, and something ought to be published on the subject. Here are a few attempts to supply the want. But they scream a little too loud. They forever want to tell somebody "the facts of life." Like the old lady who wakened her confessor at two in the morning, to confess her one sin, which was committed fifty years ago, they "likes to talk about it." Their liberalism is a tight little doctrine which 'keeps its hottest hatred for liberals of other stripes. Towards the arch-Tories of the world they are more than friendly. Their pacifism objects to the shedding of blood in any formal manner. But a bomb tossed nonchalantly into a crowd, or the shooting of unarmed men in the back—since these require no degrading drill nor discipline on the part of the performers—are perfectly tolerable to them. To keep their own skins whole and safe is their notion of the noblest conduct—and they call themselves "idealists" forty times a day. Their novelists hold up the slacker, the sneak, and the deserter for sympathy and admiration; their story-tellers discuss their own bodily functions as if they were old grannies gossiping in a sanatarium, or wheezy clubmen with disordered livers. And this senile chatter is hailed, in *The Purple Pagan,* as "the cry of youth."

On the whole, the worst thing about them is their complexions. They are as sallow as their paintings, as puffy and muddy as their clay and wax figurines. Old Mr. Falcon, with his bright blue eyes and pink cheeks, looks as if he could give Morris ten yards in a hundred yard dash. Morris, I believe, claimed exemption in 1918, not because he objected to putting bullets into other men nor was afraid some other man might put a bullet into him. But the thought of being made to get up early and take some exercise revolted his proud soul. His personal freedom to remain a little greasy looking was in danger. An hour's drill and a shower-bath would brighten his views on politics, art, and literature. But he would denounce me as a militarist and a slave to militarism if I told him so. And he would smile a sad, greenish smile to show what he thinks of the mental equipment of cheerful persons.

As for the comparative liberality of their literary notions —I suppose it must be admitted that *The Purple Pagan* is much narrower than Miss Cary. They both have their crotchets. Miss Cary disapproved of "Pecks' Bad Boy" for persons of my age, and so inspired me with an unholy desire to read it. She did or she did not—I really cannot remember —keep solely for her older readers a little book by Grant Allen, called "The Woman Who Did," which (laughable to recall) was then sold, after whispered conversations and with a great show of secrecy, by newsboys on the trains. Today it sits neglected on the book-shelves, middle-aged, obscure, and only occasionally sought for its Aubrey Beardsley title-page.

The Purple Pagan is still devoted to the theory that to be in trouble with the police is the sign of the artist. The proprietor of that gaudy shop always patronizes Poe, not on account of his poetry, for that is diametrically opposed to all the Pagan's ideas of verse-making, but because of his enjoyment of the belief that Poe was a drunkard. Nothing could be more amusing than to have Poe come back, sit at his editorial desk for a week, and release the torrent of his critical rage upon the *vers librists* and others of their stripe.

Miss Cary first brought to my notice the fact that the current *Lippincott's Magazine* had in it a yarn of a new and admirable detective who dosed himself with cocaine and owned a friend named Watson. At about that time there appeared in the same magazine a weird story, slightly sweet, slightly sickish, called "The Picture of Dorian Gray." Miss Cary said that the author was a donkey, but that he could write. She lent me a novel called "Tess of the d'Urbervilles," but at that time it seemed to me to have "too much scenery" in it. Aside from a murder and a hanging there was little to attract me. Miss Cary had not yet heard—and neither had any one of us—of an Irish critic named Shaw; perhaps a curious, thin book named "The Time Machine," by H. G. Wells, had come to her library. If so, knowing my tastes, she certainly passed it on to me. Mark Twain had just published a book—with delightful illustrations—which I enjoyed then as I have never been able to enjoy it since. It was "The Connecticut Yankee." Miss Cary talked less about liberalism but believed in it rather more than the Purple man does. She allowed authors freedom in choice of subject; he would pin them down to a pretty narrow range. The themes of both "Othello" and "Macbeth" were great themes in her opinion; *The Purple Pagan* would vote for "Othello" and despise the theme of "Macbeth." She cared not at all about the politics of a novelist or poet, but he would insist that even the writer of nursery rhymes must believe in Communism, or whatever cure-all he happened to favor at the moment. If Miss Cary were Czar, I think it would be an easy sort of tyranny, but one has only to look at the fanatical eyes of *The Purple Pagan* to know that his firing-squads would never stop until they had cleared the earth of all who did not share his beliefs, down to his last economic or artistic dogma.

"LORNA DOONE" *

By William Lyon Phelps

THE air of Devon and Somerset is full of literary germs. The best advice a London hack could give to a Gigadibs would be *Go west, young man.* The essential thing is to establish a residence south of Bristol, grow old along with Wessex, and inhale the atmosphere. Thousands of reverent pilgrims, on foot, on bicycle, and in automobile, are yearly following the tragic trails of Mr. Hardy's heroines; to a constantly increasing circle of interested observers, Mr. Eden Phillpotts is making the topography of Devon clearer than an ordnance map; if Mrs. Willcocks writes a few more novels like *The Wingless Victory* and *A Man of Genius,* we shall soon all be talking about her—just wait and see; and in the summer season, when soft is the sun, the tops of coaches in North Devon and Somerset are packed with excited Americans, carrying Lornas instead of Baedekers. To the book-loving tourists, every inch of this territory is holy ground.

Yet the author of our favourite romance was not by birth a Wessex man. Mr. Richard D. Blackmore (for, like the creator of *Robinson Crusoe,* his name is not nearly so well known as his work) first "saw the light" in Berkshire, the year being 1825. But he was exposed to the Wessex germs at the critical period of boyhood, actually going to Blundell's School at Tiverton, a small town in the heart of Devonshire, fourteen miles north of Exeter, at the union of Exe and

*From *Essays on Modern Novelists;* copyright, 1910, by The Macmillan Company. Reprinted by permission of the author and the publishers.

Lowman rivers. To this same school he sent John Ridd, as we learn in the second paragraph of the novel:—

"John Ridd, the elder, churchwarden, and overseer, being a great admirer of learning, and well able to write his name, sent me, his only son, to be schooled at Tiverton, in the County of Devon. For the chief boast of that ancient town (next to its woolen staple) is a worthy grammar-school, the largest in the west of England, founded and handsomely endowed in the year 1604 by Master Peter Blundell, of that same place, clothier."

From this institution young Blackmore proceeded to Exeter College, Oxford, where he laid the foundations of his English style by taking high rank in the classics. Like many potential poets and novelists, he studied law, and was called to the bar in 1852. But he cared little for the dusty purlieus of the Middle Temple, and not at all for city life: his father was a country parson, as it is the fashion for English fathers of men to letters to be, and the young man loved the peace and quiet of rural scenery. He finally made a home at Teddington, in Middlesex, and devoted himself to the avocation of fruit-growing. On this subject he became an authority, and his articles on gardening were widely read. Here he died in January, 1900.

His death was mourned by many thousand persons who never saw him, and who knew nothing about his life. The public always loves the makers of its favourite books; but in the case of Mr. Blackmore, every reader of his masterpiece felt a peculiarly intimate relation with the man who wrote it. The story is so full of the milk of human kindness, its hero and heroine are so irresistibly attractive, and it radiates so wholesome and romantic a charm, that one cannot read it without feeling on the best possible terms with the author— as if both were intimate friends of long standing. For *Lorna Doone* is a book we think we have always been reading; we can hardly recall the time when it had not become part of our literary experience; just as it takes an effort to remember that there were days and years when we were not even aware of the existence of persons who are now indissolubly close. They have since become so necessary that we imagine life before we knew them must really have been more barren than it seemed.

Like many successful novelists, Mr. Blackmore began his literary career by the publication of verse, several volumes of poems appearing from his pen during the years 1854-1860. Although he never entirely abandoned verse composition, which it was only too apparent that he wrote with his left hand, the coolness with which his Muse was received may have been a cause of his attempting the quite different art of the novel. It is pleasant to remember, however, that in these early years he translated Vergil's *Georgics;* combining his threefold love of the classics, of poetry, and of gardening. Of how much practical agricultural value he found the Mantuan bard, we shall never know.

Contrary to a common supposition, *Lorna Doone* was not his first story. He launched two ventures before his master-piece—*Clara Vaughan* in 1864, and *Cradock Nowell* in 1866. These won no applause, and have not emerged from the con-genial oblivion in which they speedily foundered. After these false starts, the great book came out in 1869, with no blare of publisher's trumpets, with scanty notice from the critics, and with no notice of any kind from the public. In the preface to the twentieth edition, and his various prefaces are well worth reading, the author remarked:—

"What a lucky maid you are, my Lorna! When first you came from the Western Moors nobody cared to look at you; the 'leaders of the public taste' led none of it to make test of you. Having struggled to the light of day, through obstruction and repulses, for a year and a half you shivered in a cold corner, without a sun-ray. Your native land disdained your voice, and America answered, 'No child of mine'; knowing how small your value was, you were glad to get your fare paid to any distant colony."

The *Saturday Review* for 5 November, 1870, uttered a few patronising words of praise. The book was called "a work of real excellence," but the reviewer timidly added, "We do not pretend to rank it with the acknowledged masterpieces of fiction." On the whole, there is good ground for gratitude that the public was so slow to see the "real excellence" of *Lorna.* A sudden blaze of popularity is sometimes so fierce as to consume its cause. Let us spend a few moments in devout meditation, while we recall the ashes of "the book of the year." The gradual dawn of Lorna's fame has assured her of a long and fair day.

Possibly one of the reasons why this great romance made so small an impression was because it appeared at an unpropitious time. The sower sowed the seed; but the thorns of Reade and Trollope sprang up and choked them. These two novelists were in full action; and they kept the public busy. Realism was strong in the market; people did not know then, as we do now, that *The Cloister and the Hearth* was worth all the rest of Charles Reade put together. Had *Lorna Doone* appeared toward the end of the century, when the Romantic Revival was in full swing, it would have received a royal welcome. But how many would have recognised its superiority to the tinsel stuff of those recent days, full of galvanised knights and stuffed chatelaines? For *Lorna* belongs to a class of fiction with which we were flooded in the nineties, though, compared with the ordinary representative of its kind, it is as a star to a glow-worm. Readers then enjoyed impossible characters, whose talk was mainly of "gramercy" and similar curiosities, for they had the opportunity to "revel in the glamour of a bogus antiquity." But an abundance of counterfeits does not lower the value of the real metal; and *Lorna* is a genuine coin struck from the mint of historical romance. In the original preface its author modestly said:—

"This work is called a 'romance,' because the incidents, characters, time, and scenery are alike romantic. And in shaping this old tale, the writer neither dares, nor desires, to claim for it the dignity or cumber it with the difficulty of an historic novel."

In warmth and colour, in correct visualisation, and in successful imitation of the prose of a bygone day (which no one has ever perfectly accomplished), it ranks not very far below the greatest of all English historical romances, *Henry Esmond.*

Lorna Doone is practically one more illustration of Single-Speech Hamilton. After its appearance, its author wrote and published steadily for thirty years; but the fact remains that not only is *Lorna* his best-known work, but that his entire reputation hangs upon it. Many of his other stories are good, notably *Cripps the Carrier* and *Perlycross;* the latter has a most ingenious plot; but these two now peacefully repose with their mates in undisturbed slumber at dusty library corners. They had an initial sale because they came from the hand that created *Lorna;* then they were lost in the welter of ephemeral literature. Mr. Blackmore offered his buyers all sorts of wares, but, after a momentary examination, they declined what was "just as good," and returned to their favourite, which, by the way, was never his; he ranked it third among his productions.

For this novel is not only one of the best-loved books in English fiction, and stands magnificently the severe test of rereading, it is bound to have even more admirers in the future than it has ever yet enjoyed; it is visibly growing in reputation every year. It may be interesting to analyse some of its elements, in order to understand what has given it so assured a place. The main plot is simplicity itself. It is a history, however, that the world has always found entertaining, the history of the love of a strong man for a beautiful girl. They meet, he falls in love, he rescues her from peril, she goes up to London, becomes a great lady, returns, is dangerously wounded on her wedding-day, recovers, and they live happily for ever after—*voilà tout.* A very simple plot, yet the telling fills two stout volumes, with the reader's interest maintained from first to last.

It is told in the first person—the approved method of the historical romance. Professor Raleigh has admirably pointed out the virtues and defects of the three ways of composing a novel,—direct discourse by the chief actor, the exclusive employment of letters, and the "invisible and omniscient" impersonal author.[1] It is interesting to note, in passing, that our first English novelist, Defoe, adopted the first method; Richardson, our second novelist, took the second; and Fielding, our third novelist, took the third. Now, the great advantage of having John Ridd speak throughout is the gain in reality and vividness; it is as though we sat with him in the ingle, and obtained all our information at first hand. What is lost by narrowness of experience is made up in intensity; we follow him breathlessly, as Desdemona followed Othello, and he has every moment our burning sympathy. We participate more fully in his joys and sorrows, in the agony of his suspense; we share his final triumph. He is talking directly to us, and John Ridd is a good talker. He is the kind of man who appeals to all classes of listeners. He has the gentleness and modesty that are so becoming to great physical strength; the love of children, animals, and all helpless creatures; reverence for God, purity of heart, and a noble slowness to wrath. Such a man is simply irresistible, and we are sorry when he finishes his tale. The defect in this method of narration, which Mr. Blackmore has employed with such success, is the inevitable defect in all stories written in this manner, as Professor Raleigh has observed: "It takes from the novelist the privilege of killing his hero." When John Ridd is securely bound, and the guns of hostile soldiers are levelled at his huge bulk, with their fingers actually on the triggers, we laugh at ourselves for our high-beating hearts; for of course he is unkillable, else how could he be talking at this very moment?

[1] *The English Novel*, Chapter VI.

The plot of *Lorna Doone,* which, as we have observed, is very simple, is, nevertheless, skilfully complicated. It is not a surprise plot, like that of *A Pair of Blue Eyes;* we are not stunned by the last page. It is a suspense plot; we have a well-founded hope that all will come right in the end, and yet the author has introduced enough disturbing elements to put us occasionally in a maze. This artistic suspense is attained partly by the method of direct discourse; which, at the same time, develops the character of the hero. Big John repeats incidents, dwells lengthily on minute particulars, stops to enjoy the scenery, and makes mountains of stories out of molehills of fact. The second complication of the plot arises from the introduction of characters that apparently divert the course of the story without really doing so. There are nineteen important characters, all held well in hand; and a conspicuous example of a complicating personage is little Ruth Huckaback. She interferes in the main plot in an exceedingly clever way. The absorbing question in every reader's mind is, of course, Will John marry Lorna? Now Ruth's interviews with the hero are so skilfully managed, and with such intervals of time between, that on some pages she seems destined to be his bride. And, admirably drawn as her character is, when her artistic purpose in the plot is fully accomplished, she quietly fades out, with the significant tribute, "Ruth Huckaback is not married yet."

There is also a subsidiary plot, dovetailed neatly into the main building. This is the story of the attractive highwayman, Tom Faggus, and his love for John's sister, Annie. Many pages are taken up with the adventures of this gentleman, who enters the novel on horseback (what a horse!) at the moment when the old drake is fighting for his life. Besides our interest in Tom himself, in his wild adventures, and in his reformation, we are interested in the conflict of his two passions, one for the bottle, and one for Annie, and we wonder which will win. This subsidiary love story is still further complicated by the introduction of young De Whichehalse; and in the struggle between John Ridd and the Doones, both Tom Faggus and the De Whichehalse family play important parts. It is interesting, too, to observe how events that seem at the time to be of no particular importance, turn out later to be highly significant; when, at the very beginning of the long story, the little boy, on his way home from school, meets the lady's maid, and shortly after sees the child borne away on the robber's saddle, we imagine all this is put in to enliven the journey, that it is just "detail"; long afterwards we find the artistic motive. In fact, one of the most notable virtues of this admirable plot is the constant introduction of matters apparently irrelevant and due to mere garrulity, such as the uncanny sound, for example, which prove after all to be essential to the course of the narrative.

As for the characters, they impress us differently in different moods. For all John Ridd's prodigious strength, marvellous escapes, and astounding feats, his personality is so intensely human that he seems real. His *soul,* at any rate, is genuine, and wholly natural; his bodily activity—the extraction of Carver's biceps, the wrenching of the branch from the tree, the hurling of the cannon through the door—makes him a dim giant in a fairy story. When we think of the qualities of his mind and heart, he comes quite close; when we think of his physical prowess, he almost vanishes in the land of Fable. I remember the comment of an undergraduate—"John Ridd is as remote as Achilles; he is like a Greek myth."

The women are all well drawn and individualised—except the heroine. I venture to say that no one has ever seen Lorna in his mind's eye. She is like a plate that will not develop. A very pretty girl with an affectionate disposition, —what more can be said? But so long as a Queen has beauty and dignity, she does not need to be interesting; and Lorna is the queen of this romance. John's mother and his two sisters are as like and unlike as members of the same family ought to be; they are real women. Ruth Huckaback and Gwenny Carfax are great additions to our literary acquaintances; each would make an excellent heroine for a realistic novel. They have the indescribable puzzling characteristics that we call feminine; sudden caprices, flashes of unexpected jealousy, deep loyal tenderness, unlimited capacity for self-sacrifice, and in the last analysis, Mystery.

The humour of the story is spontaneous, and of great variety, running from broad mirth to whimsical subtlety. The first concerted attack on the Doones is comic opera burlesque; but the scenes of humour that delight us most are those describing friendly relations with beast and bird. The eye of the old drake, as he stared wildly from his precarious position, and the delight of the ducks as they welcomed his rescue; above all, Annie's care of the wild birds in the bitter cold.

"There was not a bird but knew her well, after one day of comforting; and some would come to her hand, and sit, and shut one eye, and look at her. Then she used to stroke their heads, and feel their breasts, and talk to them; and not a bird of them all was there but liked to have it done to him. And I do believe they would eat from her hand things unnatural to them, lest she should be grieved and hurt by not knowing what to do for them. One of them was a noble bird, such as I had never seen before, of very fine bright plumage, and larger than a misselthrush. He was the hardest of all to please; and yet he tried to do his best."

Whatever may be the merits of Mr. Blackmore's published verse, there is more poetry in *Lorna Doone* than in many volumes of formal rime. The wonderful descriptions of the country in shade and shine, in fog and drought, the pictures of the sunrise and the falling water, the "tumultuous privacy" of the snow-storms,—these are all descriptive poems. Every reader has noticed the peculiar rhythm of the style, and wondered if it were intentional. Hundreds of sentences here and there are perfect English hexameters; one can find them by opening the book at random, and reading aloud. But this peculiar element in the style goes much farther than isolated phrases. There are solid passages of steady rhythm, which might correctly be printed in verse form.[1]

Mr. Blackmore's personal character was so modest, unassuming, and lovable, that it is not difficult to guess the source of the purity, sweetness, and sincerity of his great book. If he were somewhat surprised at the utter coldness of its first reception, he never got over his amazement at the size and extent of its ultimate triumph. In the preface to the sixth edition, he said:—

"Few things have surprised me more, and nothing has more pleased me, than the great success of this simple tale. . . . Therefore any son of Devon may imagine, and will not grudge, the writer's delight at hearing from a recent visitor to the west, that *'Lorna Doone,* to a Devonshire man, is as good as clotted cream, almost!'

"Although not half so good as that, it has entered many a tranquil, happy, pure, and hospitable home; and the author, while deeply grateful for this genial reception, ascribes it partly to the fact that his story contains no word or thought disloyal to its birthright in the fairest county of England."

Mr. Blackmore lived long enough to see an entirely different kind of "local colour" become conventional, where many a novelist, portraying his native town or the community in which he dwelt, emphasised with what skill he could command all its poverty, squalor, and meanness; the disgusting vices and malignant selfishnes of its inhabitants; and after he had thus fouled his nest by representing it as a mass of filth, degradation, and sin, he imagined he had created a work of art. The author of *Lorna Doone* had the satisfaction of knowing that he had inspired hundreds of thousands of readers with the love of his favourite west country, and with an intense desire to visit it. And being, like John Ridd, of a forgiving nature, he forgave America for its early neglect

[1] A writer in the *Atlantic Monthly* notes especially the closing paragraph of Chapter XXVIII, and parts of Chapter XXIX.

of his story; for being informed of the supremacy of *Lorna Doone* in the hearts of American undergraduates, he remarked, in a letter to the present writer, "The good word of the young, who are at once the most intelligent and the most highly educated of a vast intellectual nation, augurs well for the continuance—at least for a generation—of my fortunate production."

MONEY *

By Agnes Repplier

"As the world is, and will be, 't is a sort of duty to be rich,"
wrote Lady Mary Wortley Montagu; and her words—which
sound almost ascetic in our ears—were held to be of doubtful
morality in the godless eighteenth century which she adorned
and typified. Even Lady Mary endeavoured to qualify their
greed by explaining that she valued money because it gave
her the power to do good; but her hard-headed compatriots
frankly doubted this excusatory clause. They knew perfectly
well that a desire to do good is not, and never has been, a
motive power in the acquisition of wealth.

Lady Mary did render her country one inestimable service;
but her fortune (which, after all, was of no great magnitude)
had nothing whatever to do with it. Intelligent observation, dauntless courage, and the supreme confidence which
nerved her to experiment upon her own child,—these qualities
enabled her to force inoculation upon a reluctant and
scandalized public. These qualities have lifted mankind out
of many a rut, and are all we shall have to depend on while
the world rolls on its way. When Aristotle said that money
was barren, he did not mean that it was barren of delights;
but that it had no power to get us to any place worth reaching,
no power to quicken the intellectual and spiritual potencies
of the soul.

The love of gold, the craving for wealth, has not lain dor-

* From *Points of Friction;* copyright, 1920, by Houghton Mifflin
Company. Reprinted by permission of, and special arrangements
with, the publishers, Houghton Mifflin Company.

mant for ages in the human heart, waiting for the twentieth century to call it into being. It is no keener now than it has always been, but it is ranker in its growth and expression, being a trifle over-nourished in our plethoric land, and not subjected to keen competing emotions. Great waves of religious thought, great struggles for principles and freedom, great births of national life, great discoveries, great passions, and great wrongs,—these things have swayed the world, wrecking and saving the souls of men without regard for money. Great qualities, too, have left their impress upon the human race, and endowed it for all the years to come.

The genius which in the thirteenth century found expression in architecture and scholasticism, which in the sixteenth and seventeenth centuries found expression in art and letters, finds expression to-day in applied science and finance. Industrial capitalism, as we know it now, is the latest development of man's restless energy. It has coloured our times, given us new values in education, and intruded itself grossly into the quiet places of life. We should bear with it patiently, we might even "admire it from afar," if only we were sometimes suffered to forget. "Money talks," and, by way of encouraging its garrulity, we talk about money, and in terms of money, until it would sometimes appear as if the currency of the United States were the only thing in the country vital enough to interpret every endeavour, and illustrate every situation.

Here, for example, is an imposing picture in a Sunday paper, a picture full of dignified ecclesiastics and decorous spectators. The text reads, "Breaking ground for a three-million-dollar nave." It is a comprehensive statement, and one that conveys to the public the only circumstance which the public presumably cares to hear. But it brings a great cathedral down to the level of the million-dollar club-houses, or boat-houses, or fishing-camps which are described for us in unctuous and awe-stricken paragraphs. It is even dimly suggestive of the million-dollar babies whom reporters follow

feverishly up and down Palm Beach, and who will soon have
to be billion-dollar babies if they want to hold their own. We
are now on terms of easy familiarity with figures which used
to belong to the abstractions of arithmetic, and not to the
world of life. We have become proudly aware of the infinite
possibilities of accumulation and of waste.

For this is the ebb and flow of American wealth. It is
heaped up with resistless energy and concentration; it is
dissipated in broken and purposeless profusion. Every class
resents the extravagance of every other class; but none will
practise denial. The millionaire who plays with a yacht and
decks his wife with pearls looks askance upon the motor and
silk shirt of the artisan. The artisan, with impulses and ambitions as ignoble and as unintelligent as the millionaire's, is
sullenly aware that, waste as he may, the rich can waste
more, and he is still dissatisfied. There is no especial appeal
to manhood in a silk shirt, no approach to sweetness and light.
It represents an ape-like imitation of something not worth
imitating, a hopeless ignorance of the value and worth of
money.

A universal reluctance to practise economy indicates a
weakness in the moral fibre of a nation, a dangerous absence
of pride. There is no power of the soul strong enough to induce thrift but pride. There is no quality stern enough to bar
self-indulgence but the overmastering dictates of self-respect.
There is no joy that life can yield comparable to the joy of
independence. A nation is free when it submits to coercion
from no other nation. A man is free when he is the arbiter
of his own fate. National and individual freedom have never
come cheap. The sacrifice which insures the one insures the
other; the resolution which preserves the one preserves the
other. When Andrew Marvell declined the bribe offered him
"out of pure affection" by the Lord Treasurer, saying he had
"a blade-bone of mutton" in his cupboard which would suffice
for dinner, he not only held his own honour inviolate, but he
vindicated the liberty of letters, the liberty of Parliament,

and the liberty of England. No wonder an old chronicler says that his integrity and spirit were "dreadful" to the corrupt officials of his day.

There are Americans who appear to love their country for much the same reason that Stevenson's "child" loves the "friendly cow":

> "She gives me cream with all her might
> To eat with apple tart."

When the supply of cream runs short, the patriot's love runs shorter. He holds virulent mass-meetings to complain of the cow, of the quality of the cream, and of its distribution. If he be an immigrant, he probably riots in the streets, not clamouring for the flesh-pots of Egypt—that immemorial cry for ease and bondage—inasmuch as the years of his thraldom had been softened by no such indulgence; but simply because the image of the cow is never absent from his mind, or from the minds of those to whom he looks for guidance. The captain of industry and the agitator, the spendthrift and the spendthrift's wife who fling their money ostentatiously to the four winds of heaven, the working-man and the working-woman who exact the largest wage for the least labour, all are actuated by the same motive,—to get as much and to give as little as they can. It is not a principle which makes for citizenship, and it will afford no great help in the hour of the nation's trial. Material progress and party politics are engrossing things; but perhaps Francis Parkman was right when he said that if our progress is to be at the mercy of our politics, and our politics at the mercy of our mobs, we shall have no lasting foundation for prosperity and well-being.

The tendency to gloat over the sight and sound of money may be less pervasive than it seems. It may be only a temporary predisposition, leaving us at heart clean, wise, and temperate. But there is a florid exuberance in the handling of this recurrent theme which nauseates us a little, like very

rich food eaten in a close room. Why should we be told that
"the world gapes in wonder" as it contemplates "an Aladdin
romance of steel and gold"? The world has had other things
to gape over in these sorrowful and glorious years. "Once a
barefoot boy, now riding in a hundred-thousand-dollar private car." There is a headline to catch the public eye, and
make the public tongue hang watering from its mouth. That
car, "early Pullman and late German Lloyd," is to the
American reader what the two thousand black slaves with jars
of jewels upon their heads were to Dick Swiveller,—a vision
of tasteful opulence. More intimate journalists tell us that
a "Financial Potentate" eats baked potatoes for his luncheon,
and gives his friends notebooks with a moral axiom on each
page. We cannot really care what this unknown gentleman
eats. We cannot, under any conceivable circumstance, covet
a moral notebook. Yet such items of information would not
be painstakingly acquired unless they afforded some mysterious gratification to their readers.

As for the "athletic millionaires," who sport in the open
like—and often with—ordinary men, they keep their chron-
iclers nimble. Fashions in plutocracy change with the changing times. The reporter who used to be turned loose in a
nabob's private office, and who rapturously described its
"ebony centre-table on which is laid a costly cover of maroon-
coloured silk plush," and its panelled walls, "the work of a
lady amateur of great ability" (I quote from a newspaper of
1890), now has to scurry round golf-links, and shiver on the
outskirts of a polo-field. From him we learn that young New
Yorkers, the least and lowest of whom lives in a nine-hundred-
thousand-dollar house, play tennis and golf like champions,
or "cut a wide swathe in polo circles with their fearless riding." From him we learn that "automobile racing can show
its number of millionaires," as if it were at all likely to show
its number of clerks and ploughmen. Extravagance may be
the arch-enemy of efficiency, but it is, and has always been,
the friend of aimless excess.

When I was young, and millionaires were a rarity in my unassuming town, a local divine fluttered our habitual serenity by preaching an impassioned sermon upon a local Croesus. He was but a moderate sort of Croesus, a man of kindly nature and simple vanities, whom his townspeople had been in the habit of regarding with mirthful and tolerant eyes. Therefore it was a bit startling to hear—from the pulpit— that this amiable gentleman was "a crown of glory upon the city's brow," and that his name was honoured "from the Golden Gate to New Jersey's silver sands." It was more than startling to be called upon to admire the meekness with which he trod the common earth, and the unhesitating affability with which he bowed to all his acquaintances, "acknowledging every salute of civility or respect," because "like another Frederick II of Prussia," he felt his fellow-citizens to be human beings like himself. This admission into the ranks of humanity, however gratifying to our self-esteem, was tempered by so many exhortations to breathe our millionaire's name with becoming reverence, and was accompanied by such a curious medley of Bible texts, and lists of distinguished people whom the millionaire had entertained, that we hardly knew where we stood in the order of creation.

Copies of this sermon, which was printed "in deference to many importunities," are now extremely rare. Reading its yellow pages, we become aware that the rites and ceremonies with which one generation worships its golden calf differ in detail from the rites and ceremonies with which another generation performs this pious duty. The calf itself has never changed since it was first erected in the wilderness,—the original model hardly admitting of improvement. Ruskin used to point out gleefully a careless couple who, in Claude's picture of the adoration of the golden calf, are rowing in a pleasure boat on a stream which flows mysteriously through the desert. Indifferent to gold, uninterested in idolatry, this pair glide smoothly by; and perhaps the river of time bears them through centuries of greed and materialism to some hidden haven of repose.

Saint Thomas Aquinas defines the sin of avarice as a "desire to acquire or retain in undue measure, beyond the order of reason." Possibly no one has ever believed that he committed this sin, that there was anything unreasonable in his desires, or undue in their measure of accomplishment. "Reason" is a word of infinite flexibility. The statisticians who revel in mathematical intricacies tell us that Mr. John D. Rockefeller's income is one hundred dollars a minute, and that his yearly income exceeds the lifetime earnings of two thousand average American citizens, and is equivalent to the income of fifty average American citizens sustained throughout the entire Christian era. It sounds more bewildering than seductive, and the breathless rush of a hundred dollars a minute is a little like the seven dinners a day which Alice in Wonderland stands ready to forego as a welcome punishment for misbehavior. But who shall say that a hundred dollars a minute is beyond the "order of reason"? Certainly Saint Thomas did not refer to incomes of this range, inasmuch as his mind (though not without a quality of vastness) could never have embraced their possibility.

On the other hand, Mr. Rockefeller is responsible for the suggestion that Saint Paul, were he living to-day, would be a captain of industry. Here again a denial is as valueless as an assertion. It is much the habit of modern propagandists—no matter what their propaganda may be—to say that the gap between themselves and the Apostles is merely a gap of centuries, and that the unlikeness, which seems to us so vivid, is an unlikeness of time and circumstance, not of the inherent qualities of the soul. The multiplication of assets, the destruction of trade-rivalry, formed—apparently—no part of the original apostolic programme. If the tent-maker of Tarsus coveted wealth, he certainly went the wrong way about getting it. If there was that in his spirit which corresponded to the modern instinct for accumulation, he did great injustice to his talents, wasting his incomparable energy on labours which—from his own showing—left him too often homeless, and naked, and hungry. Even the tent-making, by which he earned his bread, appears to have been valuable to him for the same reason that the blade-bone of mutton was valuable to Andrew Marvell,—not so much because it filled his stomach, as because it insured his independence.

"L'amour d'argent a passé en dogme de morale publique," wrote George Sand, whose words have now and then a strange prophetic ring. The "peril of prosperity," to borrow President Hibben's alliterative phrase, was not in her day the menace it is in ours, nor has it ever been in her land the menace it has been in ours, because of the many other perils, not to speak of other interests and other ideals, filling the Frenchman's mind. But if George Sand perceived a growing candour in the deference paid to wealth, to wealth as an abstraction rather than to its possessor, a dropping of the old hypocrisies which made a pretence of doubt and disapproval, a development of honoured and authorized avarice, she was a close observer as well as a caustic commentator.

The artlessness of our American attitude might disarm criticism were anything less than public sanity at stake. We appeal simply and robustly to the love of gain, and we seldom appeal in vain. It is not only that education has substituted the principle of getting on for less serviceable values; but we are bidden to purchase marketable knowledge, no less than marketable foodstuffs, as an easy avenue to fortune. If we will eat and drink the health-giving comestibles urged upon us, our improved digestions will enable us to earn larger incomes. If we will take a highly commended course of horse-shoeing or oratorio-writing, prosperity will be our immediate reward. If we will buy some excellent books of reference, they will teach us to grow rich.

"There are one thousand more millionaires in the United States than there were ten years ago," say the purveyors of these volumes. "At the present rate of increase, the new millionaires in the next few years will be at least twelve hundred. *Will you be one of them?"* There is a question to ask a young American at the outset of his career! There is an incentive to study! And by way of elucidating a somewhat doubtful situation, the advertisers go on to say: "Typical men of brains are those who have dug large commercial enterprises out of a copper mine, or transformed buying and selling into an art. You must take a leaf from the experience of such men if you would hold positions of responsibility and power."

Just how the reference books—chill avenues of universal erudition—are going to give us control of a copper mine or of a department store is not made clear; but their vendors know that there is no use in offering anything less than wealth, or, as it is sometimes spelled, "success," as a return for the price of the volumes. And if a tasteful border design of fat moneybags scattering a cascade of dollars fails to quicken the sales, there is no tempting the heart of man. Our covetousness is as simple and as easily played upon as was the covetousness of the adventurers who went digging for buried treasures on the unimpeachable authority of a soothsayer. The testimony offered in a New Jersey court that a man had bought some farmland because the spirit of a young negro girl had indicated that there was money hidden beneath the soil; the arraignment before a Brooklyn magistrate of two Gipsy women, charged with stealing the cash they had been commissioned to "bless," are proof, if proof were needed, that intelligence has not kept pace with cupidity.

The endless stories about messenger boys and elevator men who have been given a Wall Street "tip," and who have become capitalists in a day, are astonishingly like the stories which went their round when the South-Sea Bubble hung iridescent over London. Mankind has never wearied of such tales since Aladdin (one of Fortune's fools) won his easy way to wealth. Even the old dime novel with "Dare-Devil Dick," or "Jasper, the Boy Detective," for a hero, has been transmogrified into a "Fame and Fortune," series, with "Boys That Make Money," figuring vaingloriously on the title-page. Gone is the Indian brave, the dauntless young seaman who saved the American navy, the calm-eyed lad who held up a dozen masked ruffians with one small pistol. In their place we have the boy in the broker's office who finds out that "A. and C." stock will double its value within ten days; or the exploits of a group of juvenile speculators, who form a "secret syndicate," and outwit the wisest heads on Wall Street. The supremacy of youth—a vital feature of such fiction—is indicated when the inspired messenger boy gives a "pointer" to an old and influential firm of brokers, who receive it with glistening eyes and respectful gratitude. "I did not tip you in expectation of any compensation," observes the magnanimous and up-to-date young hero. "I simply felt it was my duty to prevent you from losing the profit that was bound to come your way if you held on a few days longer."

Our newspapers have told us (we should like to know who told the newspapers) that high prices are popular prices. It is fitting and proper that people who own the wealth of the world should pay a great deal for everything they buy. Shoppers with their purses full of money are affronted by any hint of cheapness or economy. This may be true, though it reminds me a little of a smiling Neapolitan who once assured me that his donkey liked to be beaten. One cannot, without entering into the mind of a donkey or of a rich American, deny the tastes imputed to them; but one may cherish doubts. It is true that "record prices" have been paid for every luxury, that the sales of furriers and jewellers have been unprecedented in the annals of our commerce, that the eager buying of rare books, pictures, and curios, flung on the markets by the destitution of Europe, has never been surpassed. One might wish that destitution anywhere (Vienna is not so far from New York that no cry of pain can reach us) would dim our pleasure in such purchases. This does not seem to be the case. " 'T is man's perdition to be safe," and 't is his deepest and deadliest perdition to profit by the misfortunes of others.

An American rhapsodist, singing the pæan of money in the pages of the "Bankers' Magazine," says in its mighty name: "I am the minister of war and the messenger of peace. No army can march without my command. Until I speak, no ship of trade can sail from any port."

"Until I speak"! Always the emphasis upon that powerful voice which is so mute and inglorious without the compelling mind of man. When President Cleveland said that if it took every dollar in the Treasury, and every soldier in the United States army, to deliver a postal card in Chicago, that postal card should be delivered, he was perhaps glad to think that the nation's wealth, like the nation's force, could be used to fulfil the nation's obligations. But back of wealth, and back of force, was purpose. When man lays hand upon the "hilt of action," money stops talking and obeys.

Mr. Shane Leslie, shrinking sensitively from that oppressive word, "efficiency," and seeking what solace he can find in the survival of unpractical ideals, ventures to say that every university man "carries away among the husks of knowledge the certainty that there are less things saleable in heaven and earth than the advocates of sound commercial education would suppose." This truth, more simply phrased by the Breton peasant woman who said *"Le bon Dieu ne vend pas ses biens,"* has other teachers besides religion and the classics. History, whether we read it or live in it, makes nothing clearer. Mr. Henry Ford is credited with saying that he would not give a nickel for all the history in the world; but though he can, and does, forbear to read it, he has to live in it with the rest of us, and learn its lessons first-hand. No one desired the welfare—or what he conceived to be the welfare—of mankind more sincerely than he did; and he was prepared to buy it at a handsome figure. Yet Heaven refused to sell, and earth, inasmuch as the souls of men are not *her* possessions, had nothing worth his purchase.

The price of war can be computed in figures; the price of peace calls for another accountant. The tanker, Gold Shell, which first crossed the "forbidden" zone did more than a score of peace ships could have done to secure the civilization of the world. Its plain sailors who put something (I don't know what they called it) above personal safety, and their plain captain who expressed in the regrettable language of the sea his scorn of German pirates, were prepared to pay a higher price than any millionaire could offer for their own and their country's freedom. We know what these men risked because we know what agonizing deaths the sailors on the tanker, Healdton, suffered at Germany's hands. The Gold Shell seamen knew it too, and met frightfulness with fearlessness. The world is never so bad but that men's souls can rise above its badness, and restore our fainting faith.

Mohammed prayed that he might be found among the poor on the Judgment Day,—a prayer echoed by Saint Bernard, who took some pains to insure its being answered. Yet, as a mere abstraction, of what worth is poverty? The jewel in the toad's head is as glittering as adversity is sweet. One has been well likened to the other. Bishop Lawrence, undismayed by the most humiliating page of our country's history, seized a crucial moment in which to say very simply and gallantly that Americans are not wedded to ease, or enthralled by wealth. The time has come to prove him in the right. God will not sell us safety. We learned this much in the winter of 1917, when we dug our mail out of an American steamer, and asked Britain—Britain burdened with debt and bleeding at every pore—to carry it over the sea. For our own sake, no less than for the world's sake, we must show that we coin money in no base spirit, that we cherish it with no base passion. The angel who looked too long at heaven's golden pavement was flung into hell.

TRADITION *

By Stuart P. Sherman

To LENGTHEN the childhood of the individual, at the same time bringing to bear upon it the influences of tradition, is the obvious way to shorten the childhood of races, nations, classes, and so to quicken the general processes of civilization. Yet in the busy hum of self-approbation which accompanies the critical activities of our young people, perhaps the dominant note is their satisfaction at having emancipated themselves from the fetters of tradition, the oppression of classical precedent, the burden of an inherited culture. By detaching the new literature from its learned past they are confident that they are assuring it a popular future. Turn to any one of half a dozen books which discuss the present movement, and you will learn that people are now discovering, for example, "often to their own surprise," that they can read and enjoy poetry. That is because poetry has been subjected to "democratization." The elder writers, such as Shakespeare, Milton, Emerson, and Longfellow, constantly gravelled them with strange and obsolete phrases, like "multitudinous seas incarnadine," and like "tumultuous privacy of storm." The ancient writers sent them to out-of-the-way reference books to look up obscure legends about Troy, not the city where collars are made, and old stuff about war in heaven, and the landing at Plymouth Rock. It is therefore a relief to countless eager young souls that Mr. Mencken has dismissed all this as "the fossil literature taught in colleges," and that

* From *Americans;* copyright, 1922, by Charles Scribner's Sons. Reprinted by permission of the author and the publishers.

Mary Austin insists that native verse rhythms must be "within the capacity of the democratically bred." It is a joy to hear from Mr. Untermeyer that modern readers of poetry may now come out from the "lifeless and literary storehouse" and use life itself for their glossary, as indeed they may—or the morning's newspaper.

Those who encourage us to hope for crops without tillage, learning without study, and literary birth without gestation or travail are doubtless animated by a desire to augment the sum of human felicity; but one recalls Burke's passionate ejaculation: "Oh! no, sir, no. Those things which are not practicable are not desirable." To the new mode of procuring a literary renascence there may be raised one objection, which, to minds of a certain temper, will seem rather grave: all experience is against it. Such is the thesis recently argued by an English critic, Mr. H. J. Massingham, who reviews with mingled amusement and alarm the present "self-conscious rebellion against tradition." In the eyes of our excited young "cosmopolitans," whose culture has a geographic rather than an historical extension, Mr. Massingham's opinions will of course appear to be hopelessly prejudiced by his Oxford breeding, his acquaintance with the classics, his saturation in Elizabethan literature, and his avowed passion for old books in early editions, drilled by the bibliomaniac worm, "prehistoric" things, like Nares' *Glossary* and Camden's *Remains*. But it is not merely the opinion of our critic that is formidable: "The restoration of the traditional link with the art of the past is a conservative and revolutionary necessity." It is not the supporting opinion of Sir Joshua Reynolds: "The only food and nourishment of the mind of an artist is the great works of his predecessors." Sir Joshua, too, was prejudiced by his position as a pillar of the robust English classicism of George III's time. It is not even the opinion of Henry James, whom Mr. Massingham proclaims the profoundest critic since Coleridge, and who even our own irreverent youth seem to suspect should be mentioned respectfully: "It takes an endless amount of history to make even a little tradition and an endless amount of tradition to make even a little taste and an endless amount of taste, by the same token, to make even a little tranquillity."

The formidable arguments against the radical engineers of renascence are just the notorious facts of literary history. The fact that a bit of the "fossil literature taught in colleges," the story of Arthur, written in Latin by a Welsh monk in the twelfth century, has flowered and fruited in poetry, painting, and music generation after generation pretty much over the civilized world. The fact that Chaucer and his contemporaries, in whom poetry had a glorious rebirth, had previously devoured everything in what Mr. Untermeyer would call the "lifeless and literary storehouse" of the Middle Ages. The fact that the Elizabethans, to quote Mr. Massingham's vigorous phrase, flung themselves on tradition "like a hungry wolf, not only upon the classics but upon all the tradition open to them." The fact that Restoration comedy is simply a revival of late Caroline in the hands of men who had studied Molière. The fact that the leaders of the new movement in the eighteenth century, when they wished to break from the stereotyped classicism, did not urge young people to slam the door on the past, but, on the contrary, harked back over the heads of Pope and Dryden to the elder and more central tradition of Milton, Shakespeare, and Spenser; and sluiced into the arid fields of common sense, grown platitudinous, the long-damned or subterranean currents of mediæval romance. The fact that "Childe Harold," "Adonais," "The Eve of St. Agnes," "The Cotter's Saturday Night," and "The Castle of Indolence" were all written by imitators of Spenser or by imitators of his imitators. The fact, to omit the Victorians, that Mr. W. B. Yeats, the most skilful living engineer of literary renascence, set all his collaborators to digging around the roots of the ancient Celtic tree before we enjoyed the blossoming of the new spring in Ireland. The fact that John Masefield, freshest and most tuneful voice in England, is obviously steeped to the lips in the poetry of Byron, Shakespeare, Spenser, and Chaucer.

Why is it that the great poets, novelists, and critics, with few exceptions, have been, in the more liberal sense of the world, scholars—masters of several languages, students of history and philosophy, antiquarians? First of all because the great writer conceives of his vocation as the most magnificent and the most complex of crafts. He is to be his own architect, master-builder, carpenter, painter, singer, orator, poet and dramatist. His materials, his tools, his methods are, or may be, infinite. To him, then, the written tradition is a school and a museum in which, if he has a critical and inventive mind, he learns, from both the successes and the failures of his predecessors, how to set to work upon his own problems of expression. As Mr. Yeats is fond of pointing out, the young poet may find Herbert and Vaughan more helpful to him than the work of his own contemporaries, because the faults in the elder poets, the purple patches that failed to hold their color, will not attract and mislead him.

But tradition is more than a school of crafts. It is a school of mood and manners. The artist who is also a scholar cannot fail to discover that what distinguishes all the golden periods of art, what constitutes the perpetual appeal of the masters, is a kind of innermost poise and serenity, tragic in Sophocles, heroic in Michelangelo, skeptical in Montaigne, idyllic in Sidney, ironic in Fielding. This enviable tranquillity reigns only in a mind that, looking before and after, feels itself the representative of something outlasting time, some national ideal, some religious faith, some permanent human experience, some endless human quest. Nothing begets this mood and manner, the sovereign mark of good breeding in letters, like habitual association with those who have it, the majority of whom are, in the vulgar sense of the word, dead. Izaak Walton, a minor writer in whose work there is a golden afterglow of the great age, calls, in one of his Angler's

Dialogues, for "that smooth song which was made by Kit Marlowe, now at least fifty years ago," and for the answer to it "which was made by Sir Walter Raleigh in his younger days." If some of our modern imitators of the auctioneer and the steam calliope would now and then, instead of reading one another, step into the "lifeless and literary storehouse" and compare these "fossils" conscientiously with their own recent efforts to make verse popular! "They were old-fashioned poetry," says Piscator apologetically, "but choicely good, I think much better than the strong lines that are now in fashion in this critical age."

Out of the tranquillity induced by working in a good literary tradition develops form. The clever theorists who insist that form alone matters, that form is the only preservative element in literature, forget that form is not "self-begotten" but a product of the formative spirit. Mr. Massingham is a bit fastidious in his use of this word. He denies form, for example, to Pope and to Swinburne. Though both have technique, that is another matter. "Form," he declares, "is a vision contained and made manifest." He attributes the unproductiveness of our age in the field of satire to a vision without a traditional base, reeling and shifting in the choppy waters of contemporary opinion. His remarks on the deficiencies of Gilbert Cannan as a satirist and novelist further elucidate his idea; and they may serve also as a comment upon many of the younger writers in America:

The works of Mr. Cannan seem to say, "That is what life is —a surge of base and beautiful forces, intensified in the consciousness of man." But that is a fallacy. Life is like that to the layman, but it is the business of the artist to see a clue in it, to give it shape and order, to weld its particles into congruity. Here is where his lack of a constructive or satiric purpose growing out of and controlling the material tells to his hurt. He knows life in the raw, but the satirist would put it in the oven and dish it up. So he wanders in the dark, and we blunder after him. But we want light, if it be only from a tallow candle.

Now, many of the young writers in America are disposed to reject the English tradition as unserviceable lumber. They scorn equally the greater part of the American tradition as puritanical, effeminate, or over-intellectualized. If they seek foreign allies, it is with those who help them forget our national characteristics, our native bent and purposes, our discovered special American "genius." In what measure is the revolt due to the conduct of the movement by writers whose blood and breeding are as hostile to the English strain as a cat to water? Whatever the answer, I suspect that the young people who are being congratulated right and left on their emancipation from tradition are rather open to condolence than to felicitation. They have broken away from so much that was formative, and they suffer so obviously in consequence of the break. Their poets have lost a skill which Poe had: though they paint a little, and chant a little, and speak a great deal of faintly rhythmical prose, they have not learned how to sing. Their novelists have lost a vision which Howells had: though they have shaken off the "moralistic incubus" and they have released their "suppressed desires," they have not learned how to conceive or to present a coherent picture of civilized society. Their leaders have lost a constructiveness which a critic so laden with explosives as Emerson exhibited: though they have blown up the old highways they have not made new roads.

Am I doing the "young people" an injustice? I turn from their anthologies of verse, where I keep searching in vain for such music as the angler's milkmaid sang; and from the novels of Mr. Cabell, in whom I have not discovered that ascending sun heralded by the lookouts; to *A Modern Book of Criticism,* recently collected and put forth by Mr. Ludwig Lewisohn. The editor's desire is to show us that "a group of critics, young men or men who do not grow old, are at work upon the creation of a civilized cultural atmosphere in America." The idea resembles that, does it not? of Mr. Waldo Frank, who recently informed us that literature began

in America in 1900—or was it 1910?—at Mr. Stieglitz's
place in New York. It is related also to that recent comprehensive indictment edited by Mr. Harold Stearns and iron-
ically entitled *Civilization in the United States.* The implication is clearly that the country which developed Bradford,
Franklin, Emerson, Lincoln, Thoreau, Whitman, Mark
Twain, here and there in villages and backwoods, had no
"civilized cultural atmosphere" worth mentioning. It does
not seem quite plausible.

But let us proceed with Mr. Lewisohn. His critics:—"Like
a group of shivering young Davids—slim and frail but with
a glimpse of morning sunshine on their foreheads—they face
an army of Goliaths." The slim and shivering young Davids
turn out on investigation to be Mr. Huneker, Mr. Spingarn,
Mr. Mencken, Mr. Lewisohn, Mr. Hackett, Mr. Van Wyck
Brooks, and Randolph Bourne. It is not a group, taken as a
whole, however it may be connected with the house of Jesse,
which should be expected to hear any profound murmuring
of ancestral voices or to experience any mysterious inflowing
of national experience in meditating on the names of Mark
Twain, Whitman, Thoreau, Lincoln, Emerson, Franklin, and
Bradford. One doesn't blame our Davids for their inability
to connect themselves vitally with this line of Americans, for
their inability to receive its tradition or to carry it on. But
one cannot help asking whether this inability does not largely
account for the fact that Mr. Lewisohn's group of critics are
restless impressionists, almost destitute of doctrine, and with
no discoverable unifying tendency except to let themselves out
into a homeless happy land where they may enjoy the "color-
ful" cosmic weather, untroubled by business men, or middle-
class Americans, or Congressmen, or moralists, or humanists,
or philosophers, or professors, or Victorians, or Puritans, or
New Englanders, or Messrs. Tarkington and Churchill. A
jolly lot of Goliaths to slay before we get that "civilized cultural atmosphere."

By faithfully studying the writings of Mr. Mencken, Mr.

Lewisohn, and other "shivering young Davids," I have obtained a fairly clear conception of what a "civilized cultural atmosphere" is not. It consists of none of those heart-remembered things—our own revenue officers probing our old shoes for diamond necklaces, our own New York newspapers, and Maryland chicken on the Albany boat—which cause a native American returning from a year in Europe to exclaim as he sails up the tranquil bosom of the Hudson and rushes by a standard steel Pullman, back to the great warm embrace of his own land, "Thank Heaven, we are home again." No, it is none of these things. If, without going to Munich, you wish to know what a "civilized cultural atmosphere" really is, you must let Mr. Lewisohn describe it for you as it existed, till the passage of the Volstead act, in one or two odd corners of old New York: "The lamps of the tavern had orange-colored shades, the wainscoting was black with age. The place was filled with a soothing dusk and the blended odor of beer and tobacco and Wiener Schnitzel. *I was, at least, back in civilization.* That tavern is gone now, swept away by the barbarism of the Neo-Puritans."

To the book from which this quotation is made, Mr. Lewisohn's recently published autobiographical record, *Up Stream,* students of contemporary critical currents and eddies are much indebted. The author, like many of the other belligerent young writers who have shown in recent years a grave concern for the state of civilization in America, has ostensibly been directing his attack against our national culture from a very elevated position. He has professed himself one of the enlightened spirits who from time to time rise above the narrowing prejudices of nationality into the free air of the republic of letters, the grand cosmopolis of the true humanist. From his watch-tower—apparently "in the skies"—he has launched lightnings of derision at those who still weave garlands for their Lares and Penates, at the nationalist with his "selective sympathies," at the traditionalist with his sentimental fondness for folk-ways. Those who feel strongly attracted, as I do myself, to the Ciceronian and Stoic conception of a universal humanity and by the Christian and Augustinian vision of a universal City of God, may easily have mistaken Mr. Lewisohn for a "sharpshooter" of the next age, an outpost from the land of their heart's desire. But in *Up Stream,* Mr. Lewisohn drops the mask and reveals himself, for all his Jewish radicalism,[1] as essentially a sentimental and homesick German, longing in exile for a Germany which exists only in his imagination.

Even the purified and liberated mind of a Child of Light, living according to nature and reason, is unable to rid itself wholly of "selective sympathies." It betrays under provocation a merely "traditional emotion" for a cultural atmosphere compounded of the odors of beer, tobacco, and Wiener Schnitzel, with perhaps a whiff of Kant and a strain of Hungarian music floating through it, while two or three high philosophical spirits discuss what a poet can do when his wife grows old and stringy. I do not think it necesary to remonstrate with a man merely because his affective nature responds powerfully to a vision of felicity thus composed; but I think it a bit impractical to ask "a nation of prohibitionists and Puritans" to accept this vision as the goal of cultural efforts in America. It is a help to fruitful controversy, however,

---

[1] In a notably competent article on "The Case of Mr. Lewisohn," which appeared in *The Menorah Journal,* of June, 1922, Professor Jacob Zeitlin writes: "Whether entirely just or strongly colored, it is evident that Mr. Lewisohn's criticism of State Universities has little relevance to his character as a Jew. It indicates nothing more than that his sensitive aesthetic organism recoiled in pain from an environment that was uncongenial. And the same observation holds concerning his reaction toward American life in general. He but adds his voice to a chorus of growing volume, reiterating the now familiar burden of the crudeness and narrowness of our political and social ideas. There is ample ground for such a protest as he makes, but it is not a protest that can be identified with any recognizably Jewish outlook."

when a man abandons his absurdly insincere professions of "universal sympathy"—his purring protestation that he desires "neither to judge nor to condemn"—and frankly admits that he likes the German life, what he knows of it, and that he regards American life, what he knows of it, as "ugly and mean."

The militant hostility of alien-minded critics towards what they conceive to be the dominant traits of the national character is, on the whole, to be welcomed as provocative of reflection and as a corrective to national conceit. But the amendment of that which is really ugly and mean and basely repressive in our contemporary society is less likely to be achieved by listening to the counsels of exiled emancipators from Munich than by harking back to our own liberative tradition, which long antedates the efforts of these bewildered impressionists.

When we grow dull and inadventurous and slothfully content with our present conditions and our old habits, it is not because we are "traditionalists"; it is, on the contrary, because we have ceased to feel the formative spirit of our own traditions. It is not much in the American vein, to be sure, to construct private little anarchies in the haze of a smoking-room; but practical revolt, on a large scale and sagaciously conducted, is an American tradition, which we should continue to view with courage and the tranquillity which is related to courage. America was born because it revolted. It revolted because it condemned. It condemned because its sympathies were not universal but selective. Its sympathies were selective because it had a vision of a better life, pressing for fulfilment. That vision, and not a conception of life as a meaningless "surge of base and beautiful forces" liberated its chief men of letters. Thence their serenity, in place of that "gentle but chronic dizziness" which a critic of Young Germany, Hugo von Hofmannsthal, says "vibrates among us." Thence, too, their freedom from ancestor-worship and bondage to the letter. Listen to Emerson:

Ask not me, as Muftis can,
To recite the Alcoran;
Well I love the meaning sweet;
I tread the book beneath my feet.

Thence, too, the traditional bent of the American spirit toward modernity, toward realism. It was nearly a hundred years ago that our then-leading critic wrote in his journal: "You must exercise your genius in some form that has essential life now; do something which is proper to the hour and cannot but be done." Did he not recognize what was to be done? I quote once more from him a finer sentence than any of our impressionists has ever written: "A wife, a babe, a brother, poverty, and a country, which the Greeks had, I have." The grip and the beauty of that simple sentence are due to a union in it of an Athenian vision with Yankee self-reliance. It is the kind of feeling that comes to a man who has lived in a great tradition.

TRIVIA *

BY LOGAN PEARSALL SMITH

THE WHEAT

THE Vicar, whom I met once or twice in my walks about
the fields, told me that he was glad that I was taking an interest in farming. Only my feeling about wheat, he said,
puzzled him.

Now the feeling in regard to wheat which I had not been
able to make clear to the Vicar was simply one of amazement.
Walking one day into a field that I had watched yellowing beyond the trees, I found myself dazzled by the glow and great
expanse of gold. I bathed myself in the intense yellow under
the intense blue sky; how dim it made the oak trees and copses
and all the rest of the English landscape seem! I had not remembered the glory of the Wheat; nor imagined in my reading that in a country so far from the Sun there could be anything so rich, so prodigal, so reckless, as this opulence of
ruddy gold, bursting out from the cracked earth as from
some fiery vein below. I remembered how for thousands of
years Wheat had been the staple of wealth, the hoarded wealth
of famous cities and empires; I thought of the processes of
corn-growing, the white oxen ploughing, the great barns, the
winnowing fans, the mills with the splash of their wheels, or
arms slow-turning in the wind; of cornfields at harvest-time,
with shocks and sheaves in the glow of sunset, or under the
sickle moon; what beauty it brought into the northern landscape, the antique, passionate, Biblical beauty of the South!

SILVIA DORIA

BEYOND the blue hills, within riding distance, there is a country of parks and beeches, with views of the far-off sea. I remember in one of my rides coming on the place which was the scene of the pretty, old-fashioned story of Silvia Doria. Through the gates, with fine gate-posts, on which heraldic beasts, fierce and fastidious, were upholding coroneted shields, I could see, at the end of the avenue, the façade of the House, with its stone pilasters, and its balustrade on the steep roof.

More than one hundred years ago, in that Park, with its Italianized house, and level gardens adorned with statues and garden temples, there lived, they say, an old Lord with his two handsome sons. The old Lord had never ceased mourning for his Lady, though she had died a good many years before; there were no neighbours he visited, and few strangers came inside the great Park walls. One day in Spring, however, just when the apple trees had burst into blossom, the gilded gates were thrown open, and a London chariot with prancing horses drove up the Avenue. And in the chariot, smiling and gay, and indeed very beautiful in her dress of yellow silk, and her great Spanish hat with drooping feathers, sat Silvia Doria, come on a visit to her cousin, the old Lord.

It was her father who had sent her—that he might be more free, some said, to pursue his own wicked courses—while others declared that he intended her to marry the old Lord's eldest son.

In any case, Silvia Doria came like the Spring, like the sunlight, into the lonely place. Even the old Lord felt himself curiously happy when he heard her voice singing about the house; as for Henry and Francis, it was heaven for them just to walk by her side down the garden alleys.

And Silvia Doria, though hitherto she had been but cold toward the London gallants who had courted her, found, little by little, that her heart was not untouched.

But, in spite of her father, and her own girlish love of gold and rank, it was not for Henry that she cared, not for the old Lord, but for Francis, the younger son. Did Francis know of this? They were secretly lovers, the old scandal reported; and the scandal, it may be, had reached her father's ears.

For one day a coach with foaming horses, and the wicked face of an old man at its window, galloped up the avenue; and soon afterwards, when the coach drove away, Silvia Doria was sitting by the old man's side, sobbing bitterly.

And after she had gone, a long time, many of the old, last-century years, went by without any change. And then Henry, the eldest son, was killed in hunting; and the old Lord dying a few years later, the titles and the great house and all the land and gold came to Francis, the younger son. But after his father's death he was but seldom there; having, as it seemed, no love for the place, and living for the most part abroad and alone, for he never married.

And again, many years went by. The trees grew taller and darker about the house; the yew hedges, unclipt now, hung their branches over the moss-grown paths; ivy almost smothered the statues; and the plaster fell away in great patches from the discolored garden temples.

But at last one day a chariot drove up to the gates; a footman pulled at the crazy bell, telling the gate-keeper that his mistress wished to visit the Park. So the gates creaked open, the chariot glittered up the avenue to the deserted place; and a lady stepped out, went into the garden, and walked among its moss-grown paths and statues. As the chariot drove out again, "Tell your Lord," the lady said, smiling, to the lodge-keeper, "that Silvia Doria came back."

THE GREAT WORK

SITTING, pen in hand, alone in the stillness of the library, with flies droning behind the sunny blinds, I considered in my thoughts what should be the subject of my great Work.

Should I complain against the mutability of Fortune, and impugn Fate and the Constellations; or should I reprehend the never-satisfied heart of querulous Man, drawing elegant contrasts between the unsullied snow of mountains, the serene shining of stars, and our hot, feverish lives and foolish repinings? Or should I confine myself to denouncing contemporary Vices, crying "Fie!" on the Age with Hamlet, sternly unmasking its hypocracies, and riddling through and through its comfortable Optimisms?

Or with Job, should I question the Universe, and puzzle my sad brains about Life—the meaning of Life on this apple-shaped Planet?

MY MISSION

BUT when in modern books, reviews, and thoughtful magazines I read about the Needs of the Age, its Complex Questions, its Dismays, Doubts, and Spiritual Agonies, I feel an impulse to go out and comfort it, to still its cries, and speak earnest words of Consolation to it.

DISSATISFACTION

FOR one thing I hate Spiders—I dislike all kinds of Insects. Their cold intelligence, their empty, stereotyped, unremitted industry repel me. And I am not altogether happy about the future of the Human Race; when I think of the slow refrigeration of the Earth, the Sun's waning, and the ultimate, inevitable collapse of the Solar System, I have grave misgivings. And all the books I have read and forgotten—the thought that my mind is really nothing but a sieve—this, too, at times disheartens me.

THE SNOB

As I paced in fine company on that Terrace, I felt chosen, exempt, and curiously happy. There was a glamour in the air, a something in the special flavour of that moment that was like the consciousness of Salvation, or the smell of ripe peaches on a sunny wall.

I know what you're going to call me, Reader. But I am not to be bullied and abashed by words. And after all, why not let oneself be dazzled and enchanted? Are not Illusions pleasant, and is this a world in which Romance hangs on every tree?

And how about your own life? Is that, then, so full of golden visions?

COMPANIONS

DEAREST, prettiest, and sweetest of my retinue, who gather with delicate industry bits of silk and down from the bleak world to make the soft nest of my fatuous repose; who ever whisper honied words in my ear, or trip before me holding up deceiving mirrors—is it Hope, or is it not rather Vanity, that I love the best?

EDIFICATION

"I MUST really improve my Mind," I tell myself, and once more begin to patch and repair that crazy structure. So I toil and toil on at the vain task of edification, though the wind tears off the tiles, the floors give way, the ceilings fall, strange birds build untidy nests in the rafters, and owls hoot and laugh in the tumbling chimneys.

GREEN IVORY

WHAT a bore it is, waking up in the morning always the same person. I wish I were unflinching and emphatic, and had big, bushy eyebrows and a Message for the Age. I wish I were a deep Thinker, or a great Ventriloquist.

I should like to be refined and melancholy, the victim of a

hopeless passion; to love in the old, stilted way, with impossible Adoration and Despair under the pale-faced Moon.

I wish I could get up; I wish I were the world's greatest Violinist. I wish I had lots of silver, and first Editions, and green ivory.

ON THE FLOOR OF THE LIBRARY *

By Simeon Strunsky

Unfortunate people who never read detective novels; or, worse still, those who pick up a mystery story and wonder what in the world any one can see in the book to keep him up till 1:30 in the morning with intermittent trips to the cold meat in the ice-box; or, worst of all, those who read the first chapter and then turn to the end to see who did the killing—such unfortunates think they are sufficiently kind when they describe the habit as a mild vice, not so hard on the family as liquor or drugs, but pernicious for the eyesight. They think they are 100 per cent charitable when they tolerate the practice as one form of escape from the realities of a difficult world.

To such outsiders it is not given to understand that the "Mystery of the Chintz Room" or the "Smile of Gautama" is not an escape from the world but an initiation. They simply do not know that a select course in reading from Conan Doyle to Carolyn Wells is a guide to the institutions, culture, and life outlook of the nations from China to Chili. I have set down below a mere fragment of the picture of humanity which may be built up by devoting not more than one evening a fortnight to this field of research hitherto neglected by the sociologists. The list might easily be multiplied by twenty.

(1) The common belief that the British are an open-air people is utterly opposed to the facts. When a member of the

* From *Sinbad and his Friends;* copyright, 1921, by Henry Holt and Company. Reprinted by permission of the author and the publishers.

British nobility or upper middle classes is found dead in his bed, with a mystic Oriental symbol scrawled in blood on the sheets, the mystery is rendered all the more baffling by the fact that all the windows are hermetically sealed, the door is locked from within, the transom has not been opened for years, and the ventilators are choked up—in fact, the plumbers were scheduled to arrive on the morning after the tragedy. If it were not for that grisly Oriental symbol, the obvious conclusion would be that the victim perished for lack of a breath of fresh air. Given such a bedroom—and nearly all fatal bedrooms in our fiction are of this kind—and it is a question which is the greater puzzle: how the murderer managed to get in and escape, or how the victim managed to keep alive until the murderer got at him.

(2) Economy and resourcefulness are not among the virtues of the classes addicted to being murdered in their bedrooms or in their libraries. Twenty years after the tragedy the ghastly stain is still there on the floor. All attempts at erasing the spot in the course of twenty years have failed. What the scrubbing expense must have been, even if we reckon at a much lower rate than the prevailing scale of domestic wages to-day, is obvious. What the doctor's expenses have been in the way of treatment for nervous derangements inflicted by the ghastly stain on various members of the family is easily calculable. Yet no one in all these twenty years seems to have thought of replacing the blood-stained plank with a new one, at a trifling cost if done by day labor, and for a really insignificant sum if ordered from a collapsible bungalow manufacturer.

(3) Week-end guests in British baronial mansions or in wealthy residences on Long Island drink too much black coffee before going to bed. Then they lie awake all night. That is why about 2 in the morning they hear that queer, shuffling footfall down the hall to which at the moment they attach no particular meaning and the dread significance of which they realize only next morning when the host is found dead on

the library carpet with his eyes fixed in a ghastly stare on the ceiling.

(4)   The number of servants who have been in the employ of wealthy families addicted to violent deaths, for a period of forty years and up, and for whose fidelity the survivors can vouch as confidently as for their own husbands and wives, is truly astounding.   Here, indeed, my friends, the psychoanalysts, may find the secret of my own passion for the mystery novel.   Having in recent years never succeeded in keeping a house-worker for more than a couple of months, it is perfectly comprehensible how all my suppressed desires draw me to these faithful servants who stay forty years and then prefer to be the victims of cruel suspicion by the coroner rather than bring disgrace on the family.   It is not overstating the case to say that if only I could find a plain cook who will stay with us for forty years, I am perfectly willing to take a chance at being found at the end of the period, upon the floor of my library with the ivory-handled paper cutter through my heart. For that matter, I should welcome an unsuccessful attempt at murder if the assassin is not apprehended until he has found the paper-cutter.   As it is, I have to tear the pages open by pulling with both hands from the top.

(5)   The victims of foul play in the best British and American families never, absolutely never, cut themselves when shaving, or scrape the skin, or raise a blister.   That is how the investigator from Scotland Yard or from his private office in the Equitable Life Building is enabled to detect the cause of death in an almost imperceptible red spot under the chin which the local police have overlooked and which he immediately recognizes as the characteristic bite of the rare South American adder, *Megaloptera Bandanna*.   That method, if applied to the average man after he has shaved a second time for the theatre, would suggest that he had been done to death by the greater part of the reptilian fauna of the South American forests.

(6)   Closely allied to the preceding topic, it appears that

the principal occupation of the inhabitants of South America is the manufacture or the jealous preservation of the secret of instantaneously deadly poisons unknown to modern science and leaving no visible after-effects, excepting, of course, the corpse.

(7) Insurance premiums on the lives of the British nobility must be really enormous at Lloyd's. At least one-third of the members of the House of Lords are killed every year on the floor of their libraries or at the end of their yew walks close to the abandoned garden pavilion. But it is worse than that. If you have on the one hand the aged Duke of Beaucaire with an income of a million a year, and if you have on the other hand the third son of his fifth younger brother, who was wild at school and has lost himself somewhere on the Rand, and if you have no less than seven lives intervening between the scapegrace nephew and the ducal title, then these seven lives are sure to be wiped out by an earthquake or a fire or a marine disaster, and it only remains for the man who masquerades as the nephew (the real nephew having died of drink in Johannesburg) to come home and finish up the Duke.

(8) Nearly everybody in a mystery novel is a consummate athlete. They escape the vigilance of the detective who is disguised as a taxi-driver, or the pursuing avengers, by getting into a taxicab at one door and leaving by the other while the cab is in motion. This will interest people coming home from the theatre who have sometimes tried to open a taxi door from the inside.

(9) The wealth of Burma and Tibet in priceless jewels would be enough to pay the German indemnity ten times over. An emerald like the Eye of Gautama, a sapphire like the Hope of Asoka, a ruby like the Doom of Dhalatpur—all of them stolen from the forehead of sacred images by European adventurers—would be enough to finance British trade with Russia for the next fifty years. The fields in Burma and Tibet are cultivated entirely by women. The male popula-

tion consists solely of priests, who are off in the West for the purpose of recovering the hallowed jewels and visiting the vengeance of Brahmaputra on the sacrilegious plunderers. Usually they are disguised as elevator runners at the Savoy or the St. Regis.

People who do not know think detective fiction is a vice, whereas, it is, like Mr. H. G. Wells, a liberal education.

TALKABILITY *

A Prelude and Theme with Variations

By Henry van Dyke

"He praises a meditative life, and with evident sincerity;
but we feel that he liked nothing so well as good talk."
—*James Russell Lowell: Walton.*

I

PRELUDE—ON AN OLD, FOOLISH MAXIM

THE inventor of the familiar maxim that "fishermen must not talk" is lost in the mists of antiquity, and well deserves his fate. For a more foolish rule, a conventionality more obscure and aimless in its tyranny, was ever imposed upon an innocent and honourable occupation, to diminish its pleasure and discount its profits. Why, in the name of all that is genial, should anglers go about their harmless sport in stealthy silence like conspirators, or sit together in a boat, dumb, glum, and penitential, like naughty schoolboys on the bench of disgrace? 'Tis an Omorcan superstition; a rule without a reason; a venerable, idiotic fashion invented to repress lively spirits and put a premium on stupidity.

For my part, I incline rather to the opinion of the Neapolitan fishermen who maintain that a certain amount of noise, of certain kinds, is likely to improve the fishing, and who have a particular song, very sweet and charming, which they sing to draw the fishes around them. It is narrated, likewise, of the good St. Brandan, that on his notable voyage from Ireland in search of Paradise, he chanted the service for St. Peter's day so pleasantly that a subaqueous audience of all sorts and sizes was attracted, insomuch that the other monks began to be afraid, and begged the abbot that he would sing a little lower, for they were not quite sure of the intention of the congregation. Of St. Anthony of Padua it is said that he even succeeded in persuading the fishes, in great multitudes, to listen to a sermon; and that when it was ended (it must be noted that it was both short and cheerful) they bowed their heads and moved their bodies up and down with every mark of fondness and approval of what the holy father had spoken.

If we can believe this, surely we need not be incredulous of things which seem to be no less, but rather more, in harmony with the course of nature. Creatures who are sensible to the attractions of a sermon can hardly be indifferent to the charm of other kinds of discourse. I can easily imagine a company of grayling wishing to overhear a conversation between I. W. and his affectionate (but somewhat prodigal) son and servant, Charles Cotton; and surely every intelligent salmon in Scotland might have been glad to hear Christopher North and the Ettrick Shepherd bandy jests and swap stories. As for trout,—was there one in Massachusetts that would not have been curious to listen to the intimate opinions of Daniel Webster as he loafed along the banks of the Marshpee,—or is there one in Pennsylvania to-day that might not be drawn with interest and delight to the feet of Joseph Jefferson, telling how he conceived and wrote *Rip Van Winkle* on the banks of a trout-stream?

Fishermen must be silent? On the contrary, it is far more likely that good talk may promote good fishing.

All this, however, goes upon the assumption that fish can hear, in the proper sense of the word. And this, it must be confessed, is an assumption not yet fully verified. Experienced anglers and students of fishy ways are divided upon the question. It is beyond a doubt that all fishes, except the very lowest forms, have ears. But then so have all men; and yet we have the best authority for believing that there are many who "having ears, hear not."

The ears of fishes, for the most part, are inclosed in their skull, and have no outward opening. Water conveys sound, as every country boy knows who has tried the experiment of diving to the bottom of the swimming-hole and knocking two big stones together. But I doubt whether any country boy, engaged in this interesting scientific experiment, has heard the conversation of his friends on the bank who were engaged in hiding his clothes.

There are many curious and more or less venerable stories to the effect that fishes may be trained to assemble at the ringing of a bell or the beating of a drum. Lucian, a writer of the second century, tells of a certain lake wherein many sacred fishes were kept, of which the largest had names given to them, and came when they were called. But Lucian was not a man of especially good reputation, and there is an air of improbability about his statement that the *largest* fishes came. This is not the custom of the largest fishes.

In the present century there was a tale of an eel in a garden-well, in Scotland, which would come to be fed out of a spoon when the children called him by his singularly inappropriate name of Rob Roy. This seems a more likely story than Lucian's; at all events it comes from a more orthodox atmosphere. But before giving it full credence, I should like to know whether the children, when they called "Rob Roy!" stood where the eel could see the spoon.

On the other side of the question, we may quote Mr. Ronalds, also a Scotchman, and the learned author of *The Fly-Fisher's Entomology,* who conducted a series of experiments which proved that even trout, the most fugacious of fish, are not in the least disturbed by the discharge of a gun, provided the flash is concealed. Mr. Henry P. Wells, the author of *The American Salmon Angler,* says that he has "never been able to make a sound in the air which seemed to produce the slightest effect upon trout in the water."

So the controversy on the hearing of fishes continues, and the conclusion remains open. Every man is at liberty to embrace that side which pleases him best. You may think that the finny tribes are as sensitive to sound as Fine Ear, in the German fairy-tale, who could hear the grass grow. Or you may hold the opposite opinion, that they are

Deafer than the blue-eyed cat.

But whichever theory you adopt, in practice, if you are a wise fisherman, you will steer a middle course, between one thing which must be left undone and another thing which should be done. You will refrain from stamping on the bank, or knocking on the side of the boat, or dragging the anchor among the stones on the bottom; for when the water vibrates the fish are likely to vanish. But you will indulge as freely as you please in pleasant discourse with your comrade; for it is certain that fishing is never hindered, and may even be helped, in one way or another, by good talk.

I should therefore have no hesitation in advising any one to choose, for companionship on an angling expedition, long or short, a person who has the rare merit of being *talkable.*

II

THEME—ON A SMALL, USEFUL VIRTUE

"TALKABLE" is not a new adjective. But it needs a new definition, and the complement of a corresponding noun. I would fain set down on paper some observations and reflections which may serve to make its meaning clear, and render due praise to that most excellent quality in man or woman,—

especially in anglers,—the small but useful virtue of *talk-ability*.

Robert Louis Stevenson uses the word "talkable" in one of his essays to denote a certain distinction among the possible subjects of human speech. There are some things, he says in effect, about which you can really talk; and there are other things about which you cannot properly talk at all, but only dispute, or harangue, or prose, or moralize, or chatter.

After mature consideration I have arrived at the opinion that this distinction among the themes of speech is an illusion. It does not exist. All subjects, "the foolish things of the world, and the weak things of the world, and base things of the world, yea, and things that are not," may provide matter for good talk, if only the right people are engaged in the enterprise. I know a man who can make a description of the weather as entertaining as a tune on the violin; and even on the threadbare theme of the waywardness of domestic servants, I have heard a discreet woman play the most diverting and instructive variations.

No, the quality of talkability does not mark a distinction among things; it denotes a difference among people. It is not an attribute unequally distributed among material objects and abstract ideas. It is a virtue which belongs to the mind and moral character of certain persons. It is a reciprocal human quality; active as well as passive; a power of bestowing and receiving.

An amiable person is one who has a capacity for loving and being loved. An affable person is one who is ready to speak and to be spoken to,—as, for example, Milton's "affable archangel" Raphael; though it must be confessed that he laid the chief emphasis on the active side of his affability. A "clubable" person (to use a word which Dr. Samuel Johnson invented but did not put into his dictionary) is one who is fit for the familiar give and take of club-life. A talkable person, therefore, is one whose nature and disposition invite the easy interchange of thoughts and feelings, one in whose company it is a pleasure to talk or to be talked to.

Now this good quality of talkability is to be distinguished, very strictly and inflexibly, from the bad quality which imitates it and often brings it into discredit. I mean the vice of talkativeness. That is a selfish, one-sided, inharmonious affair, full of discomfort, and productive of most unchristian feelings.

You may observe the operations of this vice not only in human beings, but also in birds. All the birds in the bush can make some kind of a noise; and most of them like to do it; and some of them like it a great deal and do it very much. But it is not always for edification, nor are the most vociferous and garrulous birds commonly the most pleasing. A parrot, for instance, in your neighbour's back yard, in the summer time, when the windows are open, is not an aid to the development of Christian character. I knew a man who had to stay in the city all summer, and in the autumn was asked to describe the character and social standing of a new family that had moved into his neighbourhood. Were they "nice people," well-bred, intelligent, respectable? "Well," said he, "I don't know what your standards are, and would prefer not to say anything libellous; but I'll tell you in a word,— they are the kind of people that keep a parrot."

Then there is the English Sparrow! What an insufferable chatterbox, what an incurable scold, what a voluble and tiresome blackguard is this little feathered cockney. There is not a sweet or pleasant word in all his vocabulary.

I am convinced that he talks altogether of scandals and fights and street-sweepings.

The kingdom of ornithology is divided into two departments,—real birds and English sparrows. English sparrows are not real birds; they are little beasts.

There was a church in Brooklyn which was once covered with a great and spreading vine, in which the sparrows built innumerable nests. These ungodly little birds kept up such a din that it was impossible to hear the service of the sanctuary. The faithful clergy strained their voices to the verge of ministerial sore throat, but the people had no peace in their devotions until the vine was cut down, and the Anglican intruders were evicted.

A talkative person is like an English sparrow,—a bird that cannot sing, and will sing, and ought to be persuaded not to try to sing. But a talkable person has the gift that belongs to the wood thrush and the veery and the wren, the oriole and the white-throat and the rose-breasted grosbeak, the mockingbird and the robin (sometimes) ; and the brown thrush; yes, the brown thrush has it to perfection, if you can catch him alone,—the gift of being interesting, charming, delightful, in the most off-hand and various modes of utterance.

Talkability is not at all the same thing as eloquence. The eloquent man surprises, overwhelms, and sometimes paralyzes us by the display of his power. Great orators are seldom good talkers. Oratory in exercise is masterful and jealous, and intolerant of all interruptions. Oratory in preparation is silent, self-centred, uncommunicative. The painful truth of this remark may be seen in the row of countenances along the president's table at a public banquet about nine o'clock in the evening. The bicycle-face seems unconstrained and merry by comparison with the after-dinner-speech-face. The flow of tabletalk is corked by the anxious conception of postprandial oratory.

Thackeray, in one of his *Roundabout Papers,* speaks of "the sin of tall-talking," which, he says, "is the sin of schoolmasters, governesses, critics, sermoners, and instructors of young or old people." But this is not in accord with my observation. I should say it was rather the sin of dilettanti who are ambitious of that high-stepping accomplishment which is called "conversational ability."

This has usually, to my mind, something set and artificial about it, although in its most perfect form the art almost succeeds in concealing itself. But, at all events, "conversation" is talk in evening dress, with perhaps a litle powder and a touch of rouge. 'T is like one of those wise virgins who are said to look their best by lamplight. And doubtless this is an excellent thing, and not without its advantages. But for my part, commend me to one who loses nothing by the early morning illumination,—one who brings all her attractions with her when she comes down to breakfast,—she is a very pleasant maid.

Talk is that form of human speech which is exempt from all duties, foreign and domestic. It is the nearest thing in the world to thinking and feeling aloud. It is necessarily not for publication,—solely an evidence of good faith and mutual kindness. You tell me what you have seen and what you are thinking about, because you take it for granted that it will interest and entertain me; and you listen to my replies and the recital of my adventures and opinions, because you know I like to tell them, and because you find something in them, of one kind or another, that you care to hear. It is a nice game, with easy, simple rules, and endless possibilities of variation. And if we go into it with the right spirit, and play it for love, without heavy stakes, the chances are that if we happen to be fairly talkable people we shall have one of the best things in the world,— a mighty good talk.

What is there in this anxious, hide-bound, tiresome existence of ours, more restful and remunerative? Montaigne says, "The use of it is more sweet than of any other action of life; and for that reason it is that, if I were compelled to choose, I should sooner, I think, consent to lose my sight than my hearing and speech." The very aimlessness with which it proceeds, the serene disregard of all considerations of profit and propriety with which it follows its wandering course, and brings up anywhere or nowhere, to camp for the night, is one of its attractions. It is like a day's fishing, not valuable chiefly for the fish you bring home, but for the pleasant country through which it leads you, and the state of personal well-being and health in which it leaves you, warmed, and cheered, and content with life and friendship.

The order in which you set out upon a talk, the path which you pursue, the rules which you observe or disregard, make but little difference in the end. You may follow the advice of Immanuel Kant if you like, and begin with the weather and the roads, and go on to current events, and wind up with history, art, and philosophy. Or you may reverse the order if you prefer, like that admirable talker Clarence King, who usually set sail on some highly abstract paradox, such as "Civilization is a nervous disease," and landed in a tale of adventure in Mexico or the Rocky Mountains. Or you may follow the example of Edward Eggleston, who started in at the middle and worked out at either end, and sometimes at both. It makes no difference. If the thing is in you at all, you will find good matter for talk anywhere along the route. Hear what Montaigne says again: "In our discourse all subjects are alike to me; let there be neither weight nor depth, 't is all one; there is yet grace and pertinence; all there is tented with a mature and constant judgment, and mixed with goodness, freedom, gayety, and friendship."

How close to the mark the old essayist sends his arrow! He is right about the essential qualities of good talk. They are not merely intellectual. They are moral. Goodness of heart, freedom of spirit, gayety of temper, and friendliness of disposition,—these are four fine things, and doubtless as acceptable to God as they are agreeable to men. The talkability which springs out of these qualities has its roots in a good soil. On such a plant one need not look fr the poison berries of malign discourse, nor for the Dead Sea apples of frivolous mockery. But fair fruit will be there, pleasant to the sight and good for food, brought forth abundantly according to the season.

III

VARIATIONS—ON A PLEASANT PHRASE FROM MONTAIGNE

MONTAIGNE has given as our text, "Goodness, freedom, gayety, and friendship,"—these are the conditions which produce talkability. And on this fourfold theme we may embroider a few variations, by way of exposition and enlargement.

Goodness is the first thing and the most needful. An ugly, envious, irritable disposition is not fitted for talk. The occasions for offence are too numerous, and the way into strife is too short and easy. A touch of good-natured combativeness, a fondness for brisk argument, a readiness to try a friendly bout with any comer, on any ground, is a decided advantage in a talker. It breaks up the offensive monotony of polite concurrence, and makes things lively. But quarrelsomeness is quite another affair, and very fatal.

I am always a little uneasy in a discourse with the Reverend Bellicosus Macduff. It is like playing golf on links liable to earthquakes. One never knows when the landscape will be thrown into convulsions. Macduff has a tendency to regard a difference of opinion as a personal insult. If he makes a bad stroke he seems to think that the way to retrieve it is to deliver the next one on the head of the other player. He does not tarry for the invitation to lay on; and before you know what has happened you find yourself in a position where you are obliged to cry, "Hold, enough!" and to be liberally damned without any bargain to that effect. This is discouraging, and calculated to make one wish that human intercourse might be put, as far as Macduff is concerned, upon the gold basis of silence.

On the other hand, what a delight it was to talk with that old worthy, Chancellor Howard Crosby. He was a fighting man for four or five generations back, Dutch on one side, English on the other. But there was not one little drop of gall in his blood. His opinions were fixed to a degree; he loved to do battle for them; he never changed them—at least never in the course of the same discussion. He admired and respected a gallant adversary, and urged him on, with quips and puns and daring assaults and unqualified statements, to do his best. Easy victories were not to his taste. Even if he joined with you in laying out some common falsehood for burial, you might be sure that before the affair was concluded there would be every prospect of what an Irishman would call "an elegant wake." If you stood up against him on one of his favorite subjects of discussion you must be prepared for hot work. You would have to take off your coat. But when the combat was over he would be the man to help you on with it again; and you would walk home together arm in arm, through the twilight, smoking the pipe of peace. Talk like that does good. It quickens the beating of the heart, and leaves no scars upon it.

But this manly spirit, which loves

"To drink delight of battle with its peers,"

is a very different thing from that mean, bad, hostile temper which loves to inflict wounds and injuries just for the sake of showing power, and which is never so happy as when it is making some one wince. There are such people in the world, and sometimes their brilliancy tempts us to forget their malignancy. But to have much converse with them is as if we should make playmates of rattlesnakes for their grace of movement and swiftness of stroke.

I knew a man once (I will not name him even with an initial) who was malignant to the core. Learned, industrious, accomplished, he kept all his talents at the service of a perfect genius for hatred. If you crossed his path but once, he would never cease to curse you. The grave might close over you, but he would revile your epitaph and mock at your memory. It was not even necessary that you should do anything to incur his enmity. It was enough to be upright and sincere and successful, to waken the wrath of this Shimei. Integrity was an offence to him, and excellence of any kind filled him with spleen. There was no good cause within his horizon that he did not give a bad word to, and no decent man in the community whom he did not try either to use or to abuse. To listen to him or to read what he had written was to learn to think a little worse of every one that he mentioned, and worst of all of him. He had the air of a gentleman, the vocabulary of a scholar, the style of a Junius, and the heart of a Thersites.

Talk, in such company, is impossible. The sense of something evil, lurking beneath the play of wit, is like the knowledge that there are snakes in the grass. Every step must be taken with fear. But the real pleasure of a walk through the meadow comes from the feeling of security, of ease, of safe and happy abandon to the mood of the moment. This ungirdled and unguarded felicity in mutual discourse depends, after all, upon the assurance of real goodness in your companion. I do not mean a stiff impeccability of conduct. Prudes and Pharisees are poor comrades. I mean simply goodness of heart, the wholesome, generous, kindly quality which thinketh no evil, rejoiceth not in iniquity, hopeth all things, endureth all things, and wisheth well to all men. Where you feel this quality you can let yourself go, in the ease of hearty talk.

Freedom is the second note that Montaigne strikes, and it is essential to the harmony of talking. Very careful, prudent, precise persons are seldom entertaining in familiar speech. They are like tennis players in too fine clothes. They think more of their costume than of the game.

A mania for absolutely correct pronunciation is fatal. The people who are afflicted with this painful ailment are as anxious about their utterance as dyspeptics about their diet. They move through their sentences as delicately as Agag walked. Their little airs of nicety, their starched cadences and frilled phrases seem as if they had just been taken out of a literary bandbox. If perchance you happen to misplace an accent, you shall see their eyebrows curl up like an interrogation mark, and they will ask you what authority you have for that pronunciation. As if, forsooth, a man could not talk without book-license! As if he must have a permit from some dusty lexicon before he can take a good word into his mouth and speak it out like the people with whom he has lived!

The truth is that the man who is very particular not to commit himself, in pronunciation or otherwise, and talks as if his remarks were being taken down in shorthand, and shudders at the thought of making a mistake, will hardly be able to open your heart or let out the best that is in his own.

Reserve and precision are a great protection to overrated reputations; but they are death to talk.

In talk it is not correctness of grammar nor elegance of enunciation that charms us; it is spirit, *verve,* the sudden turn of humour, the keen, pungent taste of life. For this reason a touch of dialect, a flavour of brogue, is delightful. Any dialect is classic that has conveyed beautiful thoughts. Who that ever talked with the poet Tennyson, when he let himself go, over the pipes, would miss the savour of his broad-rolling Lincolnshire vowels, now heightening the humour, now deepening the pathos, of his genuine manly speech? There are many good stories lingering in the memories of those who knew Dr. James McCosh, the late president of Princeton University,—stories too good, I fear, to get into a biography; but the best of them, in print, would not have the snap and vigour of the poorest of them, in talk, with his own inimitable Scotch-Irish brogue to set it forth.

A brogue is not a fault. It is a beauty, an heirloom, a distinction. A local accent is like a landed inheritance; it marks a man's place in the world, tells where he comes from. Of course it is possible to have too much of it. A man does not need to carry the soil of his whole farm around with him on his boots. But, within limits, the accent of a native region is delightful. 'T is the flavour of heather in the grouse, the taste of wild herbs and evergreen-buds in the venison. I like the maple-sugar tang of the Vermonter's sharp-edged speech; the round, full-waisted r's of Pennsylvania and Ohio; the soft, indolent vowels of the South. One of the best talkers now living is a schoolmaster from Virginia, Colonel Gordon McCabe. I once crossed the ocean with him on a stream of stories that reached from Liverpool to New York. He did not talk in the least like a book. He talked like a Virginian.

When Montaigne mentions *gayety* as the third element of satisfying discourse, I fancy he does not mean mere fun, though that has its value at the right time and place. But there is another quality which is far more valuable and always fit. Indeed it underlies the best fun and makes it wholesome. It is cheerfulness, the temper which makes the best of things and squeezes the little drops of honey even out of thistle-blossoms. I think this is what Montaigne meant. Certainly it is what he had.

Cheerfulness is the background of all good talk. A sense of humour is a means of grace. With it I have heard a pleasant soul make even that most perilous of all subjects, the description of a long illness, entertaining. The various physicians moved through the recital as excellent comedians, and the medicines appeared like a succession of timely jests.

There is no occasion upon which this precious element of talkability comes out stronger than when we are on a journey. Travel with a cheerless and easily discouraged companion is an unadulterated misery. But a cheerful comrade is better than a waterproof coat and a foot-warmer.

I remember riding once with my lady Graygown fifteen miles through a cold rainstorm, in an open buckboard, over the worst road in the world, from *Lac à la Belle Rivière* to the Metabetchouan River. Such was the cheerfulness of her ejaculations (the only possible form of talk) that we arrived at our destination as warm and merry as if we had been sitting beside a roaring camp-fire.

But after all, the very best thing in good talk, and the thing that helps it most, is *friendship*. How it dissolves the barriers that divide us, and loosens all constraint, and diffuses itself like some fine old cordial through all the veins of life—this feeling that we understand and trust each other, and wish each other heartily well! Everything into which it really comes is good. It transforms letter-writing from a task into a pleasure. It makes music a thousand times more sweet. The people who play and sing not *at* us, but *to* us,—how delightful it is to listen to them! Yes, there is a talkability that can express itself even without words. There is an exchange of thought and feeling which is happy alike in speech and in silence. It is quietness pervaded with friendship.

Having come thus far in the exposition of Montaigne, I shall conclude with an opinion of my own, even though I cannot quote a sentence of his to back it.

The one person of all the world in whom talkability is most desirable, and talkativeness least endurable, is a wife.

ENDICOTT AND I CONDUCT AN
ORCHESTRA *

By Frances Warner

WHEN two people conduct an orchestra, there is plot
material. If the two are knit by marriage ties, the plot
thickens. Endicott and I conduct a family orchestra, he at
the piano, I playing second violin. I know more about music
than does Endicott; he is more musical than I. I keep the
time; he has the temperament. Temperament is more noble
than time, but time, I shall always insist, has its place,
perhaps nowhere more appropriately than in an orchestra.
He, at the piano, can dominate the situation more neatly
than I. In my position among the strings, however, I can
more readily organize a strike.

The rest of the "pieces" are presided over by our children,
young people of inflexible spirit and chromatic moods. Sometimes we doubt whether we have our troupe under the
rigid control which, as parents, we might expect to command.
The conductivity of an orchestra, says our son Geoffrey, varies
with the distance of the blood-relationship between artists
and conductor. When the children were little, we held the
pleasant theory that a family orchestra would draw us all
close together, standing always as a symbol of our perfect
harmony. That would be all right if the harmony would
only go to suit us all equally at the same time. As it is, our

little band, in which observers find so touching a picture of hearthside unity, suggests sometimes all the elements of guerrilla warfare.

The question most like to strain diplomatic relations is the choice of what to play. This is complicated by the fact that we each judge music by a different norm. Geoffrey, for instance, begs us not to play anything where the cornet has to rest too much. He says that he cannot keep track of a rest of more than forty-seven measures and be absolutely sure of coming in again at the right place. Every one admits that it is unfortunate when Geoffrey comes in at the wrong place. There is no smoothing over the astonishing effect of his premature trumpeting. "You cannot," says Geoffrey, "do the dumb shuffle on the cornet." For his sake, therefore, in looking over new music, we examine the cornet part for rests before we buy.

Endicott, a quorum in himself, agrees to anything except five sharps. Once seated upon the long piano bench, he is the genial patriarch at home. The girls, gracefully in league, object to extremes of any kind. They are our star performers, and must be humored at any cost. Knowing that the first violin and the 'cello are too valuable for us to lose, they exercise a cool and shameless power of veto at every turn.

I myself admire extremes. My tastes are catholic, and my choices range all the way from the "Unfinished Symphony" to "The Swing," by Sudds. The one thing in all the world that I really will not play is Schumann's "Warum," a favorite with the first violin. This worthy composition leaves me undone for days. Its insane, insistent question slides through my mind, over and over. I will not play it. I will not think about it. I will not even explain my antipathy. I have hidden the music.

Probably the assembling of an orchestra is, to the audience, a conventional and colorless affair enough. Any players of chamber music, however, who have been confined to a space that housed as many other things as does our living-room, know better. After bringing in enough dining-room chairs to seat the players, and adjusting the cross-legged music-stands, we find ourselves a little short of room. We have as yet been unable to find a type of music-stand which will not trip up long-limbed cornetists off their guard. One evening when Geoffrey, threading his way to his seat, really did lose his balance, and plunged headlong into my workbasket, one foot in the fireplace and the other still entangled in Barbara's music-stand, affairs rose to a climax.

"Everybody more than a mile high please leave the room," said Barbara, leaning over her 'cello and unweaving the legs of the stand from among her brother's feet. Any quotation from "Alice in Wonderland" is always calculated to infuriate the men of our family, and Endicott turned at once to his son's support.

"I don't see," said Endicott, "why Barbara doesn't arrange some little device for her music, just as Margaret does. Those tin spider-legs are really dangerous."

Margaret's "device" is at least not dangerous. She always pins her music to the tomato pin-cushion on the mantel, and stands aloof, compactly.

Once comfortably settled, we tune. That is one thing that we all will do. Ever since the children began to learn, when even the baby would bring his harmonica and say "Give me *M*," they have always played to pitch. For this fact, Endicott is not responsible. In the most critical attuning of our strings, Endicott will cease his obvious business of giving us "A," and will break into little improvised arpeggios and fanfares, incorrigibly. Why pianists do this will never fully appear. After the best disciplinary training that accompanist ever had, Endicott still continues to "practice his part" while the rest of us are tuning our fifths.

From my position in the orchestra, I can see the whole group reflected in the mirror over the fireplace. This helps me to conduct, and it also gives me pleasure. Barbara's 'cello is the most picturesque of all our instruments. I find something very lovable about the long, vibrant strings, and the gracious curves of its worn, dark form. A 'cello is big enough so that you can embrace it and treat it as an equal, —big enough to satisfy your love for layer on layer of velvet tone. And Geoffrey is the most picturesque of all our players. There may be men who can play a cornet with a perfectly natural cast of countenance, concealing their attention to a proper "lip" under a nonchalant expression. There is nothing nonchalant about Geoffrey's lean cheek and beetling brows. His eyes are purposeful and all his hair erect. His incalculable legs are far astray, and the very angle of his elbows has a look of do or die. Margaret, on tiptoe before her tomato pin-cushion, is perhaps not wholly at one with the group. One evening she turned briskly about, waved her violin like a brakeman's flag, and announced that somebody was out, and we'd better begin at "K."

"It was old Meggie herself," said Geoffrey fraternally. "Everybody's out of step but Meggie."

Does every amateur orchestra, I wonder, when trying new music, interrupt itself sometimes for the tentative inquiry, "Are we all at 'J'?" Now and then we have an uneasy feeling that we all are *not* at "J," and a general assurance that we are lends confidence. Another amateur pleasure of ours is in taking liberties with repeat signs. If we like the passage extremely, we mind the repeat; if we are not acutely stirred, we take the second ending. With new music, we have no way of knowing beforehand what we shall especially admire. It chances, accordingly, that the cornet and the 'cello perhaps shout in the same breath, "Repeat!" and "Don't repeat!" respectively. At such moments, it is imposible to keep the orchestra together, even with two conductors. We usually stop and have a family consultation as to who is conducting this band, anyway.

Orders of the kind just mentioned, shouted into the middle of the music, are likely to sound abrupt, not to say savage. When you have a violin beneath your chin, and a melody beneath your bow, you simply cannot converse in human tones, no matter how mild your mood. There is a certain tenseness about your voice, a dictatorial crispness about your brief request, that is likely to sound domineering. Margaret and Geoffrey, one evening, almost became permanently estranged because Geoffrey in the midst of a lovely passage took the mouthpiece of his cornet from his lips long enough to roar, "Three flats! Three flats!" for her guidance. Such stage-directions have a brusque and startling tone, as if the speaker had stood all he could from you, up to the explosion point, and must now relieve his mind. Then, too, there is of course a subtle excitement about the playing that approaches the danger mark if anything happens to spoil the spell. Little things seem vital in such moods.

But I think that the part we shall all remember is something more difficult to describe. Sometimes, of a witching night, when we all are keyed for the music, and outside circumstances behave in normal fashion, there comes an experience worth all the years of scratchy scales that went before. We are in the midst of the Larghetto, in the "Second Symphony," perhaps. I am not conducting. Neither is Endicott. Perhaps Beethoven prefers to conduct the Larghetto himself. And then, suddenly, as one sometimes on a journey becomes vividly aware of a breeze and blue distance, and firm hills beneath his feet, I really hear the chord that we are playing. It is no longer a measured flow of mingled sound, but distinct, exquisite, richly personal to me. There is the queer little rush of the accent that comes from the first violin when Margaret is really stirred; the 'cello's full response, vibrant, but soft with hidden masses of covered tone. I can feel my own little second fiddle quivering beneath my bow. There is some curious connecting of the spirit in the playing of a chord. Again and again we find it. Probably these moments are what we live for, varied though our programmes always are. In our cabinet are certain ragged folios that we try not to play too often. They live in promiscuous company: "Peer

Gynt" and the "Edinburgh Quadrille"; Massenet and Mac-Dowell; "The Red Mill"; Liszt and Bach; "The Toy Symphony" and Schumann's "Liebesgarten"—each of these has its time. Our only question is, "What next?"

At times when we have been ambitious all the evening, and Geoffrey's lip is tired, we hunt up one of the songs arranged for voice and orchestra. The "Shoogy Shoo" is one of these. Endicott then, in generous baritone, sings as he will, and the rest of us, with mutes astride our bridges, follow on. I shall not hear that song without the picture of the group in the mirror: Endicott upon the old red piano-bench, his hair silver under the lamplight, his mood transformed. He is no longer the down-trodden accompanist, to whom a measure is restraint, but the untrammeled artist creating his own rhythms. What is a measure or two among friends? Then I watch the girls, now wholly at ease, their bows moving softly, their eyes upon their muted strings. Geoffrey listens with his cornet on his knee.

After all, though music that we long to play is far beyond us, though we cannot always find all the parts, no matter how many times we search the piles; though the telephone rings and the heater blows off steam—these all are only passing discords. Some sort of music is always ready, alluring: Mr. Strauss for times of enterprise, with all our reckless hearts; the "Shoogy Shoo" for moments when strings have snapped; ancient hymns at twilight of a Sunday evening, with Endicott to sing, and now and then a guest with a fiddle of his own. After such evenings as these are over, when the children are putting away the instruments and folding the stands, and I go about locking up the house for the night, I think that I do not greatly care who really conducts that orchestra—Endicott or I.

DAYS OUT *

By Elisabeth Woodbridge

I HAD followed up her advertisement, and she stood before me in the dim hallway to which she had given me entrance. As she fingered the front door knob she told me her qualities. "Yes, mum," she concluded, "I does my work, mum. I don't never have company, and I don't never want days out."

I protested, "I always give my cook one day a week, afternoon and evening."

"Yes, mum, I know. But when I gets my work done, I likes to set right down in the kitchen. I don't want to go nowhere. If there's somethin' I need,—a spool o' cotton, or some stockin's,—why, I most gen'ally tells the lady, two-three days ahead, and then I runs out of a Saturday evenin', mebbe, fer an hour or two."

"And Sundays?" I asked faintly,—"I let my cook and waitress both go out on Sunday afternoon."

"No, I don't never go out on Sundays at all. Ye see, I likes to do my work, and when I gets through I likes to rest. That's the kind I am."

I sighed. Undoubtedly hers was a good kind, but undoubtedly I didn't want her. I had had one experience of that kind. She stayed with me two years, and in all that time was never away over a meal-hour. She was as good a creature as ever lived, but when she left, I said to myself, "Henceforth I shall *insist* on days out."

The fact is, I have an unconquerable love for my own kitchen and pantries. When I was a child they were to me realms of bliss, where I was often tolerated, often even welcomed. They still seem this to me, and—not to be tolerated at all—it is too much!

Perhaps that is an exaggeration. My cooks have usually tolerated me. They have even been polite to me. When I slink half-apologetically into the kitchen, to have a finger, so to speak, in the pie, they bring me dishes, and materials, and clear tables for me, and try to make believe I am not in the way—at least the nice ones do. But they watch me furtively. If they are self-righteous, their attitude is slightly critical, if they are self-distrustful, it is apprehensive:—what am I going to find out about their pantry? And as I am idiotically sensitive to my cook's attitude, I am conscious of this, and it spoils the fun. I slip out of my kitchen—their kitchen—and hie me to other parts of the house that seem more truly mine.

But, on the days out,—ah, those delicious days out! For the cook's outings are my innings. She is happy, too. How she works! The luncheon dishes are whisked out of the way, the kitchen is "redd up," and she flies to her room to dress. I slip out, glance up the back stairs, go to the range and poke the fire, change the draughts, shift the kettle a little, then hastily retreat to the parlor, and play the piano, with the soft pedal down, until I hear the back door shut. Then! No more piano for me! I can play the piano any time.

I walk swiftly and boldly out into the kitchen—my kitchen —MY kitchen. I perch on a table and swing my feet, in a glory of possession. What shall I make? I go over to the range again. Good fire,—good oven. 1 can make anything, anything! A feeling of power comes over me. I go to the pantry and scan its contents. I am always careful to have it well stocked on these days, that my creative impulses, no matter how freakish, may suffer no thwarting by reason of a lack of materials. I pick up the cook-book and resume my perch. I am in no special hurry. It is not yet four, and one can do almost anything between four and half-past six.

The telephone rings. I go, with my thumb in the cooky recipes. I lay the book open on the table beside me, and my eye runs over the page as I take down the receiver.

"Yes? Yes, this is Mrs. ――― Oh, Mrs. Grundy, good afternoon.― What? Another bridge? Aren't you a gay lady!―Oh, I'm so sorry. I don't play well, of course you know, but I suppose I *would* come to fill up, only you see I can't. It's my cook's day out. (I'm so glad I ordered molasses this morning!)― No, I can't change, she's gone already. (Would sugar-cookies be better, I wonder.)― Yes, of course, it *is* inconvenient sometimes, but they do want their days out, don't they?― Thank you, I'm sorry too. I hope you'll find somebody, I'm sure you will. ― Yes, good-bye." I hang up the receiver with a sigh of relief. ― Yes, I think,―ginger cookies. Hester and Tom will be in soon,―and they're so good when they're just out of the oven.

I go back, get into my big apron, give another look to my fire and my oven, and plunge in. There arises a delicious odor of spices and molasses and butter―an aroma of cooking, in short.

The front door opens and shuts, there is a stampede of feet up and downstairs. Then the kitchen door bursts open. "Oh, GOOD! It's Sarah's day out! Hester! Come on. It's Sarah's day out!"

Hester arrives. "May we make the toast?"

"May I set the table?" "What do I smell?"

"May I stir?" "May we scrape the bowl?"

"May we make griddle-cakes?"

It is like a frog-chorus in spring.

Perhaps I try to be severe.

"Griddle-cakes? Nonsense! Who ever heard of griddle cakes at night? Ginger cookies are queer enough. Besides, they don't go well together."

"No matter! Who cares! We always do nice, queer things

when Sarah is out. And we can eat up all the cookies as soon as they're done, and then they won't interfere with the cakes."

It makes really very little difference how it turns out, what things finally get cooked. The important thing is, that the cooking goes merrily on, and joy reigns.

It is, I maintain, a joy to rejoice in. I am heartily sorry for people who never do their own cooking. Cooking is an art, not only creative but social. It takes the raw materials and converts them into a product that is every way pleasing, and that brings the people who enjoy it into social harmony. The immediate products do not abide: the better they are, the more quickly they vanish; but they leave behind something spiritual and permanent. A busy mother, who was a wonderful cook, once said to me, "Sometimes it hardly seems worth while to cook things when they go fast; but then, I think, after all, they leave behind them a memory of a jolly home-table that does last, so perhaps it pays."

I am sure she was right. The memory of that home-table has lasted forty years and more, and does not yet seem to be fading.

There are other things to remember about that home, there are other things that are worth while in any home, but I think that in our modern conditions we lose too much of the pleasure that comes through doing practical things together. Almost all the physical work of our daily lives is delegated. Life is being systematized on that basis, and though there are great gains, there are also losses. The change is deeply affecting the character and quality of our hospitality. This is a big subject, and I am not going to be drawn into it too deeply. All I want to say is, that I believe we are letting ourselves be so involved in the machinery of our hospitality that we are cheated of some of its pleasures. We have submitted to certain conventions of "entertaining," and if we cannot satisfy these, we do not "entertain." What a pity! And yet, while I say this, I am aware that I too am enslaved. There are many people whom I have not the courage to invite to my house—*except* on my cook's day out. Then I am emancipated. There is no one whom I dare not invite, if I want her, when I am my own cook. Mrs. Grundy herself may come and welcome. And I believe Mrs. Grundy would have a good time. She might not ask to scrape the bowl, but I fancy she would be delighted to turn the griddle-cakes, or run out for the hot toast.

It is irresistible, this charm of doing things one's self, of doing things together. People have talked about the simple life until we are sick of the name. But we are not sick of the thing, the real thing. And our present conditions are not satisfying us. They need to be shaken up and recombined. We cannot go backward, but we can, perhaps, while accepting what is good in the new order, try to hold fast to what was good in the old. Probably it is best for me not to do all my own housework, but it would, I am convinced, be little short of a calamity if I never did any. To feel that my cook is doing her work contentedly, that she needs her wages and I need my time—this is all very well. But, like Antaeus, I must touch earth often. I yearn for the poker, I hanker for the mixing-bowl, I sigh for the frying-pan. Man does not live by bread alone, but neither does he live by taking thought alone. I love to think, and talk, and feel, but I cannot forget that I have hands which clamor to be put to use, arms which will not hang idle. It does not satisfy me to do make-believe work that does not need to be done : picture-puzzles and burnt-wood and neckties. I want real work, primitive work. Hurrah for the coalhod! Hurrah for the tea-kettle! Hurrah for the Day Out!

NOTES

Page 1

WILLIAM BEEBE was born at Brooklyn July 29, 1877. After taking his B.S. degree from Columbia he carried his scientific interest into graduate work. Since 1899 he has been honorary curator of ornithology of the New York Zoological Society and director of the British Guiana Zoological Station. He is a member of many scientific societies on both sides of the Atlantic. He has written extensively on outdoor life, especially about birds. An elaborately illustrated volume of his, *A Monograph of the Pheasants*, appeared in 1918. His two collections of essays are *Jungle Peace* (Holt, 1918) and *The Edge of the Jungle* (Holt, 1921).

Page 20

MAX BEERBOHM was born in London August 24, 1872. He was educated at Merton College, Oxford. For a number of years he has resided in Italy. In addition to being a writer he is a gifted artist, especially in caricature. Many of his drawings have been collected and have been published in book form—notably *A Book of Caricatures* and *Fifty Caricatures*, and *The Second Childhood of John Bull*. Among his books of essays are *Works of Max Beerbohm* (London, 1899), *More* (Dodd, 1899), *And Even Now* (Dutton, 1921), and *Yet Again* (Knopf, 1923.)

Page 30

HILAIRE BELLOC was born in France July 27, 1870—the son of an English mother and a French father. After being educated at Baliol College, Oxford, he served in the French field artillery. From 1906 to 1910 he was a member of the English House of Commons. He is the author of a number of children's books, of works on affairs of the day, and of a rather elaborate history of the World War. Among his best known volumes of essays are *Hills and the Sea* (Methuen, London, 1906), *On Nothing* (Dutton, 1908), *On Everything* (Dutton, 1910), *On Anything* (Dutton, 1910), *On Something* (Dutton, 1910), and *On* (Doran, 1923).

Page 37

ROBERT C. BENCHLEY was born at Worcester, Massachusetts, September 15, 1889. He graduated from Harvard with the A. B. degree in 1912. For two years after his graduation he was in the advertising department of the Curtis Publishing Company. After a year spent in industrial personnel work he became associate editor of the New York *Tribune Sunday Magazine.* Later he was editor of the New York *Tribune Graphic.* During 1919 and 1920 he was managing editor of *Vanity Fair.* Later he conducted the "Books and Other Things" column in the New York *World.* More recently he has been dramatic critic of *Life.* His two books of essays are *Of All Things!* (Holt, 1921) and *Love Conquers All* (Holt, 1922).

Page 42

RALPH BERGENGREN was born at Gloucester, Massachusetts, March 2, 1871. He took his A. B. degree from Harvard in 1893. For a number of years he contributed cartoons to the Boston *Sunday Globe.* Later he wrote editorials and dramatic criticisms for the Boston *Budget.* After serving three years on the editorial staff of the Boston Publicity Bureau he became art critic of the Boston *Advertiser.* He is the author of an attractive volume of verse for children—*Jane, Joseph, and John—their Book of Verses* (Atlantic Press, 1918)—and three volumes of essays—*The Comforts of Home* (Atlantic Press, 1918), *The Perfect Gentleman* (Atlantic Press, 1919), and *The Seven Ages of Man* (Atlantic Press, 1921).

Page 47

ALEXANDER BLACK was born in New York City February 7, 1859. He attended the public schools of Brooklyn, and in 1908 received an honorary degree of Master of Arts from St. Lawrence University. At the age of fifteen he became a reporter on the Brooklyn *Times;* later he became its literary editor. From 1905 to 1910 he was Sunday Editor of the New York *World.* Since 1913 he has been editor of the Newspaper Feature Service. To him belong the distinction of being the first to originate "picture plays"; and in 1894 he brought out the "first plays on a white sheet." He is the author of a number of novels, the most important of which are probably *The Great Desire* (Harper, 1919) and *Jo Ellen* (Harper, 1923), and of one collection of essays—*The Latest Thing and Other Things* (Harper, 1923).

Page 56

MARGARET BREUNING (Mrs. John Anderson) was born at Hawley, Pennsylvania. She was educated at Wesleyan University; later she received a diploma from L'Institut de Touraine (France). At the present time she is writing art criticisms for the New York *Evening Post*, in the columns of which originally appeared the sketches making up *You Know Charles* (Holt, 1921).

Page 59

CHARLES S. BROOKS was born June 25, 1878, at Cleveland, Ohio. After taking his A. B. degree from Yale in 1900 he entered business in Cleveland and became vice-president of the Brooks Company, printers and manufacturers of railroad stationery supplies. In addition to his duties as a business executive he finds time to offer a course in English Composition at the College for Women of Western Reserve University. Among his books are *Luca Sarto*, a novel (Century, 1920), *Frightful Plays* (Harcourt, 1922), and several volumes of essays—*Journeys to Bagdad* (Yale Press, 1915), *There's Pippins and Cheese to Come* (Yale Press, 1917), *Chimney-Pot Papers* (Yale Press, 1919), and *Hints to Pilgrims* (Yale Press, 1921). *A Thread of English Road* (Harcourt), is announced for 1924.

Page 63

HEYWOOD BROUN was born in Brooklyn December 7, 1888. After leaving Harvard in 1910 he became a reporter on the New York *Tribune*. In 1921 he joined the staff of the New York *World*, for which he is now writing dramatic criticisms. He is also dramatic editor of *Vanity Fair* and a special lecturer on drama at Columbia University. His two novels are *The Boy Grew Older* (Putnam, 1922) and *The Sun Field* (Putnam, 1923). *Seeing Things at Night* (Harcourt, 1921) and *Pieces of Hate* (Doran, 1923) are collections of essays that originally appeared, for the most part, in his column in the New York *World*.

Page 69

THOMAS BURKE was born in 1887 in London, where he now resides. After many discouragements he jumped into popularity in 1916 with his remarkable collection of stories of London's Chinatown—*Limehouse Nights*. At the present time he is acting as a literary advisor for a London publisher. *Limehouse Nights* was followed by a novel *Twinkletoes: A Tale of Limehouse* (McBride, 1918) and a second collection of short stories, *More Limehouse Nights* (Doran, 1921), the English title of which is *Whispering Windows* (London, Richards, 1921). Limehouse is the locale for his volume of poetry, *The Song Book of Quong Lee of Limehouse* (Holt, 1920). Among the books of essays and sketches, dealing for the most part with his beloved London and its environs, are *Nights in London* (Holt, 1915), *Out and About London* (Holt, 1919), *The Outer Circle* (Doran, 1921), and *The London Spy* (Doran, 1923).

Page 83

GILBERT K. CHESTERTON was born in England in 1874. After finishing the course at St. Paul's School he attended classes for a time in the Slade School of Art. His Lifework has been that of a journalist and author. He has written *Poems* (Dodd, 1915); *A Short History of England* (Dodd, 1917); *The Flying Inn*, a novel (Dodd, 1914); several volumes of detective stories— *The Innocence of Father Brown* (Dodd, 1911), *The Wisdom of Father Brown* (Dodd, 1914), and *The Man Who Knew Too Much* (Harper, 1922); many books in the field of literary biography and criticism—notably *Varied Types* (Dodd, 1903), *Dickens* (Dodd, 1906), *George Bernard Shaw* (Dodd, 1909), and *The Victorian Age in Literature* (Holt, 1913); and the following volumes of essays—*All Things Considered* (Dodd, 1908), *Tremendous Trifles* (Dodd, 1909), *Alarms and Discursions* (Dodd, 1911), *The Uses of Diversity* (Dodd, 1921), and *Fancies Versus Fads* (Dodd, 1923).

Page 87

FRANK MOORE COLBY was born at Washington, D. C., February 10, 1865. He took his A. B. degree from Columbia in 1888 and his A. M. degree in 1889. During the following year he was acting professor of history at Amherst College. After four years as lecturer and instructor in history and economics at Columbia he became professor of economics in New York University. Since 1900 he has been editor of *The New International Encyclopedia*. Among his books of essays are *Imaginary Obligations* (Dodd, 1904), *Constrained Attitudes* (Dodd, 1910), and *The Margin of Hesitation* (Dodd, 1921).

Page 94

SAMUEL MCCHORD CROTHERS was born at Oswego, Illinois, June 7, 1857. After taking his A. B. degree from Princeton in 1874 he prepared for the ministry at Union Theological Seminary and at Harvard Divinity School. He was ordained in the Presbyterian ministry in 1877 and began preaching in the Far West. In 1882 he entered the Unitarian ministry, and since 1894 he has been pastor of the First Unitarian Church of Cambridge, Massachusetts. He is also preacher to Harvard University. Many colleges and universities have bestowed honorary degrees upon him. Among his books of essays are *The Gentle Reader* (Houghton, 1903), *Among Friends* (Houghton, 1910), *Humanly Speaking* (Houghton, 1912), *The Pleasures of an Absentee Landlord* (Houghton, 1916), *The Dame School of Experience* (Houghton, 1919), and *The Cheerful Giver* (Houghton, 1923).

Page 106

JOHN GALSWORTHY was born in England in 1867. He was graduated from New College, Oxford, in 1889 with an honor degree in law. He was called to the bar in 1890. After traveling pretty much over the world he entered seriously upon his work as a writer. In three fields—novel, drama, and essay—he has been almost uniformly successful. His best known novels are probably *The Man of Property* (Scribner, 1906), *The Country House* (Scribner, 1907), *The Patrician* (Scribner, 1911), *The Dark Flower* (Scribner, 1913), and *The Forsyte Saga* (Scribner, 1922). His most successful dramas have been *Strife* (Scribner, 1909), *Justice* (Scribner, 1910), and *The Mob* (Scribner, 1914). His volumes of essays and sketches are *A Motley* (Scribner, 1910), *The Little Man and Other Satires* (Scribner, 1915), *A Sheaf* (Scribner, 1916), *Another Sheaf* (Scribner, 1919), and *Tatterdemalion* (Scribner, 1920).

Page 114

ELLWOOD HENDRICK was born at Albany, New York, December 19, 1861. He was a student at the University of Zurich, Switzerland, and studied chemistry under Victor Meyer. In 1921 he was awarded an honorary degree of Doctor of Science by Franklin and Marshall College. For many years he has been a prominent business man of New York City. At present he is consulting editor of the *Chemical and Metallurgy Engineering Magazine*. *Percolator Papers* (Harper, 1919), is a collection of his essays.

Page 133

OLIVER HERFORD was educated at Lancaster College, England, and Antioch College, Yellow Springs, Ohio. He pursued art studies at the Slade School of Art, London, and later in Paris. At the present time he is on the editorial staff of *Life*. He is the author of a long list of humorous books in verse and prose, of which the best known are probably *The Rubaiyat of a Persian Kitten* (Scribner, 1904), *Confessions of a Caricaturist* (Scribner, 1917), *This Giddy Globe* (Doran, 1919), and *Neither Here Nor There* (Doran, 1922).

Page 135

ROBERT CORTES HOLLIDAY was born at Indianapolis, Indiana, July 18, 1880. From 1899 to 1902 he was connected with the Students' Art League, of New York City. During 1903 and 1904 he was in attendance at the University of Kansas. After leaving college he was for several years a magazine illustrator and bookseller for Scribners. In 1913 he became assistant literary editor of the New York *Tribune*. During 1915 he was reporter and editor for the *Fishing Gazette*. For a time he was editor-in-chief of *The Bookman*. He is at present on the staff of *Leslie's Weekly* and is a feature writer of the Central Press Association. *Booth Tarkington* (Doubleday, 1918) and *Joyce Kilmer, a Memoir* (Doran, 1918) are two biographical volumes of his. His collections of essays include *Walking-Stick Papers* (Doran, 1918), *Peeps at People* (Doran, 1919), *Broome Street Straws* (Doran, 1919). *Men and Books and Cities* (Doran, 1920), *Turns About Town* (Doran, 1921), and *In the Neighborhood of Murray Hill* (Doran, 1923).

Page 141

BURGES JOHNSON was born at Rutland, Vermont, November 9, 1877. He took his A. B. degree from Amherst in 1899. After some experience as a reporter in New York City he became literary advisor, first of G. P. Putnam's Sons and later of Harper & Brothers. For a number of years he was on the editorial staff of *Everybody's Magazine* and of *Outing*. During 1908 and 1909 he was editor-in-chief of *Judge*. In 1919 he became editor of the Authors' League of America. Since 1915 he has been associate professor of English in Vassar College. Among his books are many volumes of verse and two collections of essays—*The Well of English and the Bucket* (Little, 1917) and *As I was Saying* (Macmillan, 1923).

Page 149

WINIFRED MARGARETTA KIRKLAND was born at Columbia, Pennsylvania, November 25, 1872. She graduated from Packer Collegiate Institute, Brooklyn, and from Vassar College. From 1898 to 1900 she was a graduate student in English in Bryn Mawr College. For a number of years she taught English in various preparatory schools for girls. She is the author of several volumes of fiction in addition to two collections of essays—*The Joys of Being a Woman* (Houghton, 1918) and *The View Vertical* (Houghton, 1920).

Page 153

STEPHEN BUTLER LEACOCK was born in England December 30, 1869. He took his A. B. degree from the University of Toronto and his Ph. D. degree from the University of Chicago. He is the holder of honorary degrees from American and English Universities. For many years he has been at the head of the Department of Political Economy in McGill University, Montreal. In 1907-1908 he made an extensive trip throughout the British empire giving lectures on Imperial Organization under the auspices of the Cecil Rhodes Trust. During the last ten years he has achieved a reputation through his writing and on the lecture platform as one of the foremost living humorists in English. He has written extensively in his chosen field of Political Economy. Among his volumes of essays, mostly of a humorous character, are *Literary Lapses* (Dodd, 1909), *Nonsense Novels* (Dodd, 1911), *Behind the Beyond* (Dodd, 1913), *Arcadian Adventures with the Idle Rich* (Dodd, 1913), *Moonbeams from a Larger Lunacy* (Dodd, 1915), *Essays and Literary Studies* (Dodd, 1916) *Further Foolishness* (Dodd, 1916), *Frenzied Fiction* (Dodd, 1917), *The Hohenzollerns in America* (Dodd, 1919), *Winsome Winnie and Other New Nonsense Novels* (Dodd, 1920), *My Discovery of England* (Dodd, 1922), and *Over the Footlights* (Dodd, 1923).

Page 167

EDWARD VERRAL LUCAS was born in England June 12, 1868. After graduating from University College he entered journalistic work on the London *Globe*. For several years he was on the staff of *Punch*. He has written many travel books and is the editor of a notable edition of the works of Charles and Mary Lamb. Among his books of essays are *Fireside and Sunshine* (Dutton, 1907), *A Boswell of Bagdad, with Diversions* (Doran, 1917), *Adventures and Enthusiasms* (Doran, 1920), and *Giving and Receiving* (Doran, 1922).

Page 170

ROBERT LYND was born in Belfast, Ireland, April 20, 1879. He was educated at the Royal Academical Institution and Queen's College, Belfast. His life work has been that of a journalist in London. He has written many books in the fields of politics and literature. Of special significance are his books upon Irish subjects—*Ireland a Nation, Home Life in Ireland, Rambles in Ireland,* and *Irish and English*. His volumes of essays are *The Art of Letters* (Scribner, 1921), *The Pleasures of Ignorance* (Scribner, 1921), *Books and Authors* (Putnam, 1922), and *Solomon in All His Glory* (Putnam, 1923).

Page 176

JOHN ALBERT MACY was born at Detroit, Michigan, April 10, 1877. He took his A. B. degree from Harvard in 1899 and his A. M. degree in 1900. After a year as instructor in English at Harvard he became associate editor of *The Youth's Companion*. At the present time he is literary editor of the New York *Nation*. Among his books are *Edgar Allan Poe* (Small, N. D.), *The Spirit of American Literature* (Doubleday, 1913), *Socialism in America* (Doubleday, 1916), and *The Critical Game*, a volume of essays (Boni, 1922).

Page 186

DONALD ROBERT PERRY MARQUIS (pronounced as spelled) was born at Walnut, a small village in Illinois, July 29, 1878. After spending a year at Knox School he entered the School of Arts in Washington, D. C. He became a reporter on the Washington *Times* and later assisted Joel Chandler Harris in magazine production in Atlanta, Georgia. Shortly after his marriage in 1909 he came to New York and joined the staff of the New York *Evening Sun*, in which he soon established his column "The Sun-Dial." There are four volumes of his poetry—*Dreams and Dust* (Harper, 1915), *Noah an' Jonah an' Cap'n John Smith* (Appleton, 1921), *Poems and Portraits* (Doubleday, 1922), and *Sonnets to a Red-Haired Lady and Famous Love Affairs* (Doubleday, 1922); a satire novel—*Hermione and Her Little Groups of Serious Thinkers* (Appleton, 1916); a collection of short stories—*Carter and Other People* (Appleton, 1921); and two volumes of essays and sketches—*Preface* (Appleton, 1919) and The *Old Soak and Hail and Farewell* (Doubleday, 1921), the last half of which is in verse. He took his column character of Clem Hawley, the bibulous but kindly "Old Soak," and wove around him a three-act comedy that proved to be one of the great New York successes of the 1922-1923 theatrical season.

Page 189

JAMES BRANDER MATHEWS was born in New Orleans February 21, 1852. He took his A. B. degree from Columbia in 1871, his LL.B. in 1873, and his A. M. in 1874. He received the honorary degree of D. C. L. from the University of the South in 1899, of Litt. D. from Yale in 1901, and of LL.D. from Columbia in 1904 and from Miami University in 1909. He was admitted to the bar in 1873 but almost immediately turned to literature. He became professor of English in Columbia in 1892, his title later being changed to that of professor of dramatic literature. He is generally recognized as one of the foremost scholars that America has produced. Some of the more important books that he has written in his chosen field of English and French drama are *A Study of the Drama* (Houghton, 1910), *Molière* (Scribner, 1910), *Shakespeare as a Playwright* (Scribner, 1913), *A Book About the Theatre* (Scribner, 1916) and *Principles of Playmaking* (Scribner, 1919). An admirable and most fascinating autobiography is his *These Many Years* (Scribner, 1917). Two collections of his short stories—*Vignettes of Manhattan* (Scribner, 1894) and *Outlines in Local Color* (Scribner, 1897)—have stood the unusual test of being reprinted after nearly thirty years—*Vignettes of Manhattan: Outlines in Local Color*, published now in one volume (Scribner, 1921). Among the more important collections of his essays are *Aspects of Fiction* (Harper, 1900), *The Historical Novel and Other Essays* (Scribner, 1901), *Parts of Speech: Essays on English* (Scribner, 1901), *Pen and Ink Papers on Subjects More or Less Important* (Scribner, 1902), *Inquiries and Opinions* (Scribner, 1907), *The American of the Future and Other Essays* (Scribner, 1909), *Gateways to Literature* (Scribner, 1912), *Essays on English* (Scribner, 1921), *The Tocsin of Revolt* (Scribner, 1922), and *Playwrights on Playmaking* (Scribner, 1923.)

Page 200

HENRY LEWIS MENCKEN was born at Baltimore, Maryland, September 12, 1880. After graduating from the Baltimore Polytechnic Institute he became a reporter. He advanced to the position of city editor and later to that of editor-in-chief of one of the Baltimore papers. He has been on the staff of the Baltimore *Evening Sun* since 1919. In 1908 he became literary critic of *The Smart Set*, and in 1914 he and George Jean Nathan became the owners and editors of this magazine. Since 1921 he has been a contributing editor of the New York *Nation*. He and George Jean Nathan are now editors of a new publication—*The American Mercury*. Mr. Mencken is the author of a number of books in the fields of literature and philosophy —especially noteworthy being *The Philosophy of Friedrich Nietzsche* (Luce, 1908), *In Defense of Women* (Knopf, 1917), *The American Language* (Knopf, 1918, revised edition 1922), and, with George Jean Nathan, *The American Credo* (Knopf, 1920, revised edition 1922). Among his volumes of essays are *A Book of Prefaces* (Knopf, 1917), *Prejudices: First Series* (Knopf, 1918), *Prejudices: Second Series* (Knopf, 1919), and *Prejudices: Third Series* (Knopf, 1922).

Page 207

ALAN ALEXANDER MILNE was born in England, January 18, 1882. He was educated at Trinity College, Cambridge. Upon leaving college he became a journalist and for a number of years was on the staff of *Punch*. More recently he has devoted himself to the writing of drama. Three of his plays have proved to be very successful here in America—*Mr. Pim Passes By* (1920), *The Dover Road* (1921) and *The Truth About the Blayds* (1921). *Not that it Matters* (Dutton, 1921) and *If I May* (Dutton, 1921) are books of essays.

Page 211

CHRISTOPHER MORLEY was born at Haverford, Pennsylvania, May 5, 1890. After taking his A. B. degree from Haverford College in 1910 he spent three years as a Rhodes scholar at Oxford University. From 1913 to 1917 he was on the editorial staff of Doubleday, Page & Company, publishers. After a year with the *Ladies' Home Journal* he joined the staff of the Philadelphia *Public Ledger*. In 1920 he entered upon his present work as editorial writer on the New York *Evening Post*. Among his books are several volumes of poetry —*Songs for a Little House* (Doran, 1917), *The Rocking Horse* (Doran, 1919), and *Chimney-Smoke* (Doran, 1921); three novels— *Parnassus on Wheels* (Doubleday, 1917), *The Haunted Bookshop* (Doubleday, 1919), and *Kathleen* (Doubleday, 1920); a collection of short stories—*Tales from a Roll-Top Desk* (Doubleday, 1921); and five volumes of essays—*Shandygaff* (Doubleday, 1918), *Mince Pie* (Doran, 1919), *Pipefuls* (Doubleday, 1920), *Plum Pudding* (Doubleday, 1921), and *The Powder of Sympathy* (Doubleday, 1923). He is also the editor of a most interesting collection of essays by present-day English and American writers—*Modern Essays* (Harcourt, 1921).

Page 221

GEORGE JEAN NATHAN was born at Fort Wayne, Indiana, February 15, 1882. He took his A.B. degree from Cornell University in 1904. The following year he spent at the University of Bologna, Italy. With his return to New York he entered upon his work as dramatic critic. Since 1908 he has been the dramatic critic of *The Smart Set*, of which in 1914 he and H. L. Mencken became owners and editors. At the present time he is co-editor with Mr. Mencken of *The American Mercury*, a new journal of art, literature, and politics. Among his volumes of essays, for the most part in the field of dramatic criticism, are *Bottoms Up* (Goodman, 1917), *Mr. George Jean Nathan Presents* (Knopf, 1917), *A Book Without a Title* (Knopf, 1918), *The Popular Theatre* (Knopf, 1918), *Comedians All* (Knopf, 1919), *The American Credo*, with H. L. Mencken (Knopf, 1921), *The Theatre, The Drama, The Girls* (Knopf, 1921), *The*

Critic and the Drama (Knopf, 1923), and *The World in Falseface* (Knopf, 1923).

Page 228

ALFRED EDWARD NEWTON was born at Philadelphia in 1863. He was educated in private schools. In 1885 he entered the electrical business and eventually became president of the Cutter Electrical & Manufacturing Company, a position he now holds. For many years he has been a collector of books, especially of first editions of authors of the eighteenth century. One of his favorite authors is Dr. Samuel Johnson, around whom he has written a delightful drama, *Dr. Johnson* (Atlantic Press, 1923). His two volumes of essays are *The Amenities of Book-Collecting and Kindred Affections* (Atlantic Press, 1920) and *A Magnificent Farce and Other Diversions of a Book Collector* (Atlantic Press, 1921).

Page 242

MEREDITH NICHOLSON was born at Crawfordsville, Indiana, December 9, 1866. He was educated in the public schools of Indianapolis. In 1901 he received the A. M. degree from Wabash College, and in 1907 the same institution conferred upon him the honorary degree of Litt. D. He resides in Indianapolis. He is the author of many novels, the best known of which are probably *The Main Chance* (Bobbs-Merrill, 1903), *The House of a Thousand Candles* (Bobbs-Merrill, 1905), *The Port of Missing Men* (Bobbs-Merrill, 1907) and *Otherwise Phyllis* (Houghton, 1913). His books of essays are *The Provincial American* (Houghton, 1912), *The Valley of Democracy* (Scribner, 1918), and *The Man in the Street* (Scribner, 1921).

Page 257

EDMUND LESTER PEARSON was born at Newburyport, Massachusetts, February 11, 1880. He took his A. B. degree from Harvard in 1902, and a degree of Bachelor of Library Science from the New York State Library School in 1904. From 1906 to 1920 he conducted the department "The Librarian" in the Boston *Transcript.* Since 1914 he has been editor of publications at the New York Public Library. He is the author of *The Believing Years* (Macmillan, 1911), *The Voyage of the Hoppergrass* (Macmillan, 1913) and *Theodore Roosevelt* (Macmillan, 1920); and of the following collections of essays—*The Old Librarian's Almanack* (Elm Tree Press, 1909), *The Library and the Librarian* (Elm Tree Press, 1910), *The Librarian at Play* (Small, 1911), *The Secret Book* (Macmillan, 1914), and *Books in Black or Red* (Macmillan, 1923).

Page 268

WILLIAM LYON PHELPS was born at New Haven, Connecticut, January 2, 1865. He took his A. B. degree from Yale in 1887, his A. M. degree from Harvard in 1891, and his Ph. D. degree from Yale in 1891. The honorary degree of Litt. D. has been conferred upon him by Brown and Colgate. After serving as an instructor in English, first at Harvard and later at Yale, he became, in 1901, Lampson professor of English Literature at Yale. He is the author of many books in his chosen field, the most noteworthy being *The Beginnings of the Romantic Movement* (Macmillan, 1893), *Browning: How to Know Him* (Bobbs-Merrill, 1915), *The Advance of the English Novel* (Dodd, 1916), *The Advance of English Poetry in the Twentieth Century* (Dodd, 1918), *Archibald Marshall* (Dodd, 1918), and *Reading the Bible* (Macmillan, 1919). *Teaching in School and College* (Macmillan, 1912), is a most delightful account of his own experiences as a teacher. His volumes of essays, for the most part on literary subjects, are *Essays on Modern Novelists* (from Macmillan, 1910), *Essays on Russian Novelists* (Macmillan, 1911), *Essays on Books* (Macmillan, 1914), *The Twentieth Century Theatre* (Macmillan, 1919), *Essays on Modern Dramatists* (Macmillan, 1921), *Some Makers of American Literature* (Marshall Jones, 1923), and *As I Like It* (Scribner, 1923).

Page 279

AGNES REPPLIER was born at Philadelphia April 1, 1858. She was educated at Sacred Heart Convent, Torresdale, Pennsylvania. In 1902 she received the honorary degree of Litt. D. from the University of Pennsylvania. For many years she has been considered one of our most distinguished women essayists. Among her volumes of essays are *Books and Men* (Houghton, 1888), *Points of View* (Houghton, 1891), *Essays in Miniature* (Houghton, 1892), *Essays in Idleness* (Houghton, 1893), *In the Dozy Hours* (Houghton, 1894), *Compromises* (Houghton, 1904), *Americans and Others* (Houghton, 1912), *Counter Currents* (Houghton, 1915), and *Points of Friction* (Houghton, 1920).

Page 291

STUART PRATT SHERMAN was born at Anita, Iowa, October 1, 1881. He took his A. B. degree from Williams College in 1903, and his A. M. and Ph. D. degrees from Harvard in 1905 and 1906 respectively. After serving for a year as instructor in English at Northwestern University he joined the English faculty of the University of Illinois and is now head of the English department. He is associate editor of the monumental *Cambridge History of American Literature.* Among his collections of essays are *On Contemporary Literature* (Holt, 1916), *Americans* (Scribner, 1922), and *The Genius of America* (Scribner, 1923).

Page 302

LOGAN PEARSALL SMITH was born at Melville, New Jersey. After spending three years at Haverford College he went to Harvard for a year and then to Baliol College, Oxford, where he took his degree in 1893. Since then he has lived in England. *Trivia* (Doubleday, 1917) and *More Trivia* (Harcourt, 1921) are two collections of his essays that some one has called his "gush of hilarious satirics."

Page 308

SIMEON STRUNSKY was born at Vitebsk, Russia, July 23, 1879. He was educated in the public schools of New York City and took his A. B. degree from Columbia in 1900. After six years as an assistant editor of *The New International Encyclopedia* he joined the editorial staff of the New York *Evening Post,* and in 1920 he became its editor-in-chief. His books of essays are *The Patient Observer* (Dodd, 1911), *Post-Impressions* (Dodd, 1914), *Belshazzar Court* (Dodd, 1914), and *Sinbad and His Friends* (Holt, 1921). *Professor Latimer's Progress* (Houghton, 1918) is his one novel.

Page 313

HENRY VAN DYKE was born at Germantown, Pennsylvania, in 1852. He graduated from Princeton in 1873. After serving as pastor of several famous Presbyterian churches he returned to Princeton in 1900 as professor of English, a position from which he recently retired. During the World War he served as our minister to Holland. Numerous volumes of poems and stories have come from his pen. "The Other Wise Man" and "The Lost Word," two of his best known stories, have been translated into almost every language on earth. Among his volumes of essays are *Little Rivers* (Scribner, 1895), *Essays in Application* (Scribner, 1905), *Days Off* (Scribner, 1907), and *Companionable Books* (Scribner, 1923).

Page 328

FRANCES LESTER WARNER (Mrs. Mayo D. Hershey) was born at Putnam, Connecticut, July 19, 1888. After taking her A. B. degree from Mt. Holyoke College in 1911 she became a teacher of English, first in several Massachusetts high schools, and later as assistant professor of English in Wellesley College. For a number of years she acted as an assistant to the editor of the *Atlantic Monthly*. She is the author of three collections of essays—*Endicott and I* (Houghton, 1919), *Life's Minor Collisions*, with her sister Gertrude Warner (Houghton, 1921), and *Groups and Couples* (Houghton, 1923).

Page 334

ELISABETH WOODBRIDGE (Mrs. Charles Gould Morris) was born at Brooklyn, June 16, 1870. Her preparatory education was secured at Packer Collegiate Institute of Brooklyn. In 1892 she took her A. B. degree from Vassar College, and in 1898 she was awarded the Ph. D. degree at Yale for graduate work in English. For a time she was a teacher of English in Packer Collegiate Institute and later became an instructor in English at Vassar. She is the author of two scholarly works—*Studies in Jonson's Comedies*, 1898, and *The Drama, its Laws and its Technique* (Allyn, 1898); and three collections of essays—*Jonathan Papers* (Houghton, 1912), *More Jonathan Papers* (Houghton, 1915), and *Days Out* (Houghton, 1917).

BIBLIOGRAPHICAL LISTS

NAMES AND ADDRESSES OF PUBLISHERS REFERRED TO IN THE BIBLIOGRAPHICAL LISTS

D. Appleton and Company, 35 West 32nd Street, New York.
Atlantic Monthly Press, 8 Arlington Street, Boston.
Bobbs-Merrill Company, Indianapolis.
Boni and Liveright, 61 West 48th Street, New York.
The Century Co., 353 Fourth Avenue, New York.
Dodd, Mead and Company, 4th Avenue and 30th Street, New York.
George H. Doran Company, 244 Madison Avenue, New York.
Doubleday, Page & Company, Garden City, New York.
E. P. Dutton & Company, 681 Fifth Avenue, New York.
Harcourt, Brace and Company, 383 Madison Avenue, New York.
Harper & Brothers, 49 East 33rd Street, New York.
Harvard University Press, Cambridge, Massachusetts.
Henry Holt and Company, 19 West 44th Street, New York.
Houghton Mifflin Company, 4 Park Street, Boston.
Alfred A. Knopf, Inc., 220 West 42nd Street, New York.
Little, Brown & Company, 34 Beacon Street, Boston.
Longmans, Green and Company, 55 Fifth Avenue, New York.
Marshall Jones Company, Boston.
Robert M. McBride Company, 7 West 16th Street, New York.
The Macmillan Company, 64 Fifth Avenue, New York.
G. P. Putnam's Sons, 2 West 45th Street, New York.
Charles Scribner's Sons, 5th Avenue and 48th Street, New York.
Small, Maynard & Company, 41 Mt. Vernon Street, Boston.
Yale University Press, New Haven, Connecticut.

VOLUMES OF ESSAYS

BARTON, BRUCE. *It's a Good Old World.* Century, 1920.
BEEBE, WILLIAM. *Jungle Peace.* Holt, 1918.
————. *The Edge of the Jungle.* Holt, 1921.
BEERBOHM, MAX. *The Works of Max Beerbohm.* Dodd, 1896.
————. *More.* Dodd, 1899.
————. *And Even Now.* Dutton, 1921.
————. *Yet Again.* Knopf, 1923.

BELLOC, HILAIRE. *On Nothing.* Dutton, 1908.
————. *On Everything.* Dutton, 1910.
————. *On Something.* Dutton, 1910.
————. *On Anything.* Dutton, 1910.
————. *This and That and the Other.* Dodd, 1912.
————. *On.* Doran, 1923.
BENCHLEY, ROBERT. *Of All Things!* Holt, 1921.
————. *Love Conquers All.* Holt, 1922.
BENNETT, ARNOLD. *How to Live on Twenty-Four Hours a Day.* Doran, 1910.
————. *Things that Have Interested Me.* Doran, 1921.
————. *Things that Have Interested Me: Second Series.* Doran, 1923.
BENSON, A. C. *From a College Window.* Putnam, 1906.
————. *Altar Fires.* Putnam, 1907.
————. *At Large.* Putnam, 1908.
————. *The Silent Isle.* Putnam, 1910.
————. *Along the Road.* Putnam, 1913.
————. *Escape and Other Essays.* Putnam, 1915.
BERGENGREN, RALPH. *The Comforts of Home.* Atlantic Press, 1918.
————. *The Perfect Gentleman.* Atlantic Press, 1919.
————. *The Seven Ages of Man.* Atlantic Monthly Press, 1921.
BLACK, ALEXANDER. *The Latest Thing and Other Things.* Harper, 1923.
BREUNING, MARGARET. *You Know Charles.* Holt, 1921.
BROOKS, CHARLES S. *Journeys to Bagdad.* Yale Press, 1915.
————. *There's Pippins and Cheese to Come.* Yale Press, 1917.
————. *Chimney-Pot Papers.* Yale Press, 1919.
————. *Hints to Pilgrims.* Yale Press, 1921.
BROUN, HEYWOOD. *Seeing Things at Night.* Harcourt, 1921.
————. *Pieces of Hate.* Doran, 1922.
BURKE, THOMAS. *Nights in London.* Holt, 1915.
————. *Out and About London.* Holt, 1919.
————. *The Outer Circle.* Doran, 1921.
————. *The London Spy.* Doran, 1923.
BURROUGHS, JOHN. *The Ways of Nature.* Houghton, 1905.
————. *Literary Values.* Houghton, 1912.
————. *Accepting the Universe.* Houghton, 1920.
————. *Under the Maples.* Houghton, 1921.
————. *The Last Harvest.* Houghton, 1922.
BURTON, RICHARD. *Forces in Fiction.* Bobbs-Merrill, 1902.
————. *Little Essays in Literature and Life.* Century, 1914.
CABELL, J. B. *Beyond Life.* McBride, 1919.
CANBY, H. S. *College Sons and College Fathers.* Harper, 1915.

CANBY, H. S. *Definitions.* Harcourt, 1922.

———. and Others. *Saturday Papers.* Macmillan, 1921.

CLARK, THOMAS A. *Discipline and the Derelict.* Macmillan, 1921.

COBB, IRVIN. *Oh, Well, You Know How Women Are!* (together with *Isn't That Just Like a Man!* by MARY ROBERTS RINEHART). Doran, 1920.

———. *Speaking of Operations.* Doran, 1915.

———. *A Plea for Old Cap Collier.* Doran, 1921.

COLBY, FRANK M. *Imaginary Obligations.* Dodd, 1904.

———. *Constrained Attitudes.* Dodd, 1910.

———. *The Margin of Hesitation.* Dodd, 1921.

COOPER, FREDERIC T. *Some American Story Tellers.* Holt, 1911.

———. *Some English Story Tellers.* Holt, 1912.

CONRAD, JOSEPH. *Notes on Life and Letters.* Doubleday, 1921.

CROTHERS, SAMUEL M. *The Gentle Reader.* Houghton, 1903.

———. *Among Friends.* Houghton, 1910.

———. *Humanly Speaking.* Houghton, 1912.

———. *The Pleasures of an Absentee Landlord.* Houghton, 1916.

———. *The Dame School of Experience.* Houghton, 1920.

———. *The Cheerful Giver.* Houghton, 1923.

DAY, CLARENCE. *This Simian World.* Knopf, 1920.

DUNNE, FINLEY. *Mr. Dooley in Peace and War.* Small, 1898.

———. *Mr. Dooley's Philosophy.* Russell, 1900.

———. *Mr. Dooley Says.* Scribner, 1905.

———. *Mr. Dooley on Making a Will and Other Necessary Evils.* Scribner, 1919.

"EAGLE SOLOMON." *See* SQUIRE, J. C.

ELLIS, HAVELOCK. *Impressions and Comments.* Houghton, 1914.

———. *Affirmations.* Houghton, 1915.

———. *Essays in War Time.* Houghton, 1917.

———. *The New Spirit.* Boni, 1921.

———. *Impressions and Comments: Second Series.* Houghton, 1921.

———. *Little Essays in Love and Virtue.* Doran, 1922.

FORSTER, E. M. *Pharos and Pharillon.* Knopf, 1923.

GALSWORTHY, JOHN. *A Motley.* Scribner, 1910.

———. *The Inn of Tranquillity.* Scribner, 1912.

———. *The Little Man and Other Satires.* Scribner, 1915.

———. *A Sheaf.* Scribner, 1916.

———. *Another Sheaf.* Scribner, 1919.

———. *Tatterdemalion.* Scribner, 1920.

GEROULD, KATHERINE. *Modes and Morals.* Scribner, 1920.

GOSSE, E. W. *Some Diversions of a Man of Letters.* Scribner, 1919.

———. *Aspects and Impressions.* Scribner, 1920.

GRANDGENT, CHARLES H. *Old and New Sundry Papers.* Harvard Press, 1920.

"GRAYSON, DAVID" (RAY STANNARD BAKER.) *The Friendly Road.* Doubleday, 1913.

HENDRICK, ELLWOOD. *Percolator Papers.* Harper, 1919.

HERFORD, OLIVER. *This Giddy Globe.* Doran, 1921.

————. *Neither Here Nor There.* Doran, 1922.

HODGINS, NORRIS. *Why Don't You Get Married?* Doran, 1923.

HOLLIDAY, ROBERT C. *Walking-Stick Papers.* Doran, 1918.

————. *Broome Street Straws.* Doran, 1919.

————. *Peeps at People.* Doran, 1919.

————. *Men and Books and Cities.* Doran, 1920.

————. *Turns About Town.* Doran, 1921.

————. *In the Neighborhood of Murray Hill.* Doran, 1923.

HUNEKER, JAMES. *Iconoclasts: A Book of Dramatists.* Scribner, 1905.

————. *Ivory Aples and Peacocks.* Scribner, 1915.

————. *Bedouins.* Scribner, 1920.

————. *Variations.* Scribner, 1922.

HUSBAND, JOSEPH. *America at Work.* Houghton, 1915.

HUXLEY, ALDOUS. *On the Margin.* Doran, 1923.

INGE, W. R. *Outspoken Essays.* Longmans, 1920.

————. *Outspoken Essays: Second Series.* Longmans, 1922.

JOHNSON, BURGES. *As I Was Saying.* Macmillan, 1923.

————. *The Well of English and the Bucket.* Little, 1917.

KERFOOT, J. B. *How to Read.* Houghton, 1916.

KIRKLAND, WINIFRED. *The Joys of Being a Woman.* Houghton, 1918.

————. *The View Vertical.* Houghton, 1920.

LEACOCK, STEPHEN. *Literary Lapses.* Dodd, 1909.

————. *Nonsense Novels.* Dodd, 1911.

————. *Behind the Beyond.* Dodd, 1913.

————. *Arcadian Adventures with the Idle Rich.* Dodd, 1913.

————. *Moonbeams from the Larger Lunacy.* Dodd, 1915.

————. *Frenzied Fiction.* Dodd, 1913.

————. *Essays and Literary Studies.* Dodd, 1916.

————. *Further Foolishness.* Dodd, 1916.

————. *The Hohenzollerns in America.* Dodd, 1919.

————. *Winsome Winnie and Other New Nonsense Novels.* Dodd, 1920.

————. *My Discovery of England.* Dodd, 1922.

————. *Over the Footlights.* Dodd, 1923.

————. *College Days.* Dodd, 1923.

LITTLE, P. *Books and Things.* Harcourt, 1919.

LUCAS, E. V. *Fireside and Sunshine.* Dutton, 1907.
———. *A Boswell of Bagdad, with Diversions.* Doran, 1917.
———. *Adventures and Enthusiasms.* Doran, 1920.
———. *Giving and Receiving.* Doran, 1922.
LYND, ROBERT. *The Art of Letters.* Scribner, 1921.
———. *The Pleasures of Ignorance.* Scribner, 1921.
———. *Books and Authors.* Putnam, 1922.
———. *Solomon in All His Glory.* Putnam, 1923.
MCFEE, WILLIAM. *Harbours of Memory.* Doubleday.
———. *An Ocean Tramp.* Doubleday.
MACHEN, ARTHUR. *Hieroglyphics.* Knopf, 1923.
MACY, JOHN. *The Critical Game.* Boni, 1922.
MARQUIS, DON. *Prefaces.* Appleton, 1919.
MATTHEWS, BRANDER. *Aspects of Fiction.* Harper, 1900.
———. *The Historical Novel and Other Essays.* Scribner, 1901.
———. *Parts of Speech: Essays on English.* Scribner, 1901.
———. *Pen and Ink Papers on Subjects More or Less Important.* Scribner, 1902.
———. *Inquiries and Opinions.* Scribner, 1907.
———. *The American of the Future and Other Essays.* Scribner, 1909.
———. *Gateways to Literature.* Scribner, 1912.
———. *Essays on English.* Scribner, 1921.
———. *The Tocsin of Revolt.* Scribner, 1922.
———. *Playwrights on Playmaking.* Scribner, 1923.
MAUGHAM, W. SOMERSET. *On a Chinese Screen.* Doran, 1922.
MENCKEN, H. L. *A Book of Prefaces.* Knopf, 1917.
———. *Prejudices: First Series.* Knopf, 1918.
———. *Prejudices: Second Series.* Knopf, 1920.
———. *Prejudices: Third Series.* Knopf, 1923.
MEYNELL, A. C. *Second Person Singular.* Oxford Press, 1921.
MILNE, A. A. *If I May.* Dutton, 1921.
———. *Not That It Matters.* Dutton, 1921.
MORE, PAUL ELMORE. *Shelburne Essays;* I-IX Series. Putnam and Houghton, V. D.
MORLEY, CHRISTOPHER. *Shandygaff.* Doubleday, 1918.
———. *Mince Pie.* Doran, 1919.
———. *Pipefuls.* Doubleday, 1920.
———. *Plum Pudding.* Doubleday, 1921.
———. *The Powder of Sympathy.* Doubleday, 1923.
———. (Editor). *Modern Essays.* Harcourt, 1921.
NATHAN, GEORGE JEAN. *Mr. George Jean Nathan Presents.* Knopf, 1917.
———. *A Book Without a Title.* Knopf, 1918.

NATHAN, GEORGE JEAN. *The Popular Theatre.* Knopf, 1918.
———. *Comedians All.* Knopf, 1919.
———. *The Theatre, The Drama, The Girls.* Knopf, 1921.
———. *The Circle and the Drama.* Knopf, 1922.
———. *The World in Falseface.* Knopf, 1923.
NEVINSON, H. *Essays in Freedom and Rebellion.* Yale Press, 1921.
NEWTON, A. EDWARD. *The Amenities of Book Collecting.* Atlantic Press, 1920.
———. *A Magnificent Farce.* Atlantic Press, 1921.
NICHOLSON, MEREDITH. *The Provincial American.* Houghton, 1912.
———. *The Valley of Democracy.* Scribner, 1918.
———. *The Man in the Street.* Scribner, 1921.
The Notion Counter: A Farrago of Foible, being Notes about Nothing, by Nobody. Illustrated by Somebody and dedicated to Everybody. Atlantic Press, 1921.
PARK, J. EDGAR. *The Bad Results of Good Habits.* Houghton, 1920.
PEARSON, EDMUND LESTER. *The Old Librarian's Almanack.* Elm Tree Press, 1909.
———. *The Library and the Librarian.* Elm Tree Press, 1910.
———. *The Librarian at Play.* Small, 1911.
———. *The Secret Book.* Macmillan, 1914.
———. *Books in Black or Red.* Macmillan, 1923.
PERRY, BLISS. *The Amateur Spirit.* Houghton, 1904.
———. *The American Mind.* Houghton, 1912.
———. *In Praise of Folly.* Houghton, 1923.
PHELPS, WILLIAM LYON. *Essays on Modern Novelists.* Macmillan, 1910.
———. *Essays on Russian Novelists.* Macmillan, 1911.
———. *Teaching in School and College.* Macmillan, 1912.
———. *Essays on Books.* Macmillan, 1914.
———. *The Twentieth Century Theatre.* Macmillan, 1919.
———. *Essays on Modern Dramatists.* Macmillan, 1921.
———. *Some Makers of American Literature.* Marshall Jones, 1923.
———. *As I Like It.* Scribner, 1923.
PORTER, LAURA SPENCER. *Adventures in Indigence.* Atlantic Press, 1919.
REPPLIER, AGNES. *Books and Men.* Houghton, 1888.
———. *Points of View.* Houghton, 1891.
———. *Essays in Miniature.* Houghton, 1892.
———. *Essays in Idleness.* Houghton, 1893.
———. *In the Dozy Hours.* Houghton, 1894.
———. *Compromises.* Houghton, 1904.
———. *Americans and Others.* Houghton, 1912.
———. *Counter Currents.* Houghton, 1915.
———. *Points of Friction.* Houghton, 1920.

RINEHART, MARY ROBERTS. *Isn't That Just Like a Man!* (together with *Oh, Well, You Know How Women Are!* by IRVIN COBB). Doran, 1920.

ROOSEVELT, THEODORE. *History as Literature and Other Essays,* Scribner, 1913.

SAINTSBURY, GEORGE. *A Scrap Book.* Macmillan, 1922.

———. *The Cellar Book.* Macmillan, 1922.

SANTAYANA, GEORGE. *Little Essays.* Scribner, 1921.

———. *Soliloquies in England and Later Soliloquies.* Scribner, 1922.

SCARBOROUGH, DOROTHY. *From a Southern Porch.* Putnam, 1919.

SCHAUFFLER, ROBERT HAVEN. *The Joyful Heart.* Houghton, 1914.

SHARP, DALLAS L. *Where Rolls the Oregon.* Houghton, 1913.

———. *Hills of Hingham.* Houghton, 1915.

———. *The Whole Year Round.* Houghton, 1915.

———. *Roof and Meadow.* Houghton, 1918.

———. *The Magical Chance.* Houghton, 1923.

SHERINGHAM, H. T. *Ourselves When Young.* Putnam, 1922.

SHERMAN, STUART P. *On Contemporary Literature.* Holt, 1916.

———. *Americans.* Scribner, 1922.

———. *The Genius of America.* Scribner, 1923.

SMITH, LOGAN PEARSALL. *Trivia.* Doubleday, 1917.

———. *More Trivia.* Harcourt, 1921.

SMITH, C. ALPHONSO. *What Can Literature Do For Me?* Doubleday, 1913.

SQUIRE, J. C., "SOLOMON EAGLE." *Books in General.* Knopf, 1919.

———. *Books in General: Second Series.* Knopf, 1919.

———. *Life and Letters.* Doran, 1921.

———. *Essays at Large.* Doran, 1923.

STRACHEY, LYTTON. *Books and Characters.* Harcourt, 1922.

STRUNSKY, SIMEON. *The Patient Observer.* Dodd, 1911.

———. *Post-Impressions.* Dodd, 1914.

———. *Belshazzar Court.* Dodd, 1914.

———. *Sinbad and His Friends.* Holt, 1921.

STURGIS, MRS. R. CLIPSON. *Personal Prejudices.* Houghton, 1920.

TANNER, W. M. (Editor). *Essays and Essay-Writing.* Atlantic Press, 1917.

TOMLINSON, H. M. *Old Junk.* Knopf, 1920.

———. *London River.* Knopf, 1921.

TWAIN, MARK. *What Is Man? And Other Essays.* Harper, 1917.

———. *Literary Essays.* Harper, 1899.

VAN DYKE, HENRY. *Little Rivers.* Scribner, 1895.

———. *Essays in Application.* Scribner, 1905.

———. *Days Off.* Scribner, 1907.

VAN DYKE, HENRY. *Companionable Books.* Scribner, 1923.

VAN VECHTEN, CARL. *The Merry-Go-Round.* Knopf, 1918.

———. *In the Garret.* Knopf, 1920.

———. *Interpreters.* Knopf, 1920.

VINCE, CHARLES. *Wayfarers in Arcady.* Putnam, 1922.

WALKLEY, A. B. *Pastiche and Prejudice.* Knopf, 1921.

———. *More Prejudice.* Knopf, 1923.

WARNER, FRANCES. *Endicott and I.* Houghton, 1919.

———. *Groups and Couples.* Houghton, 1923.

WARNER, FRANCES, and WARNER, GERTRUDE. *Life's Minor Collisions.* Houghton, 1921.

WATERHOUSE, F. A. *Random Studies in the Romantic Chaos.* McBride, 1923.

WILSON, WOODROW. *When a Man Comes to Himself.* Harper, 1915.

———. *Mere Literature.* Houghton, 1896.

WINCHESTER, C. T. *Old Castle.* Macmillan, 1922.

WOODBRIDGE, ELISABETH. *Jonathan Papers.* Houghton, 1912.

———. *More Jonathan Papers.* Houghton, 1915.

——— *Days Out.* Houghton, 1917.